Market Relations

BTEC

BLACKWELL Business

THE OPEN LEARNING FOUNDATION

Market Relations

by:

Nick Hawkins

THE
OPEN
LEARNING
FOUNDATION

Copyright © Open Learning Foundation Enterprises Ltd 1995

First published 1995

Blackwell Publishers Ltd
108 Cowley Road
Oxford OX4 1JF, UK

238 Main Street
Cambridge, Massachusetts 02142, USA

Every effort has been made to trace all copyright owners of material used in this book but if any have been inadvertently overlooked the publishers will be pleased to make necessary arrangements at the first opportunity.

British Library Cataloguing-in-Publication Data
A CIP catalogue record for this book is available from the British Library

Library of Congress Cataloging-in-Publication Data
A catalogue record for this book is available from the Library of Congress

ISBN 0-631-19671-4

Printed in Great Britain by Alden Press

This book is printed on acid-free paper

Contents

Contents

RESOURCES

Foreword

BTEC is committed to helping people of any age to acquire and maintain the up-to-date and relevant knowledge, understanding and skills they need for success in current or future employment.

These aims are greatly enhanced by this series of open learning books for the new BTEC HND and HNC in Business Studies.

These books will provide more students with the opportunity to achieve a widely recognised national qualification in business by allowing flexible study patterns combined with an innovative approach to learning.

Our active involvement in a partnership with the Open Learning Foundation and Blackwell Publishers ensures that each book comprehensively covers the specific learning outcomes needed for a module in this Higher National programme.

Acknowledgements

Author
Nick Hawkins

Open Learning Editor: Peter Gaukroger

For the Open Learning Foundation:
Director of Programmes: Leslie Mapp
Design and Production: Stephen Moulds
Text Editor: Paul Stirner
Academic Co-ordinator: Glyn Roberts (Bradford & Ilkley
                                            Community College)
Academic Reviewers: Martin Gibson (University of Central
                                    Lancashire)

                                    Bob McClelland (Liverpool John Moores
                                    University)

The Open Learning Foundation wishes to acknowledge the support
of Bradford & Ilkley Community College during the preparation of
this workbook.

For BTEC
Dianne Billam: Director of Products and Quality Division
John Edgar: Consultant
Don Glaves: Education Adviser
Françoise Seacroft: Manager of Futures Department
Mike Taylor: Deputy Head of Department of Service Sector
                        Management, University of Brighton

For Blackwell Publishers
Editorial Director: Philip Carpenter
Senior Commissioning Editor: Tim Goodfellow
Production Manager: Pam Park
Development Editors: Richard Jackman and Catriona King
Pre-production Manager: Paul Stringer
Sub-editorial team: First Class Publishing
Reviewers: Alun Epps (Highbury College)
                Joe Bulman (West Herts College)

Copyright acknowledgments

The publishers are grateful for permission to reproduce material from the following sources:

In Section 2, Session 2, the various quotes from Richard Cassidy, business issues manager for British Gas, are from N. Hawkins, 1992, 'Open communication: British Gas and McDonald's', *Greener Marketing*, published by Greenleaf Publishing.

In Section 3, Session 1, figure 1.6 is reprinted with the permission of The Free Press, an imprint of Simon & Schuster, from *Diffusion of Innovations* by Everett M. Rogers. Copyright © 1962 by The Free Press.

The classification system and figure 1.1 in Section 4, Session 1 are from Philip Kotler, *Marketing Management: Analysis, Planning, Implementation, and Control*, 8th edition, © 1994, pp. 211, 349. Reprinted by permission of Prentice Hall, Upper Saddle River, New Jersey.

Figure 2.1 in Section 4, Session 2 is reprinted with the permission of The Free Press, an imprint of Simon & Schuster, from *Competitive Strategy: Techniques of Analysing Industries and Competitors* by Michael E. Porter. Copyright © 1980 by The Free Press.

In Section 4, Session 2, figure 2.2 showing the Boston Consulting Group's product portfolio matrix is reproduced from B Medley, 'Strategy and the business portfolio', *Long Range Planning*, February 1977, p.12, Elsevier Science Ltd.

Figure 2.4 in Section 4, Session 2 is from Theodore Levitt, 'Exploit the product life cycle', *Harvard Business Review*, November/December 1965.

The publishers wish to thank Cadbury Ltd for the material used in the case study describing the launch of Spira.

Introduction

Welcome to this workbook for the BTEC module Market Relations.

This is a book specifically designed for use by students studying on BTEC Higher National programmes in Business, Business and Finance, Business and Marketing and Business and Personnel. However, it can be also used by people who wish to learn about this aspect of business.

How to use the workbook

Please feel free to:

○ write notes in the margins

○ underline and highlight important words or phrases.

As you work through this module, you will find activities have been built in. These are designed to make you stop to think and answer questions.

There are four types of activities.

Memory and recall These are straightforward tests of how much text you are able to remember.

Self-assessed tasks (SATs) These are used to test your understanding of the text you are studying or to apply the principles and practices learnt to a related problem.

Exercises These are open-ended questions that can be used as a basis for classroom or group debate. If you do not belong to a study group, use the exercises to think through issues raised by the text.

Assignments These are tasks set for students studying at a BTEC centre which would normally require a written answer to be looked at by your tutor. If you are not following a course at college, the assignments are still a useful way of developing and testing your understanding of the module.

There are answer boxes provided below each activity in this module. Use these boxes to summarise your answers and findings. If you need more space, use the margins of the book or separate sheets of paper to make notes and write a full answer.

Managing tasks and solving problems ✔

EXAMPLE ACTIVITY

As an 'icebreaker' try this exercise.

List three products you bought recently. Why did you buy them rather than competing brands?

Commentary...

You could have brought a particular make of jeans because they are the height of fashion. In the supermarket, you might have chosen an own-brand detergent because it was significantly cheaper. The batteries you brought may have been the most expensive on offer but they have a reputation for long life. The point to note is that consumers' needs and perceptions of products are key elements in developing a market strategy.

The emphasis of the workbook is to provide you with tasks that relate to the general operating environment of business. The work that you do on these tasks enables you to develop your BTEC common skills and a skills chart is provided at the end of this introduction for you to note your practice of each skill. One sheet is probably not enough, so cut this sheet out and photocopy it when you require new sheets.

Aims of the workbook

This workbook looks at how organisations satisfy the needs of their customers and stakeholders, and their social responsibilities. It provides an understanding of the approaches of marketing-orientated businesses and describes how to collect data and analyse the market-place.

The book has four sections which are designed to cover the learning outcomes (as shown in bold in the boxes below) for this core module. These are as given in the BTEC publication (code 02–104–4) on the Higher National programmes in Business Studies. Where appropriate, BTEC's suggested content may be reordered within the sections of this book.

SECTION ONE: MARKETING ORIENTATION

On completion of this section, you should be able to:

> ▶ **evaluate the effectiveness of a production and marketing orientation as the basis for business operations under different conditions**

> ▶ **identify and analyse relationships within the marketing system**

> ▶ **identify and evaluate how business environmental forces affect marketing**

Content

Marketing and the marketing concept: definitions of marketing; the origins of the marketing concept and its development; how to distinguish between needs, wants and demands; the concept of relationship marketing and the benefits of working in partnerships.

Marketing and the business environment: the workings of the market system; the environment in which businesses must operate and how it can be affected by global events; DEPICTS analysis of the factors influencing the business environment.

SECTION TWO: STAKEHOLDERS AND SOCIAL RESPONSIBILITIES

On completion of this section, you should be able to:

> ▶ **identify and assess the aspirations of stakeholders**

> ▶ **review the effectiveness of approaches by organisations to satisfy stakeholders**

> ▶ **identify the social responsibilities of marketing and evaluate organisational responses**

Content

Stakeholders and marketing communications: the groups that influence company policy and balancing conflicts of interest between them; the stakeholder model of corporate behaviour; public relations as a communication tool and why companies publicise their activities; the importance of favourable publicity; press coverage and press releases.

Responsibility to society: marketing ethics and the issues of ethical advertising and marketing behaviour; the relationship between marketeers and society and the impact on businesses of consumers' values and beliefs; why companies must be environmentally aware and responsive; consumerism as a force in the market.

SECTION THREE: ANALYSING THE MARKET

On completion of this section, you should be able to:

> ▶ **investigate and report on the organisation's position in its market**

▶ **select and use appropriate data collection methods**

▶ **identify, evaluate and apply analytical techniques**

Content

Competitive position: how markets can be segmented and the variables used to analyse this segmentation; lifestyle segmentation and targeting groups; product positioning and strategies for influencing how consumers think about products and services; the cycle of adoption of new products.

Types of data: gathering data for marketing research; the market research process and test marketing; using data to develop a business strategy; finding and using secondary data.

Survey planning: the main types of survey and sampling methods; how to conduct a survey; interview techniques and questionnaire design.

Analytical techniques: the importance of analysing data; calculating mean, mode and median values; distribution and measures of spread; time series analysis; correlation to establish associations between sets of data.

SECTION FOUR: THE COMPETITIVE PROCESS

On completion of this section, you should be able to:

▶ **analyse the interaction of market forces**

▶ **analyse features of consumer, industrial and service markets**

▶ **identify and describe key features of alternative marketing and other competitive strategies**

Content

Market features: what you need to know about competitors; the differences between industrial and consumer markets; the behaviour of consumers and industrial buyers; the development and marketing of services.

Strategies: the Porter five-forces model of industrial competitiveness; the Boston Consulting Group's approach to strategic planning; stages in a product's life cycle; the decision-making framework of the Ansoff product–market matrix.

Market Structure: regulation of markets and businesses; perfect competition, oligopoly and monopoly; competition within the public services; public sector organisations and customer-centred operations.

In working through the BTEC Higher National programme in Business Studies, you will practise the following BTEC common skills:

Managing and developing self	✔
Working with and relating to others	✔
Communicating	✔
Managing tasks and solving problems	✔
Applying numeracy	✔
Applying technology	✔
Applying design and creativity	✔

You will practise most of these skills in working through this module.

Recommended reading

Kotler, Philip, 1994, *Marketing Management: Analysis Planning, Implementation and Control*, 8th edition, Prentice Hall International.

Christopher, Martin, Payne, Adrian and Ballentyne, David, 1991, *Relationship Marketing – Bringing Quality Customer Service and Marketing Together*, Butterworth Heinemann.

Doyle, Peter, 1994, *Marketing Management and Strategy*, Prentice Hall International.

Dibb, Sally and Simkin, Lyndon, 1994, *The Marketing Casebook – Cases and Concepts*, Routledge.

Pearson, David and Fifield, Paul, 1995, *The CIM Diploma Case Study Book 1995–96*, 2nd edition, Butterworth Heinemann in conjunction with the Chartered Institute of Marketing.

PERIODICALS

Student members of the Chartered Institute of Marketing can receive *Marketing Business*, a magazine published by the CIM. It covers the latest thinking and activity throughout the world of marketing.

The *Journal of Marketing Management*, also published by the CIM, is the UK's best-known specialist marketing journal. It offers an in-depth analysis of the field.

Name

Module

BTEC Skill	Activity No./Date	Activity No./Date	Activity No./Date	Activity No./Date	Activity No./Date	Activity No./Date
Managing and developing self						
Working with and relating to others						
Communicating						
Managing tasks and solving problems						
Applying numeracy						
Applying technology						
Applying design and creativity						

Marketing Orientation

Marketing and the marketing concept

Objectives

After participating in this session, you should be able to:

▶ define marketing

▶ explain the differences between production, sales management and marketing orientation

▶ distinguish between needs, wants and demand

▶ understand the concept of relationship marketing

▶ explain the benefits that arise from entering into partnerships.

In working through this session, you will practise the following BTEC common skills:

Managing and developing self	✔
Working with and relating to others	
Communicating	✔
Managing tasks and solving problems	✔
Applying numeracy	
Applying technology	
Applying design and creativity	

Introduction to marketing

Although you have probably not studied marketing before, it is almost certain that you are familiar with the term. Marketing is a dynamic and wide-ranging subject. It is highly practical in that it influences not only what businesses actually do, but how well they do it. It is also a subject which has attracted a lot of attention from academics. They have developed theories and models which can help to explain and develop the marketing-based approach to business.

Given the scope of marketing, it is not surprising that you come into contact with aspects of it every day of your lives.

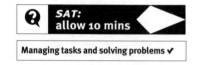

SAT:
allow 10 mins

Managing tasks and solving problems ✔

ACTIVITY 1

Write down five ways in which you come into contact with various aspects of marketing from the moment you wake up until you retire at night on a typical day.

Commentary...

Most of you will have thought of the choices available to you, the purchases you make, and the advertisements that you see or read.

For example, when you wake up you decide what to eat – cereals, a cooked breakfast or toast. If you choose a cereal, what kind of cereal should it be – cornflakes, porridge, muesli or one of the many other varieties?

Do you watch early morning television? If so, which channel do you choose? Is it to be breakfast television or GMTV? On ITV or Channel 4, you will see television advertising – these advertising messages are aimed specifically at the breakfast audience. Do you listen to the radio? Which station do you choose? If it is a commercial station, then you will hear radio advertising.

Are you ready to have a wash and brush your teeth? Do you use a facial scrub, a washing cream or soap? Which is your favourite brand? Do you use a toothpaste which fights cavities, freshens breath or both? Is it a gel or a paste? Which flavour do you use? Do you use dental floss? Is it waxed or unwaxed?

Have you time to read the paper before leaving for college? Which one is it to be? Why do you read it? Some tabloid papers (such as the *Star, Mirror* and *Sun*) contain a lot of advertising in them.

Ready for college? Do you travel by car, train, bus, taxi, bicycle or on foot? On your journey, you might talk to friends about fashion, music, football, environmental issues and so on. You might change your views as a result of these conversations.

On your way to college, you might see advertising on billboards and posters. Shops and businesses display names, logos and messages to catch your attention. It is impossible to take in all the messages directed at you.

It is lunchtime. Do you eat on the premises? If so, is it to be the canteen or a snack from a vending machine? Do you choose a hot meal, a sandwich, or do you bring your own food? If you go outside, is it to a snack bar, a restaurant, a pub or a fish and chip shop? Your choice is of critical importance for these businesses as they battle for your custom.

Having arrived home from college (possibly reading an evening newspaper on the way) you switch on the television. Apart from anything else, the news may interest you. It might feature corporate strategies, business expansion, consumer trends, unemployment, trade figures and company executives explaining their corporate plans. Political and technical changes are presented in relation to the future of society.

In the evening, you decide to go out. The pub? A nightclub? The cinema? A football match? Once again the choice of entertainment is yours – at a price.

You arrive home and are ready for bed. You take one last look at the television, again more adverts, possibly a programme on business. How about a final drink? Tea, coffee or cocoa? And so to sleep.

You can see that, as a customer, you have immense power. The actions of customers determine which companies and products succeed and, conversely, those which fail. Size is no guarantee of success. Unilever, a very large UK company making soap and detergents, has been forced to take a product called 'Persil Power' off the market. This is because it has been conclusively proved to damage clothes over a series of washes. If the product was not withdrawn from sales, angry customers might not have trusted any of the company's products again. This would have led to enormous losses in profits.

FIGURE 1.1: *The marketing approach.*

Figure 1.1 shows the range of functions which are covered by the term marketing. The marketing approach incorporates and integrates all these functions. Here is a brief overview of some key issues in each area.

New products and services

Firms try to guarantee their future survival by developing new products and services. They need to ask some key questions: What benefits do consumers require? Is it technically feasible? How quickly will it date?

Pricing

How much will customers pay? What are the costs that must be covered? Is there a link between price and quality?

Distribution

What is the most effective way to distribute products? Can distribution be streamlined to save costs?

Packaging

How can the company use less packaging? Can this reduction become part of an environmental campaign? Does the product need to be tamperproof?

Advertising

Which media should be used (press, television, radio, cinema, posters)? How can the target audience be reached with effective messages at a reasonable cost? Should the advertising be based on humour, or not?

Sales promotion

Would the product benefit from in-store displays and demonstrations? Should the product have special offers?

Public relations

Companies need to concentrate on communication and publicity.

Sponsorship

Is it worthwhile to sponsor a sports event to increase awareness? Should the company sponsor a worthy cause?

Sales

This is only one aspect of marketing – some people think marketing is only about sales, but this is not so. Issues in this area include sales force size and sales territory planning.

After-sales service

What happens if the product breaks down or the service is poor? Warranties and guarantees may be offered, as may telephone hot-line emergency numbers.

Competitive analysis

Who are the main competitors? What are their strengths and weaknesses?

Business analysis and planning

How quickly should the company expand? What financial controls need to be in operation?

Marketing research

What is the size of the market? What do customers think about the service the company offers?

It can be seen that marketing encompasses a wide range of functions. It has a vital role to play in developing successful businesses.

Marketing definitions

Before examining the components of a marketing orientation in some detail, it is necessary to attempt to define marketing. This is not easy, as numerous definitions exist. However, many definitions stress the same fundamental points.

> **!?!** The Chartered Institute of Marketing offers this definition:
> '**Marketing** is the management process responsible for identifying, anticipating and satisfying customer requirements profitably.'

This definition shows how wide-ranging marketing is, and how it covers far more than just selling. Let us pick out some of the key words in the definition to show the breadth of coverage. **Identify** – this implies the need to undertake market research. **Anticipate** – this means predicting customer requirements, and improving and adapting products and services. **Satisfy** – this means ensuring that the customer is happy with the price, performance, design and quality of the product or service offered.

> **True marketing starts out with the customers, their demographics, related needs and values. It does not ask: What do we want to sell? It asks: What does the customer want to buy? It does not say: This is what our product or service does. It says: These are the satisfactions the customer looks for.**
>
> Peter Drucker, 1991, *Management,* London: Pan, p.59.

ACTIVITY 2

Review these two definitions (by the Chartered Institute of Marketing and Peter Drucker) and write down their central feature in the box below.

SAT:
allow 5 mins

Managing tasks and solving problems ✔

Commentary...

Customer orientation or the emphasis on how to provide customers with both current and future needs is the central feature of a marketing philosophy. This means the organisation must be integrated so that marketing becomes the aim of the whole company rather than a specific department.

EXCHANGE AND VALUE

Marketing is a social and managerial process by which individuals and groups obtain what they need and want through creating, offering and exchanging products of value with others.

Philip Kotler, 1994, *Marketing Management*, 8th edn, New Jersey: Prentice Hall International, p.6.

The customer pays a price for a given article, but customers are also giving the company their loyalty and trust. If customers are pleased with what the company provides then they may reward it with a lifetime of loyal custom; over time their purchases add up to a considerable sum. Think of a bank which recruits customers as students and receives their loyal custom over a lifetime. Many students take up well-paid jobs and demand a range of financial products throughout their lives. The bank will not lose these customers if it fulfils their needs competently, thus minimising the costly business of recruiting new customers.

The same issues apply to business. Banks are not only concerned with individual accounts but with obtaining and holding company accounts too. When a company prices a given product or service, it has to be confident that the customer will consider that price good value, taking into account quality, reliability and competitive alternatives.

The key to a successful exchange relationship is that both parties are totally satisfied with the price paid. Then the relationship is likely to be a long-term one. The Arthur Daley character might sell a dodgy car to a trusting customer once, but never again. This is a one-off sale to a gullible customer.

Figure 1.2 shows several critical propositions in a marketing orientation. Companies that fully incorporate all four components can be described as fully marketing oriented but many firms are only part of the way to achieving this state.

1 Customers and their requirements are given absolute priority when plans and strategies are devised.

2 Long-term, mutually beneficial exchange relationships are considered to be critical.

3 The whole organisation is integrated around marketing. Marketing becomes the 'hub' of the organisational 'wheel'.

4 Marketing is felt to be the best organisational defence against competitive attack, and proactive method of attracting new customers and developing new markets.

Note: the use of all four components implies a strong marketing orientation using less than all four implies a weaker orientation.

FIGURE 1.2: *The crucial components of a marketing orientation.*

ACTIVITY 3

Reread the Chartered Institute of Marketing definition of marketing. Do you feel it takes into account all the points in figure 1.2? Suggest a fuller definition of marketing.

SAT:
allow 10 mins ?

Communicating ✔

Managing tasks and solving problems ✔

Commentary...

The strength of the Chartered Institute of Marketing definition is its focus on the customer. However, given the developments in the pace of technological change, and in the growth of competition on a world-wide scale, it can be argued that the definition does not pay sufficient attention to the competitive aspect. The actions of companies must take competitors into account because they are a very important factor when making key decisions such as whether to enter a given market. Hence, the words 'taking the actions and reactions of competitors fully into account' could be added to the end of the Chartered Institute of Marketing definition.

The origins and development of the marketing concept

Differences of opinion exist as to the exact nature of the development of the marketing concept. However, a mainstream view has emerged. The Scottish economist Adam Smith in his work *An Inquiry into the Nature and Causes of The Wealth of Nations* (1776) wrote: 'Consumption is the sole end of all production.' This was a far-sighted way of thinking at a time when the key emphasis was on increasing productive capacity to satisfy the massive demand for goods and services as the Industrial Revolution began to gather pace.

THE ORIGINS AND DEVELOPMENT
OF THE MARKETING CONCEPT

Let us now examine how this production orientation was replaced by a sales management orientation, which has been replaced in some companies by a marketing orientation. (It is, however, important to remember that many businesses are still basically production or sales management oriented.)

PRODUCTION ORIENTATION

In the so-called production era, which ran from the Industrial Revolution in the late eighteenth century until the early part of the twentieth century in the UK, the emphasis was on the production of standard products at the lowest possible unit cost. For example, furniture and household goods were produced in huge quantities to standard designs. This maximised the profits of ambitious entrepreneurs who sold their products to people in the rapidly growing towns and cities. Indeed, from an economic viewpoint, given that there was an excess demand over supply for goods, it could be argued that it was sensible to concentrate on supply-side issues. These issues included taking advantage of economies of scale, negotiating low prices by bulk buying of components, and reducing costs by increased machine and labour efficiency. The net result was increased profits. The individual customer still had sovereignty, in that they could buy or not buy from whom they liked, but there was always another customer to replace them. Professor Michael Baker refers to a production orientation as a 'take it or leave it' attitude (Marketing Education Group Conference Paper; New Product Development and Marketing Strategy, Lancaster, July 1974, p.108, pp.108—19), for precisely this reason.

SALES MANAGEMENT ORIENTATION

Gradually, customers became wealthier and more discerning and began to realise that they had the power to choose from a widening range of options. The philosophy of Henry Ford, that a customer can have 'any colour as long as it is black' is of little use if the competition offers red and green as well as black. From the early twentieth century, many companies decided to move to a sales management orientation. This can be summarised as 'selling what the company can make'. It is characterised by two main approaches: the hard sell and product differentiation.

The hard sell

This implies financial incentives to increase sales. These include money-off offers, more-for-less bargains, and so on. Think of the present day price wars in the airline, newspaper and supermarket businesses to see how this can affect a company's profit. The hard sell is a very short-term solution to the strategic issue of conducting business profitably. If the current newspaper price war continues, it is almost certain that at least one newspaper will go into liquidation. Most businesses try not to become involved in costly price wars, but in a recession many companies find that they can only survive by aiming for the hard sell.

Product differentiation

Here, a firm seeks to develop some distinguishing feature of its product or service and to avoid head-on price competition with suppliers of similar products or services. Marketeers refer to these distinguishing features as unique selling propositions – watch out for them when you watch television adverts. For example, the advert for Mr Sheen furniture polish stresses how a new anti-static agent helps it to clean more effectively than ever before.

The main aim of a sales management orientation is to make an attempt to sell those products which a company can make effectively. Notice how this is an improvement on the 'take it or leave it' approach of a production orientation. The realisation is that competitive pressure makes it important to actually sell the product rather than waiting for someone to buy it.

MARKETING ORIENTATION

The marketing orientation was first developed in America in the late nineteenth century and the early twentieth century. A marketing orientation is built on the philosophy that supply issues should be less important than demand issues. This can be seen in figure 1.3, which highlights the key factors. Understanding the nature of demand, and being able to influence demand has to take top priority. A major task of marketing management is to induce consumers to demand more of a company's product or service, and to place a higher value on it.

THE ORIGINS AND DEVELOPMENT

OF THE MARKETING CONCEPT

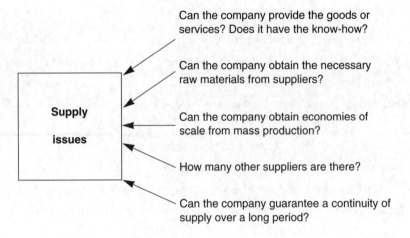

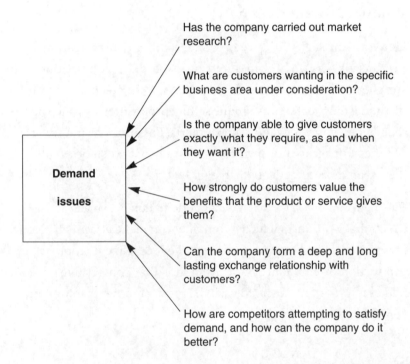

FIGURE 1.3: *Demand and supply considerations.*

After the end of rationing in the 1950s, consumers in the UK began to enjoy an immense choice. Since then, many UK businesses have moved to a marketing orientation. The key management task is to understand the requirements of the customers. The emphasis is on 'making only what can be sold' – the direct opposite of a production orientation, and a clear improvement upon trying to sell customers products and services which they do not really want. Making only what the customers want to buy means that companies should not have to resort to the hard-sell tactics of price cutting and discounting. The marketing orientation is more likely to achieve the right exchange relationship.

At the pre-production stage, a marketing orientation means that firms spend time and money on various forms of market research to understand the requirements of customers for particular categories of goods and services. When Cadbury's launched the successful Wispa Bar in the early 1980s, it researched and planned all aspects of the customer requirements, the product and packaging, and the communications policy. The company used full-page newspaper advertisements to promote the bar. It became a major success.

Finally, when a company adopts a marketing orientation, it is important that its organisational structure is integrated – so that marketing becomes the central focus of the organisation – and that it has effective interactions between areas such as production, finance and personnel.

FIGURE 1.4: *An advertisement from Daewoo's 1995 campaign illustrating the marketing orientation. (continues overleaf)*

THE ORIGINS AND DEVELOPMENT
OF THE MARKETING CONCEPT

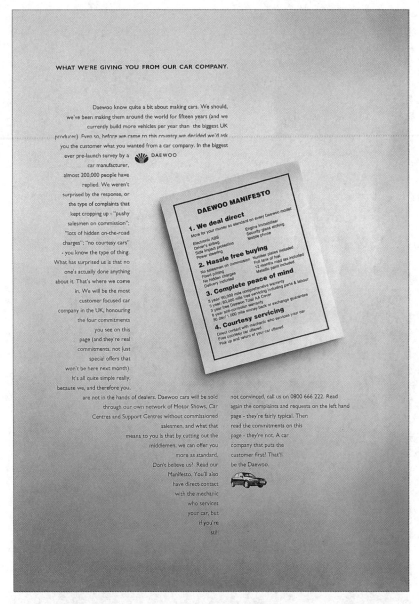

FIGURE 1.4: *Daewoo's advertisement (continued)*

**SAT:
allow 15 mins**

Managing tasks and solving problems ✔

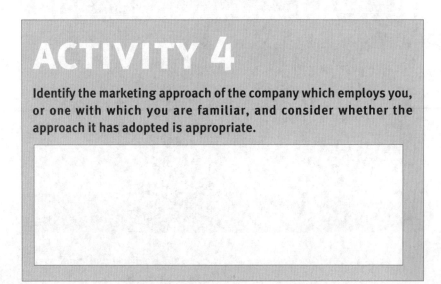

ACTIVITY 4

Identify the marketing approach of the company which employs you, or one with which you are familiar, and consider whether the approach it has adopted is appropriate.

Commentary...

The key differences between the orientations can be summed up as

- ◉ production – a supply-side approach, 'take it or leave it'

- ◉ sales – selling products actively once they have been produced

- ◉ marketing – demand-side issues are crucial.

Considering whether the approach adopted by the company you chose is appropriate asks you to make a subjective judgement. Without carrying out a good deal of market research, it is not possible to answer the question fully. It is likely, however, in view of our previous discussions on the three orientations, that you have made the judgement that the market orientation will be the 'best' approach in instances where purchasing power and consumer goods are concerned. The same judgement is also likely to apply to suppliers of business or industrial products, because many of the same consumer issues apply in suitability for purpose, quality and so on.

Needs, wants and demand

To fully understand the significance of a marketing orientation, it is important to distinguish between needs, wants and demand. A **need** is an absolute necessity to maintain life. Air, food, water, clothing and shelter are needs and, in the industrialised world, these absolute essentials are often taken for granted.

NEEDS, WANTS AND DEMAND

Consumer choice and preferences play a major role in satisfying **wants**. Wants are an extension of needs, and it is very difficult to separate customers' perceptions of what is a need and what is a want. Wants are not essential. They can be defined as consumer desires backed up by an ability and willingness to pay for them. Wars and famines show people with real needs – there is no question of wants in such instances.

Wants are physically non-essential, but they become psychologically essential to a given consumer. Consumers who have achieved their ambition to own a Rolls-Royce have exercised their choice to own a fast luxurious car. It has a number of functional benefits such as speed and comfort, but is also confers on them the status and recognition that arises from a visual symbol of their wealth. They have backed up their want for a luxurious fast car and its associated benefits with the means and willingness to pay. It would be very difficult for these customers to substitute a Mini for the Rolls-Royce, even though they perform the same basic function.

A **demand** is created when consumers show a willingness to pay the set price for a product or service. Consumer wants are becoming increasingly sophisticated due to constantly rising expectations and increased purchasing power, and once consumer wants are achieved, they assume the same psychological status as needs. It is very difficult for consumers to give up something which they have taken for granted. As people become wealthier, the boundaries between needs and wants become blurred. Most people in the UK consider clothes a need. A fashion conscious teenager might consider Levi 501s to be a need rather than a want, in order to maintain a certain self-image.

A want only becomes important in marketing terms when it is supported by an ability and willingness to pay the price of satisfying it. Many people dream of wants which are unattainable. See how the football pools use this to attract customers. In effect, they are saying to customers: 'Now you can have all of your wants without having to compromise on essential purchases.' This is a powerful and emotive communications device. The National Lottery uses the same approach to encourage people to buy a ticket for £1 in the hope of becoming a millionaire.

THE FUTURE

Given the rate of technological innovation, and our human ingenuity in designing and creating ever more sophisticated ways of doing things, the prediction of future consumer lifestyles and trends is important for companies. Think of the recent growth of Direct Line Insurance and First Direct. These are both financial service companies organised to provide a first-class service via the telephone for the customer. They offer speed and convenience without the need to visit a bank or insurance office. The telephone network and a customer information system have made these services possible.

Consider the number of people in the UK who are divorced or single. A product like Menumaster, a frozen main meal is 'created for the way you live today'. It promises speed, convenience, health and an active lifestyle. It is essentially targeted at people who live alone, and who have a busy social life. It gives these people specific benefits in a simple, easy-to-use form. They are low in calories, the ingredients are healthy, and they can be cooked quickly in the microwave.

In the near future, home shopping and entertainment services may make the traditional ways of shopping and consumer spending obsolete. Television will become an interactive medium which will allow consumers to buy from home by viewing products on the screen. Should you want entertainment, you would call up videos from a massive computerised video library. Convenience is the key, and consumers will pay extra for this as an alternative to going out.

Home shopping could become the accepted way of shopping. Businesses who are threatened in this way (such as high street shops and video stores) need to address their competitive response now. For example, high street shops could offer free home delivery as part of their service. Video stores could consider selling more than videos, perhaps wine and snacks to offer 'a great night in'. Notice how this response from video stores would threaten the local pub trade, and the local small shops. They, in turn, would need to consider their competitive response.

Creativity and innovation in meeting the requirements of consumers will be increasingly important as competition becomes increasingly global. People involved in marketing must constantly evaluate the way in which products and services are perceived by consumers. They have to be responsive to changes in society and they have to ensure that consumers can afford to translate their wants into a specific demand for their product or service. Young boys often want a fast car such as a Ferrari, but most people who buy such cars are wealthy men in their late thirties. Marketeers must constantly focus on the reality of the purchasing decisions made by consumers. This is why it is such a practical and pragmatic subject.

BEWKES LIMITED

Bewkes Limited is a company which prides itself on tradition. Founded in 1847, it is a manufacturer of sticky sweets such as mintballs and gobstoppers. This type of product is known in the trade as sugar confectionery. Polo mints, produced by Rowntree are perhaps the best known sugar confectionery product in the UK. The segment of the market is showing minimal growth overall. The chocolate confectionery market (products like Flake and Mars Bar) is growing at nearly 4 per cent per year. The snackfood market (crisps, nuts, etc.) is growing at nearly 8 per cent per annum. Products such as KitKat and ice-cream bars have 'crossover' appeal; they are bought as both a chocolate confection and a snack.

The board of directors of Bewkes Limited met recently to discuss the present market situation. It is not good. The company only operates in the sugar confectionery market and its products are aimed at young people under 12 years of age. It does not export, nor does it have a marketing manager. Sales are down from £5 million per annum to £4 million per annum in the last year, and the factory is operating at only 50 per cent of its productive capacity. The company has begun to lose money. Half of the 250 staff are threatened with redundancy. One of the board members argued that the company is set in its ways, and is not paying enough attention to market conditions. The chairman replied that the company, in his opinion, 'makes the best sweets in the country' and has 'very loyal staff', including 'superb sales representatives'. He went on to say that the company had 'always pulled through'. The finance director made the following statement to the board: 'In view of the grave situation, and with several of our products making losses, this could be the last board meeting of Bewkes Limited.'

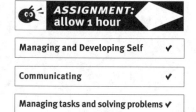

ASSIGNMENT:
allow 1 hour

Managing and Developing Self	✔
Communicating	✔
Managing tasks and solving problems	✔

ACTIVITY 5

Bewkes Limited has decided to appointed a marketing manager. Acting as the new marketing manager, draw up a short initial report for your board of directors. Making use of the material in this session, your report should:

- **diagnose where you feel Bewkes Limited is going wrong in its approach to marketing**

- **describe the essential steps that you feel that this company should take to develop a marketing orientation.**

Produce a 600-word report for submission to your tutor and summarise your findings in the box below.

Relationship marketing

> **!?!** **Relationship marketing** brings together quality issues and customer service management within a marketing orientation. This is done both to attract customers and to maintain their loyalty over a protracted period in the face of severe competition.

The relationship marketing process seems set to dominate the way in which firms try to enhance their competitive position as we approach the next century. It encompasses a number of complementary perspectives, with the aim of achieving synergy between them. Synergy means that the whole becomes greater than the sum of the parts. For example, when an airline such as British Airways attempts to provide an improved level of customer service, it has to involve its employees and, perhaps, upgrade its operational methods and information systems.

Relationship marketing has three key aspects.

- The emphasis is on a move from all forms of one-off sales transactions towards a **long-term relationship** approach aimed at maximising **customer retention rates**. The high street banks have regularly been accused of poor customer service; in the face of this criticism, Barclays has recently stressed the relationship approach in its recent press advertising.

- In addition to customers, the organisation becomes concerned with the development of **relationships with other external markets**. American Professor Shelby Hunt (guest lecturer, MEG Conference, 4 July 1994, Coleraine, N. Ireland) has described ten such relationships split into four types of partnerships –

supplier partnerships, internal partnerships, buyer partnerships and lateral partnerships (see figure 1.5).

● Relationship marketing is based on the recognition that quality, customer service and marketing activities should all focus on one central issue: **satisfying the customer**.

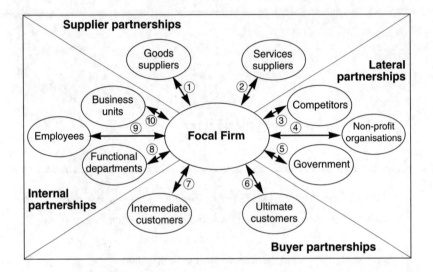

FIGURE 1.5: *Key exchanges in relationship marketing.*

INTERNAL PARTNERSHIP

Internal partnerships are often grouped together under the term internal marketing. This approach treats employees as **internal customers**; people who buy the product or service are the external customers.

Internal marketing brings together four key disciplines:

1. human resource management

2. marketing

3. training

4. behavioural sciences.

The aim is to match the needs and values of the workforce with the aims and objectives of the organisation in order to achieve the objectives of the company effectively. This matching is done by making sure that everyone in the organisation is committed to quality and customer service. In Japanese companies, this is the normal way of carrying out the business of the firm. In the UK, this process is likely to develop rapidly over the next ten years. The very latest term for this process is **TIMAQ: total integration of marketing and quality**.

You may have heard of the quality standards BS5750 or ISO9000. BS5750 is the accepted quality assurance standard in the UK and ISO9000 is the international equivalent. To obtain BS5750 certification, companies must undergo a detailed evaluation of their processes and products by an approved quality inspector. Firms who achieve these standards have to go through a rigorous process to show how quality is built into products and services through investment in training and equipment, and by a customer focus – they are carrying out internal marketing by another name. All kinds of firms, of all sizes, aim for the quality standard BS5750. When you see business programmes on television, you will notice how often quality issues are stressed by the participants.

ACTIVITY 6

Imagine that you have visited a fast-food restaurant such as McDonald's. Examine what aspects of customer service and quality are important to you. List the key points below.

SAT:
allow 15 mins ②

Managing tasks and solving problems ✔

Commentary...

In terms of customer service, you would want a friendly greeting and courtesy. You would not expect to be interrupted during your meal. If you have a complaint, you would expect it to be dealt with in a reasonable manner. Being a fast-food outlet, you would expect to be served quickly. (The company expects you to consume it quickly to create table space for others.) In terms of quality, you want nutritious, well-prepared food, without too many additives. You want the chips to be crisp and not greasy, and any salads or dressings to be crisp and fresh. You will set the price of this against your own value of it. If you feel it is good value, you will probably return.

Business units

Business units are different parts of a company operating with individual profit responsibility. Large companies, in particular, are normally divided into different business units. For example, the computer company, IBM UK, has nine identifiable business units for corporate customer accounts:

1. banking

2. insurance

3. retail

4. local government

5. national government

6. utilities

7. transport and communications

8. production and engineering

9. oil, pharmaceuticals and chemicals.

The aim of this nine-way split is to be more responsive in the market place, and to satisfy customers according to their specific requirements.

As part of an internal partnership approach to the whole company, it is essential that the activities of different business units are carefully co-ordinated. For example, in the search for new product ideas within a company every functional department would be expected to make an input in one way or another. This could be via a suggestion scheme, or involvement in a planning meeting or a brainstorming session. Every department in the organisation has to have its focus on the ultimate customer.

SUPPLIER PARTNERSHIPS

Supplier partnerships are critical within the context of a relationship marketing process. Suppliers and their customers are increasingly looking to develop long-term co-operation – this is in direct contrast to an adversarial approach in which each side aims to gain the better deal. In terms of a trade-off, the aim is to give both sides equal benefits from a mutually beneficial exchange relationship.

Companies rely on suppliers to deliver the raw materials and components they need to make the products that the final customer will want to buy. For example, a car manufacturer needs steel, wheels, electrical parts and other items such as upholstery and radiators. It needs to ensure a regular supply of these items, at the right price and of an acceptable quality.

A company like Nissan attempts to save money by eliminating the piles of stocks of components it carries; it operates a JIT (just-in-time) policy. Stocks are constantly being used, and new supplies are ordered only as and when required – this greatly reduces stock holding costs. This means there is an absolute need for an excellent relationship between Nissan and its suppliers. Such a partnership between a firm and its suppliers is called a **co-makership** or a **vendor partnership**.

We can take a further example of a lateral supplier partnership from Japan. The **keiretsu** are groups of companies that form corporate families. They are bound together by mutual shareholding or other financial and business links (shared research or product development deals, for example), and they co-operate with each other very closely. Because Toyota's keiretsu includes Koito Manufacturing, a car parts company, Koito has special privileges when supplying parts to Toyota; other companies find it difficult to compete with this unique situation.

LATERAL PARTNERSHIPS

Companies who sell equipment of an infrastructural nature, such as nuclear reactors, telephone systems and defence equipment have to understand the importance of political links. In practice, regulatory bodies often provide a clear link between firms and the government. For example, the gas, water and electricity companies are carefully regulated and their profits are monitored to ensure that the customer is not paying an excessive price for these utilities. It is important that these companies put across their point of view to the government on issues such as investment and future business strategy.

Competitors actions have to be monitored and carefully evaluated, in order to see how they affect the organisation. Companies need to investigate possible areas in which collaborations or mergers could be beneficial. With the formation of the single European market, the possibilities for such alliances seem set to increase. For example, to avoid a price war, the major firms in the oil industry do not compete on price. The major firms in the airline industry would prefer not to have too much competition on any particular routes following deregulation, as that could lead to fierce price wars. The bad relationship between Virgin and British Airways could be said to be damaging to them both, as it prevents them from negotiating on issues such as on which routes to compete.

Relationship marketing is rather like a marriage. The marriage of the firm and its partners thrives on co-operation, commitment and trust. Professor Shelby Hunt has pointed out that relationship marketing implies that managers of firms should:

1. choose partners carefully

2. structure partnerships carefully

3. allow time for relationship growth

4. maintain open lines of communication

5. maintain a corporate culture that is trustworthy.

BUYER PARTNERSHIPS

Relationship marketing is important because firms want to keep customers for life. This minimises the costs of recruiting new customers, and it guarantees firms a steady income from customers over time.

Very small businesses such as hairdressers, newsagents and tobacconists have always known that to stay in business they have to keep a loyal base of regular customers. Notice how the owner will often call you by your first name, and will ask how you and your family are doing. This is good manners and very good business. Relationships are the key to commercial success at every level.

Let us take the example of Mrs Jones. Mrs Jones shops at her local supermarket and spends £30 each week on groceries. One day, a check-out assistant is very rude to her – she feels deeply aggrieved. Despite having shopped at the store for four years, she decides to take her custom to a competitor. This might not sound so serious; the supermarket has only lost the custom of one person. However, if we take a **lifetime customer value approach**, and assume that Mrs Jones has another 30 years of loyal grocery shopping left, then on a weekly 30 average bill, she might be expected to spend a further £46,800 at the store, ignoring effects of inflation. Having felt aggrieved by poor customer service, Mrs Jones may tell relatives and friends about it. If two of those decide to switch their allegiance and if they too spend £30 each week, then assuming a 30-year shopping life, the supermarket has lost £140,400 in potential revenue. The effect is not trivial at all, and this is why internal marketing, in the form of a focus on customer service, is imperative in the battle to retain loyal customers.

It is important that businesses understand the lifetime value of a loyal customer. Equally valuable is a corporate account. If we take the example of a company awarding its corporate account to an airline, it is important that the airline maintains a dialogue with the corporate buyer who actually made the purchase. The airline must ensure that corporate passengers receive a first class service both in the air and on the ground. (Corporate passengers are often regular flyers and they will be critical of poor service.) The airline must endeavour to understand the needs of the corporate flyers. For example, the airline could have special arrangements with hotel groups, restaurants and theatres to sell a total corporate work and entertainment package. This is the relationship theme in action again.

Marketing then is about customers, competition, profit and survival. Indeed, one American expert summed it up when asked what marketing was about he replied, 'everything' (Regis McKenna, 1991, *Harvard Business Review*).

RELATIONSHIP MARKETING

Communicating ✔

Managing tasks and solving problems ✔

ACTIVITY 7

In a recent two-page advertisement in the quality press for the Marriott Hotel group, one page shows a picture of a dark rain-lashed street with a waiter entering a car. Underneath the picture, it says: 'Based on a true story which took place in Bristol, March 1993.' The next page gives a brief description in quotation marks, to make it appear as if a guest is speaking. It says: 'I couldn't sleep without my favourite bedtime drink. But the tireless Marriott waiter didn't rest until he'd found it.' It then tells how, on finding none of the drink in stock, the waiter drove off to fulfil the order. It took him 30 minutes, and he made no special charge to the guest for the time it took. The quote then concludes: 'I understand Marriott staff often go out of their way for the benefit of their guests. They call it empowerment. It's the reason why I'll never tire of recommending Marriott Hotels to friends and colleagues of mine.'

Critically assess what this advertisement is trying to achieve. In particular, say how it brings in a relationship approach. Summarise your findings in 150 words and note your key findings in the box below.

Commentary...

It would be correct to say that the aim of all advertising is to increase awareness and encourage the purchase of the product or service. This advertisement is very carefully presented to appeal to people who might stay in hotels when travelling, as part of their jobs, as well as on holidays.

It is also presenting an important image of customer care. The waiter did not say: 'We have no drink X, how about drink Y?' Instead, he took time to make sure the customer received what he had asked for.

The benefit to the organisation lies in the fact that this satisfied customer is now an advocate of the company. (Remember Mrs Jones at the supermarket? She was the opposite of a loyal customer, as she positively encouraged friends to go elsewhere.) The Marriott advocate is likely to return the commitment and loyalty shown by the waiter by telling friends. If only a few friends visit and are pleased, then they may tell other friends. This kind of word of mouth advocacy is far more effective than advertising. This is why the words 'based on a true story' are important.

The company has now set very high standards of customer service expectations which it must maintain if it is not to create disappointed customers who will then choose to stay in other hotels.

TRADITIONAL VERSUS NETWORK COMPETITION

One of the main reasons why Shelby Hunt argues that relationship marketing is growing in importance is the change from traditional competition to network competition. There is a clear shift towards maximising value to the customer, through a whole chain of firms involved in the production and delivery of products and services (the network). This contrasts with traditional competition is which each firm would compete with every other firm. The key change is that companies are attempting to forge much stronger links with their suppliers, advertising agencies and dealers.

Figure 1.6 illustrates the traditional view of competition. Notice how there is competition across every level in the competitive hierarchy from raw materials suppliers to automobile buyers. Now look at how the relationship marketing approach encourages the development of network competition, as illustrated in figure 1.7. See how the five hierarchies are now transformed into three groupings. These are Ford, Nissan and Volkswagen, and their relationships with various intermediaries in their supply and distribution chain. Notice how this approach stresses the need for all of the relationships to be managed effectively, and for all of the partners to gain benefits from the relationship. This makes for much stronger competition with its rivals owing to the specific advantages gained from the development of a network of relationships.

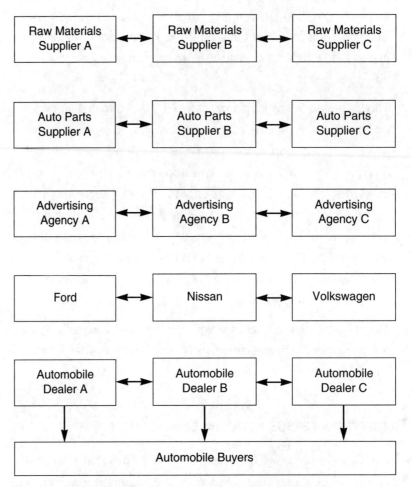

FIGURE 1.6: *The traditional view of competition.*

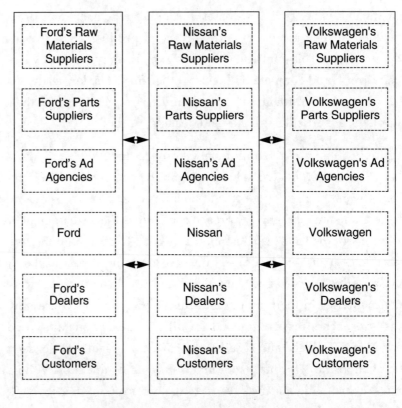

FIGURE 1.7: *The network view of competition.*

Two of the specific advantages that Ford, Nissan and Volkswagen gain from the network approach to competition are:

- Security of supplies of raw materials and components which are of guaranteed quality standards.

- A unique relationship with their advertising agencies which will enable them to communicate effectively with their target audiences. For example, each company will have unique ways of developing its corporate and brand images, and of stressing the unique selling propositions of their cars.

Not only do Ford, Nissan and Volkswagen gain from the relationship network but so do their suppliers and advertising agencies. They obtain longer-term contracts which allow them to plan their business strategy with greater certainty. This long-term approach enables them to develop synergistic solutions to problems with members of the car companies, without the fear of being replaced by competitors until they have been given an opportunity to put solutions to problems into operation. Of course, if a major problem, such as poor quality components persisted, then it is inevitable that the relationship would be terminated by the car company before it lost the loyalty of its customers.

summary

This session has introduced marketing and explored the concepts of marketing orientation and relationship marketing.

▶ Marketing is a dynamic and wide-ranging subject which incorporates and integrates a range of functions. These include new product development, pricing, distribution, packaging, advertising, public relations, competitive analysis, market research and sales.

▶ Marketing is also a social and managerial process by which individuals and groups obtain what they need and want through creating, offering and exchanging products of value with others.

▶ People in marketing must continually evaluate consumer perceptions of products and services and be responsive to changes in society.

▶ The emphasis of relationship marketing is to develop partnerships, satisfy customers and consequently maximise customer retention rates.

▶ The aim of internal partnerships is to match the needs and values of the workforce with the aims of the company by developing quality and customer service.

▶ Supplier partnerships look to develop long-term co-operation which results in a mutually beneficial relationship.

▶ Companies often see benefits arising from the formation of lateral partnerships which may involve collaboration or merger.

▶ Buyer partnerships are important to companies because they want to keep customers, and their expenditure, for life.

Marketing and the business environment

Objectives

After participating in this session, you should be able to:

▶ **explain the marketing system**

▶ **show how global events can affect the business environment**

▶ **understand the importance of DEPICTS analysis.**

In working through this session, you will practise the following BTEC common skills:

Managing and developing self	✔
Working with and relating to others	✔
Communicating	✔
Managing tasks and solving problems	✔
Applying numeracy	
Applying technology	
Applying design and creativity	

The marketing system

In 1776, Adam Smith introduced the concept of the **invisible hand** of the market. He was arguing in favour of the free market and against any form of market intervention. What is the 'invisible hand'? It is the overall purchasing decisions of consumers in the market. Their decisions affect the way firms allocate their resources. **Consumers are sovereign** in a free market economy in that they exercise their choice over what to purchase; because of this power, suppliers must make every effort to create products or services which will satisfy them. Suppliers who ignore this important fact will soon face bankruptcy because consumers will not want to buy what they produce. This is the harsh reality of the free market.

Marketeers see the market as the set of existing or potential customers who are willing to satisfy their requirement for given products or services by exchanging money for them. This brings us back to one of the cornerstones of the marketing system. The capitalist, or market, system is based on buyers and sellers freely negotiating terms of exchange.

Marketeers see the collection of sellers as the industry. For example, they speak of the chemical industry, the steel industry and the soft drinks industry. These industries contain all the firms who want to sell that particular product, but many companies operate in different industries. For example, brewing companies such as Whitbread have substantial property interests and Unilever is internationally famous for soaps and detergents, but it also owns food companies and a chemical business.

Figure 2.1 illustrates the interaction that takes place between customers and firms. Firms conduct market research to understand customer requirements, and they communicate with customers by using advertising and promotion campaigns. Customers compare the deals offered by a particular firm to those of its competitors and, if they are suitably impressed, they will buy. The firm sets the price, but consumers ascertain the value to them. If the customers are satisfied by the value given to them, then the relationship with the firm will be a long-term one. If the customers feel that they did not obtain sufficient value in exchange for their money, then a one-off transaction will have occurred. Marketeers want to have long-term relationships with consumers, not one-off transactions.

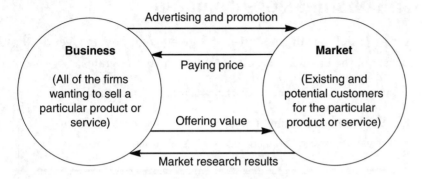

FIGURE 2.1: *The marketing system.*

ACTIVITY 1

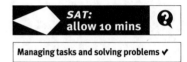

SAT:
allow 10 mins

Managing tasks and solving problems ✔

List three products or services that you bought recently. (Examples of services might include hair stylists, cinemas, night-clubs.) Why did you buy them and how did they satisfy your requirements better than competitive offerings?

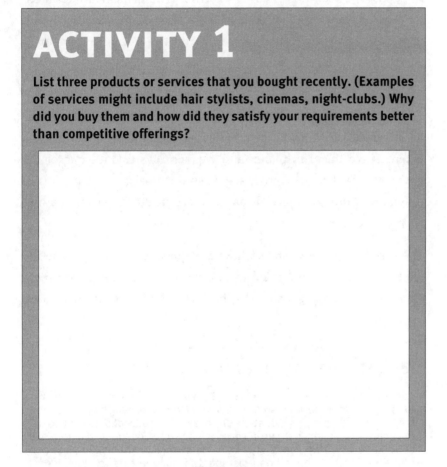

Commentary...

Some examples could be a decision to watch one football team because you feel it plays more attractive football than its rivals. You might buy one cola instead of another because you prefer the taste. You visit one night-club over another because you prefer the atmosphere. You chose to see one film instead of another because you felt it would be more exciting. No doubt you have many other examples. The main point is that consumer choice is the key to a market economy.

The business environment

It is essential that the activities of a given company are seen in the context of the business environment in which it operates.

> **\?/** The **business environment** is made up of a set of external influences over which a firm usually has very little control.

If the business environment is predictable, it could be taken for granted. However, this is rarely the case. The business environment must be constantly monitored for the threats and opportunities which it presents to firms. When scanning and evaluating the business environment, it is essential that firms look beyond superficial impacts and think carefully about multiple causes and effects.

For example, a company like British Aerospace has suffered because the break up of the Soviet Union has reduced the need for massive defence investment in planes and weapons systems to counter the Soviet threat. British Aerospace, it could be argued, might have diversified into commercial markets to guard against this having such a major impact.

The case study below shows how a major event – in this case the Gulf War – can have numerous and varied effects on the business environment, and major strategic impacts on individual firms who are affected.

MULTIPLE EFFECTS OF THE 1990 GULF WAR

The invasion of Kuwait by Iraq in 1990 was a potential disaster for the Western world. It threatened to cut off a source of oil which was vital for the efficient running of industries. It threatened total destabilisation of the political situation in an area which is known to be highly volatile. This could have led to the possibility of a nuclear conflict. The economic order of the world would have been disrupted for many years, and business confidence would have plummeted, sparking off a global recession, mass unemployment and hyper-inflation. Of course, none of this happened. The military victory was reasonably swift, and the financial markets stood up surprisingly well. Allied casualties were light. Iraq suffered heavy military losses and its economy became severely disrupted.

Any firms that had scanned the political horizon in advance may have been able to detect the possibility of a conflict. Some companies – such as shipping and holiday firms – removed both personnel and financial assets from the Middle East as a precaution.

Some firms did well out of the Gulf War as their products came into heavy demand. Examples include uniform makers, tent manufacturers, armament makers, field dressing suppliers and field ration suppliers. Some heavy engineering firms from the Border region of Scotland fared badly; they lost contracts and assets in Iraq. The transatlantic airline business, already affected by over-capacity and recession, was damaged still further by the threat of hijackings and bombing. The slump in the number of tourists to the UK, particularly of wealthy American tourists, led to a severe reduction in numbers staying in London hotels and visiting musicals and plays in the West End. Many musicals and plays closed, and hotels and airlines began to cut prices and add extra services to stay in business.

Even when the Gulf War had finished, problems and opportunities existed. There were ecological problems following the use of eco-terrorism in the form of deliberate oil pollution by the Iraqi army. This created a major business opportunity for firms specialising in oil cleaning equipment, and a severe threat to both the fishing and tourist industries in the region.

The rebuilding of the Kuwaiti infrastructure provided new opportunities for many British companies specialising in buildings, engineering and telecommunications. For those Scottish engineering firms who lost out in Iraq, the rebuilding of Kuwait presented a vital commercial opportunity.

In the meantime, several uniform makers, tent manufacturers and field ration suppliers experienced financial problems as their products were no longer needed. Members of Parliament called for a strategic review of the UK defence industry. The military threat from the Soviet Union has reduced, but there are many other regions of instability in the world. This has led to the need for a flexible, cost-effective armed force backed by the latest technological weapons systems.

ACTIVITY 2

SAT:
allow 15 mins

Managing tasks and solving problems ✔

Consider a situation in which a major disaster had global consequences. The nuclear reactor incident at Chernobyl in the Soviet Union in the late 1980s is an example. This released a large cloud of radioactive material which spread across Europe. Note down at least five varied effects this had on the business environment.

Commentary...

Some of the effects of the disaster at Chernobyl on the business environment are listed here:

- It put pressure on all nuclear energy producers to show that their plants were safe, as politicians and pressure groups called for reassurance and urgent action.

- Farmers became increasingly worried about radioactive fall-out damaging their crops and devastating their livestock. For example, the Norwegian government banned reindeer farmers from selling the meat due to contamination and, in the UK, the Government introduced emergency procedures and measures while scientists took regular measurements on highland areas.

- Environmentally friendly ways of generating heat – such as solar and wind power – became more popular in the eyes of worried consumers.

- Firms that made anti-radioactive clothing and footwear saw a massive increase in demand in Europe, especially from farmers and forestry workers.

- Specialist manufacturers of nuclear generators found that their specific advice in areas such as design was needed to seal the site of the incident.

- In the Soviet Union itself, many people died or became very ill from radioactive poisoning and this led to the whole region being evacuated because it was uninhabitable. This devastated the local economy.

You may have listed different factors to these. The key point is that wars and major disasters introduce massive uncertainty into the business environment within which firms operate.

DEPICTS analysis

Given the importance of monitoring the forces in the business environment, it is essential that these forces can be assessed. Sometimes the factors used in the examination of the business environment are called **PEST factors**.

- Political-legal

- Economic

- Socio-cultural

- Technological

Useful though this is, it can lead to several important factors being overlooked. Figure 2.2 shows a more detailed model of the business environment called **DEPICTS**.

- Demographic

- Economic

- Political

- Infrastructure

- Competitive

- Technological

- Socio-legal

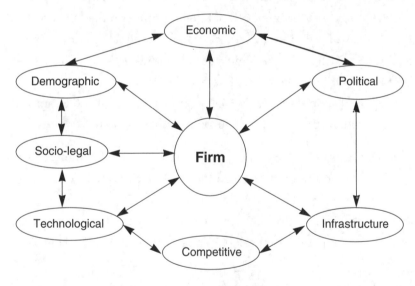

FIGURE 2.2: *The business environment.*

Let us see how each of these factors can affect companies.

DEMOGRAPHIC

Demographics is concerned with the scientific study of populations. It includes factors such as birth and death rates, marriage and divorce rates, age structure, and racial, ethnic and religious backgrounds. These factors are of immense relevance to marketeers who have to analyse and predict trends if they are to continue to give customers exactly what they want, and if companies are to make realistic profits by doing so.

DEPICTS ANALYSIS

For example, in the UK, a declining birth rate means that there are now less people in the youth category of 18- to 24-year-olds. Many companies that relied on providing products and services for this age group have targeted older age groups. The clothes company Burton is one example.

Insurance and record companies are keen to provide services and products for a wide variety of age groups, but cinema audiences are mainly aged under 25 years old, so it is vital for film makers to understand the tastes of this audience.

People tend to live longer now, often enjoying 15 or 20 years of active retirement. With more people inheriting property and owing private pensions and investments, there are many more well-off older people. Many holiday firms target this particular group of 55- to 80-year-olds, as do garden centres, book clubs, and golf and fishing societies.

With the world gradually becoming much more integrated due to increased travel and sophisticated communications, many companies will have to consider international demographic trends. Europe has the slowest population growth in the world, and the population is ageing. By 2015, various demographic studies estimate that 23 per cent of the UK population will be over 60. Switzerland will have 30 per cent of its population over 60. In contrast, Portugal and Spain will have less than 20 per cent of their populations over 60.

Although most of Europe's youth populations are shrinking due to the fall in the number of births in the 1970s, Ireland will see a rise in the number of 15- to 24-year-olds by some 10–15 per cent by the late 1990s. Japan had a baby boom in the mid-1970s and this will increase the number of people in the 20–29 age group by the mid-1990s.

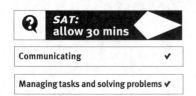

SAT: allow 30 mins	
Communicating	✔
Managing tasks and solving problems	✔

ACTIVITY 3

Imagine you are a marketing executive employed in the following UK companies:

(a) a company selling fashionable training shoes

(b) a company selling expensive family cars

(c) a company selling insurance products.

Identify the key demographic groups these companies should target and the marketing considerations that need to be taken into account. Write a 150-word report and summarise your findings in the box below.

Commentary...

For fashionable training shoes, the target group is young males in the 13–25 age group. This would be the main fashion-conscious market for this product. For the younger age segment, who are not in full-time employment, the price of the product would be carefully weighed against the amount of street credibility particular brands confer. This type of product can go out of fashion quickly.

For family cars, there are two main considerations: the number of family groups in the UK; and their socio-demographic characteristics. Remember, this is an expensive car, so wealthy families with two or more children would be the target group. Research into the product features desired by the target group would be important, so data on occupation, income, lifestyle and personality would be evaluated.

For insurance products, an insurance company must apply the appropriate product to the correct target group. For example, think of the different needs of pensioners and students. Studying the number of people buying houses and cars and having families will be critical. Insurance companies look at insurance needs over the family life cycle. For example, a couple in their early thirties who have three young children, will have a completely different set of priorities from an older couple whose children have left home. Factors such as disposable income and the need to make future plans, change according to age.

ECONOMIC

Global considerations

All businesses are affected by economic considerations. The state of the economy needs to be monitored carefully by firms to identify trends which can be seen as either favourable or unfavourable. Every UK firm will be influenced in some way by the single European market of some 375 million consumers. With the creation of an open market between all member states, British businesses are encouraged to see the single European market as the home market. Clearly, firms in the UK will have both an export opportunity and a threat from competitive imports.

With the development of an increasingly global market, the need to monitor the state of foreign economies is also critical for many organisations. For example, companies such as Guinness and ICI trade in over one hundred countries and, if there is recession in, say, the USA, Germany and Japan, this may mean reduced demand for British goods in those countries, leading to lost revenue and possible redundancies.

The British economy must be seen in the context of the world economy. It is vital to Britain that agreements such as the **General Agreement on Tariffs and Trade (GATT)** made by the major industrial nations proceed smoothly. The GATT agreements are important because they regulate the volumes of world trade, and the controls and barriers to trade between nations. For example, the luxury car manufacturer Rolls-Royce expects China to be its main market within the next 15 years, as China is expected to become one of the largest international trading economies, second only to the USA.

With regard to the world economy, companies that rely on importing raw materials from abroad constantly have to plan for price fluctuations. The prices of raw materials can be affected by poor harvests or depleted natural reserves. For example, Cadbury's has to plan its bulk purchases of African cocoa for chocolate production to ensure that consumers are not hit by sharp price rises. Coffee producers face a similar problem.

Lower wage rates in the Far East and Eastern Europe have a direct relevance to British manufacturers. Textile manufacturers, pneumatic equipment manufacturers, consumer electronics companies and car manufacturers all claim that the low wage rate in those areas gives foreign imports an unfair price advantage over British produced goods. Many companies now try to produce goods in low labour cost areas, but these areas must have the necessary labour skills and advanced technology. Most of the silicon chips in the world are produced in the Philippines and Taiwan for this reason. Economists call this **global sourcing** of supplies.

ACTIVITY 4

Identify a company (excluding the examples just given) which has to be aware of global economics. State the issues it has had to face. It might be useful to conduct your research for this activity at the library, using, for example, newspapers or journals.

SAT: allow 20 mins	❓

Managing and developing self	✔
Managing tasks and solving problems	✔

Commentary...

Here are some further examples of companies that must take into account global economic considerations.

- ● Nescafé, like Cadbury's, attempts to plan its coffee purchases to minimise price rises caused by poor harvests.

- Toyota, the Japanese car manufacturer, has constructed a car plant in the UK to overcome import restrictions with the European Union.

- British Steel has made considerable improvements in productivity to compete with foreign steel producers (in what has, over the past decade, been a shrinking market). Foreign producers are often subsidised by their governments.

Domestic considerations

There are many domestic economic considerations which are vitally important to UK firms, and it is the role of marketeers to ensure that companies are kept aware of them. You will have heard of the expressions, **'consumer confidence'** and, **'business confidence'**, on the television news, and seen them mentioned in the press. These reflect the general state of economic trends. In this respect, the stock market values of firms indicate the general 'confidence level' of investors. Factors such as the rate of inflation, wage increases, levels of economic growth and the balance of trade with the rest of the world are crucially important.

Generally speaking, governments try to create stable economic conditions within which business can flourish. Key economic goals are low inflation, low wage increases, and a 'tight' monetary policy (higher, rather than lower, interest rates). This cannot always be achieved, and sometimes businesses must operate in difficult periods of economic recession. For example, producers of high-priced luxury products such as champagne often see the demand for their products fall during prolonged recessions. In recessions and situations with poor economic prospects, consumers become more cautious in their spending habits. In the recent past, nervous consumers have saved 'for a rainy day' in ever-increasing numbers. House prices tend to fall as people worry over the security of their employment.

Marketing managers have to assess how the industries within which they operate are likely to be affected by changing economic circumstances. Here, we can note some general trends:

- The construction, tourist and machine tool industries are very closely linked to the general state of the economy as a whole.

- Spending on items such as cosmetics tends to be maintained in a recession because people still want to look good.

● People tend to switch from expensive food items to cheaper substitutes in a recession. For example, consumers often buy a cheaper supermarket 'own label' product rather than more expensive branded one when spending power is reduced.

Marketeers must measure these relationships and take precautionary measures to protect their products and services from competition at such times. One of the slogans in a campaign for Fairy Liquid washing-up liquid says: 'A few more pence makes a lot more sense.' This stresses the value of the product to the consumer; it emphasises the amount of washing that can be achieved in comparison with cheaper (own-label) brands. This is an excellent communications strategy in times of recession. It reassures existing users of the product and encourages own-label users to switch to the branded product.

POLITICAL

Most analysts agree that political factors are the most important component of the business environment. This is because political decisions often have immense bearing on all other factors in the business environment. Political decisions usually become law and place statutory requirements on firms. For example, laws relating to the sale of goods clearly specify the minimum legal obligations of firms covering issues such as product information and product quality.

The world scene has seen immense political change recently. In 1990, Germany reunified. The break up of the Soviet Union followed the ending of the Cold War between the USA and Russia. The Gulf War and its aftermath has had major political consequences. More recently, there have been moves for peace in the Middle East and the cessation of violence in Northern Ireland in favour of political action.

Interpreting what these political changes might mean for firms is very difficult. The Gulf War seemed to show that the world was not necessarily becoming safer and that it was too soon to run down the UK defence industry. The UK defence industry itself was quick to seize upon this point and make its claim to be both a major exporter for the UK and a major employer. In keeping with most industries, defence companies pay Members of Parliament to act as political advisers. They keep the industry informed about any new legislation which might affect it and, in this way, it tries to influence the political process, and not merely respond to it. Similarly, the tobacco industry uses political lobbying in its fight to be allowed to continue

DEPICTS ANALYSIS

sponsoring sports events and using poster advertising in the UK. Environmental pressure groups such as Greenpeace have also lobbied to ensure that environmental issues are near the top of the political agenda of all of the major parties.

In the UK, the Conservatives have been in power since 1979. They have adopted policies which have attempted to control inflation as a priority. These 'tight money control' or **monetarist policies** involve a market approach to resource allocation (the 'invisible hand' of Adam Smith). A Labour government, if elected, may intervene more to stimulate the economy by investing in roads, railways and house building. The question is: Would more interventionist policy help, or hinder, the British economy? It would create jobs and provide wages which could be spent on goods and taxes, but would it increase inflation by expanding the money supply and pulling in foreign imports? This is an open question, but it is clearly an important example of how political influences create ripple effects throughout the economy and society.

Firms must constantly appraise these economic and political issues when devising their marketing strategies – politics and the economy are closely interlinked. For example, if the cease-fire in Northern Ireland becomes permanent, the tourist industry could pick up dramatically. Foreign firms will be more likely to set up in Northern Ireland if the threat of violence is removed.

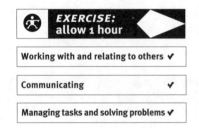

EXERCISE: allow 1 hour

Working with and relating to others ✔

Communicating ✔

Managing tasks and solving problems ✔

ACTIVITY 5

In groups of four, imagine you are representatives of the tobacco industry worried about possible legal restrictions on sponsorship and cigarette advertising. How would you attempt to increase your political representation? What arguments would you use to influence Members of Parliament and convince them that restrictions would not be in the best interests of the country?

Prepare a five-minute presentation to be given to the class. Summarise the main points of your presentation in the box below.

Commentary...

You would do well to enlist the active support of credible spokespersons. These should be well-known politicians if possible. Margaret Thatcher has such a role with the Philip Morris Tobacco Company.

Politicians who represent constituencies with a large number of tobacco-related jobs would be natural supporters, as redundancies might cost them votes at the next election – politicians are very pragmatic.

The first draft of a proposed Bill is called a Green Paper. It is a consultation document. At the Green Paper stage, when bills are being discussed and amendments are still possible, these spokespersons should be raising the following key points:

(a) The tobacco industry is already making voluntary restrictions on its promotional activities, such as not using billboards near schools whenever possible and being willing to increase the size of health warnings on cigarette packets.

(b) Smokers are voters and have the same rights as anyone else.

(c) Jobs would be lost if demand for cigarettes were to fall.

(d) The country would then lose tax revenues from the tobacco industry.

(e) A reduction in profits would mean the industry would

have to cut back on research and development into safer cigarettes.

(f) Popular sports might suffer if sponsorship support had to be withdrawn; this would affect both smokers and non-smokers.

Note that you should aim to put across the tobacco companies point of view as persuasively as you can. The health arguments and costs of treatment for smoking-related illness play no part in the arguments from your side. You are stressing the positive side of your case with a view to preventing legal restrictions being imposed.

INFRASTRUCTURE

The infrastructure is the underlying capital investment of a society. It includes transportation and communication systems, water, gas and electricity provision, sewers and drain maintenance, and health and education provision. Many firms depend either directly or indirectly on a healthy infrastructure for their survival in business:

- The channel tunnel provides a major opportunity for the soon-to-be privatised railway industry to compete with road hauliers, ferries and planes for lucrative freight and passenger markets to France.

- The switch to digital telephone technology has created a very lucrative market for companies involved in the production of fibre optic cables.

Investment in infrastructure to create jobs produces an increase in disposable income. This can lead to an extension in the demand for services such as retailing, food provision and entertainment and leisure. Service industries keep a close check on the 'health' of the infrastructure as it affects consumer incomes and confidence. For construction, transportation and communication firms, the levels of employment, inflation and 'business confidence' all play a part in how their markets will develop and they must be prepared to meet threats and grasp opportunities whenever they arise.

COMPETITIVE

Section 4 is devoted to an in-depth appraisal of the competitive process. This illustrates the vital importance of this particular force for understanding the business environment. Every firm has rivals in its particular market and, on a wider scale, there is the question of the competitive position of entire industries. Firms need to know their own competitive position and be able to evaluate the competitive position of their rivals.

TECHNOLOGICAL

In 1941, during the Battle of Britain, the Spitfire was considered a superb fighter plane. It represented leading-edge technology. It had a top speed of 320 mph. In 1969, Apollo 11 travelled to the moon at 20,000 mph. The television pictures that came back were seen by more people than had ever watched a broadcast before. Technological changes are a major influence on how we live. Imagine what a man or woman aged 90 today has seen in the way of technological changes. Now consider how those changes have affected every aspect of life.

ACTIVITY 6

Identify five technological changes that have occurred during the last 90 years. Consider how they have affected aspects of life. Write down your key points in the box below.

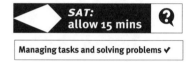

SAT:
allow 15 mins

Managing tasks and solving problems ✔

Commentary...

Here are just a few examples:

- Medical diagnosis and treatments, along with better lifestyle and diets, allow us to live longer.

- The atomic bomb and ballistic missiles have changed warfare.

- Radar has improved navigation.

- The motor car and aeroplane have revolutionised travel.

- Television, cinema and video have changed leisure activities.

- The silicon chip has encouraged the development of incredibly powerful computers which have apparently a limitless range of uses.

- Fibre optic cables have revolutionised tele-communications by enabling enormous amounts of digital information to be sent down telephone lines.

- Desktop publishing has changed the newspaper industries.

You have grown up in a technological age. Yet, the next 50 years could see changes that will make the way people work, travel and live their daily lives now, seem totally primitive and old-fashioned.

Companies must keep pace with technological developments in their industry, and assess how relevant they are for them. For example, virtual reality systems allow people to 'travel the world' and experience many different sensations without leaving their own homes. This could greatly expand the leisure market. It poses a serious threat to computer game manufacturers, whose products might seem tame or old-fashioned by comparison. Theme parks will rapidly develop new rides using virtual reality technology.

In air travel, pilots could soon become obsolete as increasingly sophisticated computers are used to control the flight of planes. However, research shows that a pilot provides vital reassurance to passengers, so the pilot-less plane does not seem to be a serious commercial proposition. The technology is not the issue – the key is to provide consumers with exactly what they require.

Technology is helping to make the world a **global village**. Affluent consumers increasingly expect high-quality product and service standards. More people travel abroad, broadening their horizons, and wanting a better lifestyle. The economic, social and cultural differences that exist in the world will provide a challenging period for politicians, as poor people become aware of how wealthy people live, and desire a better life of their own.

Technological changes could lead to serious problems for the world. If people live longer, become wealthier, and have more children, then the world population growth will soar. This will put a huge strain on the natural resources of the world. Without finding and developing new sources of energy and foodstuffs, the world will find itself unable to sustain its population. The regular famines that affect parts of Africa remind us of this.

One advance in the development of new foodstuffs is **genetic engineering**. This allows natural plants and foodstuffs to be laboratory reared and modified, to grow faster and possibly taste better. Some people see this as a threat to the poorer countries of the world. For example, American scientists have developed an artificial pyrethrum daisy which has all the essential characteristics of the natural plant grown in Kenya. The extract of the plant is used in the manufacture of agrochemicals for the farming industry. At present, Kenya exports 80 per cent of its crop to the USA and earns millions of dollars in foreign currency as a result. This market could close if the farming industry opts for the genetic product, which can be grown in a controlled laboratory environment.

ACTIVITY 7

In groups of four, discuss how the five products listed below could change by the year 2050, due to developments in science and technology.

1. Television

2. Washing machines

3. Cars

4. Books

5. Sweets

Summarise your conclusions in the box below.

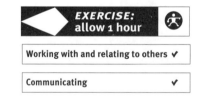

EXERCISE:
allow 1 hour

Working with and relating to others ✔

Communicating ✔

Commentary...

Televisions could have cinemascope screens. They could have concert clarity sound systems. They could be totally interactive allowing people to shop and call up entertainment services from home. People could be able to use the television to show interactive distance learning material from pre-school ages to Masters level degrees. The number of channels could be infinite as the world television networks become integrated. Headphones could be worn for automatic translations of foreign programmes.

The **washing machine** could become an incredibly complex piece of equipment, exploiting extremely powerful silicon chips. Coming in a range of sizes, washing machines could automatically sort, wash, rinse, dry and even iron clothes. Sophisticated sensors could use the least amount of water at the lowest temperature. The water could be recycled by a special unit. Machines could run on mains electricity or solar or wind power generated electricity. They could be designed to never need repair.

Cars could become sophisticated personal transportation systems, but highly efficient public transportation systems could provide serious competition. Those cars that do exist could be designed to use the least fuel, travel at maximum safe speed in all conditions and could only be driven by a sophisticated computer system with an infallible fail-safe mechanism.

Books as we know them could become a rarity. Very powerful CD-ROMs (compact disc, read only memories) could enable all materials to be fully interactive. Lights, sound effects and sophisticated graphics could exist alongside text as the CD is placed into the computer. For example, the complete works of Shakespeare on CD could come with interactive material on the history, art and sports of the period. Many interactive fiction books could allow the reader to choose the ending of their choice, or even select a given plot line. Educational materials could be completely interactive allowing testing to be carried out via interactive television without the student having to leave home.

Sweets as they exist today might disappear due to increased awareness of tooth decay and the dangers of being overweight. Healthy sweets could be developed. These could have no fat or sugar, but a subtle, totally harmless taste activator which allows the purchaser to feel they are eating the sweet of their dreams.

Notice how we can only attempt to predict the future. Right now, no one **knows** what the future holds. However, all firms must do this if they are to produce products that people will want to buy, when the only limit to what might be produced in the future is our own imagination.

Socio-legal

The socio-legal factors which operate in the business environment are very important for several reasons:

- Social-legal factors reflect the attitudes of consumers towards issues.

- The pressure exerted upon both government and companies by the force of consumer opinion influences what becomes law, and what is produced or not produced.

- The attitudes of consumers can change and so it is important that a company monitors socio-legal trends carefully if it wants its products and services to fit the current requirements of society.

We used arguments from the tobacco industry to illustrate political lobbying, but it is important to remember that there is another side to the debate. The health risks of smoking are being widely publicised by ASH (Action on Smoking and Health lobby). The costs to the economy of illnesses and deaths from cigarette smoking are often stressed. As a result of social pressure, legislation has been enacted which prohibits smoking in some public places, strictly limits the advertising of tobacco products and imposes fines on shopkeepers who sell cigarettes to children under the age of 16.

Tobacco companies respond to these restrictions in a variety of ways.

- They continue to lobby politicians.

- They export to parts of the world in which smoking is still regarded as glamorous and sophisticated, and where the industry is less strictly regulated.

- They diversify into new products. For example, the Alfred Dunhill company was once heavily dependent upon tobacco products for the majority of its revenue, but over the last 50 years it has diversified into male toiletries, fashion accessories, and leisure and sports wear.

The anti-smoking climate of opinion helps other companies who are marketing quit-smoking pills, gums, patches and lotions. Even hypnotists see an upsurge in business from desperate smokers determined to quit.

Another socio-legal issue is environmentalism. This has risen from being a minor issue to something no business should ignore. More manufacturers now claim to be 'green', although consumers question whether these claims are justified. For example, many supermarkets withdrew so called 'dolphin friendly' tuna when it was found that there were no checks on how it was caught. Stringent environmental monitoring by consumers has also encouraged firms to use less packaging in products.

Increasing crime rates have expanded the market for theft deterrents. Companies like Chubb, which markets safes, locks, infra-red devices, bars and alarms have benefited from an increased demand for security products. (Much of the increased demand for such products is caused by the spiralling cost of household insurance premiums or by the requirements demanded by the insurance companies.)

ACTIVITY 8

Identify three consumer responses to rising crime, and describe how they could affect particular businesses.

Commentary...

Examples may include the following ideas:

1. There may be an increase in the purchase of security products and services – security guards and guard dogs could be used for more premises.

2. Some people may avoid going out at night. This could reduce the business for night-clubs, pubs, restaurants, cinemas and theatres. But, an increase in the purchase of home entertainment services would benefit video stores and CD-ROM manufacturers.

3. People might try to avoid being a target by purchasing less extravagant products. This could adversely affect the sales of expensive cars and jewellery, but it could also increase the sales of fake jewellery and smaller cars.

Another social-legal factor concerns general **standards** of public taste and decency, e.g. stereotyping in advertising which is now closely monitored. The Advertising Standards Authority exists to ensure that all advertising is 'decent, legal, honest and truthful'.

For example, a Benetton advertising campaign raised issues of bad taste, attracting complaints from civil rights groups. One billboard poster, in particular, showed a black girl as having 'devil-like' horns, and an intended photograph of ex-American President Ronald

Reagan, with AIDS-related skin cancer. Such sensationalist publicity stunts often backfire on companies despite the free media attention they generate as consumers are quick to see through them. The moral and ethical values of the company are also brought into question.

Companies that target their products at young people have to be aware of what is considered 'in' at any given time. Many young consumers are difficult to reach with conventional advertising messages because they are cynical about the process of advertising and are sceptical about claims. Many cinema advertisements are aimed at the young, the 18–30 age group being the main cinema audience. They try to use 'shocking' messages to overcome audience inertia. For example, they show gratuitous violence of the kind seen in many modern films. This is a two-edged strategy which might lead to the advertisements being given attention but the specific message being ignored. The yuppies (young upwardly mobile professionals) of the 1980s have been replaced by more caring role models. Anything with a 'yuppie' feel is already rather a cliché for greed, self-interest and an intolerance of others.

As an example of advertising pitched at the young, consider the ice-cream market. Ben and Jerry's ice-cream is the number one product in the expensive quality segment of the market in America and its main competitor is Häagen-Dazs. Häagen-Dazs, well-known in the UK as a yuppie product, was launched in the UK in the 1980s primarily aimed at young professionals. It is a fashion product as much as a food product. The Häagen-Dazs image was one of success, sophistication and sex. Ben and Jerry's has a totally different image. Humour is at the heart of it – even the advertising is deliberately amateurish. This may have more world-wide appeal as an environmentally friendly, funny, experience. The very factor that led to the success of Häagen-Dazs – sophistication – could undermine it when sophistication is no longer an especially desirable attribute to the target audience.

The socio-legal factors in the environment are very important, and firms must take account of them when planning their strategies.

summary

This session has dealt with the business environment.

> ▶ Consumers are sovereign in a free market economy. Suppliers must ensure that their products and services meet consumers' needs; otherwise they may face bankruptcy.

> ▶ The business environment is unpredictable. Companies must constantly monitor it for threats and opportunities.

> ▶ One framework which companies can use to monitor the forces in the business environment is DEPICTS analysis. This model covers demographic, political, infrastructure, competitive, technological and socio-legal factors.

Stakeholders and social responsibilities

Stakeholders and marketing communications

Objectives

After participating in this session, you should be able to:

▸ discuss the claims of stakeholder groups on companies

▸ understand why companies need to balance conflicts of interest

▸ show how companies use public relations within their communications strategies

▸ understand why companies publicise their activities

▸ explain the key aspects of press releases.

In working through this session, you will practise the following BTEC common skills:

Managing and developing self	✔
Working with and relating to others	
Communicating	✔
Managing tasks and solving problems	✔
Applying numeracy	
Applying technology	
Applying design and creativity	

Stakeholders

Stakeholders are the different groups who have a legitimate interest in the activities of a company. They form a wide-ranging cross-section as shown in figure 1.1. You should note that it is important for a firm to form an effective relationship with each of these stakeholders if it hopes to achieve its overall objectives. This is yet another facet of the relationship marketing approach discussed in Section 1.

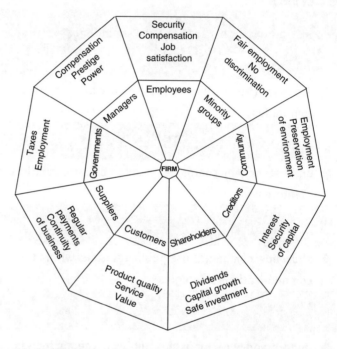

FIGURE 1.1: *Stakeholders and their expectations. Reproduced from* Marketing Management and Strategy *by Peter Doyle, 1994, by permission of the publisher Prentice Hall International, Hemel Hempstead.*

Over the last 20 years, managers have been expected to understand that there is a wide diversity of expectations among the stakeholders of an organisation.

- **Shareholders** expect good dividends and high ethical standards.

- **Employees** expect rising wages and better working conditions as well as further training and education.

- **Customers** expect products to be of high value to them. This means that the products should be high quality, provide value for money and that after-sales services and guarantees must be comprehensive.

- **Local residents** expect a pollution-free environment, as do consumers in other countries. No one wants the acid rain or radiation produced elsewhere.

A firm has to arrange its activities so as to achieve the correct balance with each stakeholder group. This is extremely difficult to achieve as stakeholders vary both in their own aims and in the relative importance and influence on the managers who set the overall objectives. One of the main problems is a **conflict of interest**. For example, the shareholders (people who actually own part of the wealth of the firm in the form of shares which are valued on the stock market) want a high return on their investment, while the local community wants the firm to concentrate on making sure that profits are not achieved at the expense of the physical environment. This balance between business objectives and environmental and social responsibility is important; it is also difficult to judge.

Managers must attempt to set priorities which take into account the relative strength of the different stakeholder groups. They need to achieve a mutually beneficial exchange relationship with each group. The power of stakeholders is very important. Strong stakeholders can put pressure on a firm to increase its value offer to them. Weak stakeholders exert less pressure, and have to be satisfied with far less. For example, institution shareholders who own large blocks of shares are in a position to exert considerable pressure on companies. Maurice and Charles Saatchi were ousted from the Saatchi organisation by a group of shareholders. The need to take account of powerful shareholders' requirement for higher dividends may have to be offset by holding levels of remuneration of employees, who may be seen as a less powerful group.

We now concentrate on four important stakeholder groups:

1. customers

2. employees (who include executives and managers)

3. minority groups

4. suppliers

and briefly examine each group in turn.

CUSTOMERS

Customers are **sovereign** in a market economy. If customers' expectation levels are not met, their ultimate weapon is to withdraw their custom from a given firm. We have seen how marketing-oriented firms aim to satisfy customers by meeting their expectations in order to retain their loyalty. If a company attempts to increase its rewards to other stakeholders, without taking customers into account, then there is likely to be a conflict of interest.

Let us take the example of the privatised utilities such as gas, electricity and water. The senior executives of these organisations have enjoyed massive increases in their salaries since privatisation and shareholders have seen handsome increases in the value of their investment. However, customers have complained of increased prices and of reduced service. Water meters have proved to be extremely unpopular with large families, for example. But, at the moment, customers have no real choice over who supplies them. This may change in the future, and the increased competition should act in the interest of customers by keeping prices down and service levels high.

At present, the consumer pressure groups in these industries monitor activities and put pressure on the government. As customers are also voters, the government acts to control price increases in the interest of its own popularity. The industries complain that this restricts the amount that they can invest, and argue that it means they employ less staff. A very complex power structure is in operation.

EMPLOYEES

Salaries are the main point of issue with employees, but job security and conditions of work are also important. The general economic conditions, the nature of the work skills involved, and the strength of the trade unions are all important factors for employees. The employees are dependent upon the organisation but, if they are to be fully motivated to produce high quality goods, and to deliver top class customer service, then they have to feel they are not being exploited.

Executives and **managers** are often large shareholders in an organisation. They expect higher rewards than other employees because of their professional skills and responsibilities. If they are not rewarded to their satisfaction, they can leave the business voluntarily; often they are recruited by a competitor. The large salaries enjoyed, linked share option schemes and large golden handshakes received by executives and managers when they leave, can cause resentment among the less well paid employees. If the company is not performing to the level of shareholders' expectations, those shareholders may call for changes at boardroom level. The level of rewards at senior director level is increasingly under government scrutiny. Even in times of national pay restraint, individual companies argue that they have to offer appropriate rewards to recruit and retain talented people.

MINORITY GROUPS

Firms must take into account the needs and demands of many different minority groups. Interest groups, often described as **pressure groups**, include consumer organisations, environmental groups and single-interest groups such as anti-motorway protesters. They aim to bring pressure to bear on companies to try to force them to modify or introduce new products or change their mode of operation.

By heightening public awareness (e.g. through demonstrations or through arranging a public boycott of a firm's goods or services), pressure groups create situations which require companies to respond.

- Pressure to reduce pollution was the catalyst for legislation relating to smoke emissions from houses and factories.

- Concern about the use of scarce resources has led to the recycling of waste such as papers, plastics and metals and the use of alternative materials by manufacturers.

- Recent demonstrations have led to the severe curtailment of the transportation of live animals.

- A boycott on the purchase of its products in Germany persuaded Shell to change the decision to sink an obsolete oil platform in the North Sea.

- Public concern about testing pharmaceutical products on animals has forced companies to change production and testing methods.

Other groups are subject to **discrimination**. Companies are required by UK and European legislation and directives to adopt non-discriminatory policies. Firms need to ensure that they do not discriminate on the grounds of gender, ethnic origin, sexual orientation, religion or disability. Some companies have adopted more pro-active policies, including the provision of crèches, the introduction of job-sharing schemes, offering flexitime and career breaks for women, and producing advertising aimed at specific minority groups.

SUPPLIERS

Companies must recognise that their suppliers have a legitimate interest in their activities. Both a company and its suppliers need to understand that the benefits that can arise from a partnership based on mutual trust and respect.

A company looks to its suppliers for goods and services such as raw materials, components, office supplies and cleaning contracts. They need to ensure that contracts are of acceptable quality, delivered on time and competitively priced. In return, a company needs to acknowledge the needs of its suppliers who look for continuity of demand within reasonable time-scales, a price which enables them to make a profit and payment on time. As a consequence, it is important that companies recognise their suppliers as stakeholders and take their needs into account when balancing the interests of all the stakeholder groups.

The stakeholder model

Having looked at stakeholders in society, it is now time to examine the stakeholder model of corporate behaviour. The stakeholder model of firms' behaviour views the actions of the firm as a coalition of interests beyond the boundaries of the firm. It includes within the coalition, external groups seen to have a legitimate interest in the firm's behaviour.

Stakeholder group	Main interests
Customers	Value for money Quality products and services
Suppliers	Fair prices Security of contracts Prompt payment
Local community	Environmentally sensitive behaviour Social responsibility Employment potential Community involvement

FIGURE 1.2: *Interests of the main stakeholder groups.*

The stakeholder theory states that, for a firm to remain viable it needs to satisfy *all* stakeholder groups' interests. This again will lead to compromises between the interests of different groups and hence firms should aim at a range of satisfactory outcomes from each group's point of view.

ACTIVITY 1

Imagine you are a local authority official. The authority has decided to raise parking fees for one of its car parks. What are the potential problems that could arise for various stakeholders? Write a 150-word report for the appropriate local authority committee to consider, and summarise your points in the box below.

SAT:
allow 20 mins

Communicating	✔
Managing tasks and solving problems	✔

Commentary...

There are a few main problems:

1. People may decide to park illegally. This causes nuisance and hazards to pedestrians, residents and delivery vehicles.

2. Low income groups may not be able to afford to use the car park.

3. Cheaper alternatives may become more attractive, e.g:

   (a) using legal parking places in nearby streets, which

could cause disruption for residents who need the space to park their own cars;

(b) using car parks run by neighbouring local authorities, which could reduce custom for local shops, possibly bringing unemployment and the need for government to pay benefits.

4. Although the parking fee is to be raised, there is the possibility of a reduction in total income (due to reduced demand) which may then lead to an increase in council tax for residents.

The activity illustrates the conflicting objectives which are very much part of public service life. This makes the stakeholder model especially relevant when discussing public sector organisations.

The need to reach balanced decisions which take into account the interests of all stakeholder groups cannot be over-stressed. When the government wants to build a new road or airport, it sets up a committee of inquiry to gather evidence from the various stakeholders. There is an adjudication by the chairman of the review committee based on a complete and impartial review of the evidence. Recently, the proposed building of a new runway at Manchester Airport has received a lot of attention in the local and national media. Naturally, the airport authorities are keen to stress the extra trade and jobs the development will bring. Local groups, such as environmental groups and resident groups opposed to the venture, combine to point to noise pollution, the destruction of wildlife habitat and the reduction in property prices in the area arising from the noise and disruption.

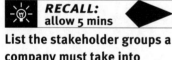

RECALL:
allow 5 mins

List the stakeholder groups a company must take into account in planning its activities and developing its marketing strategy.

Public relations

All companies need to communicate their points of view on key issues such as the environment. One expensive way of doing this is to pay for advertising in the media and on television. To reach all stakeholder groups with messages that show that the company is working for all of their interests, a firm will engage in public relations activity.

> **!?!** The Institute of Public Relations defines **public relations practice** as the deliberate, planned and sustained effort to establish and maintain mutual understanding between an organisation and its publics.

For commercial organisations, the aim of public relations is to use credible media sources to enhance the image of the company and its products or services, in the eyes of potential customers. This, they hope, will improve sales and customer loyalty. On a wider level, the whole issue of corporate communications becomes important.

The company's publics may include the government, shareholders, local councils, potential and existing employees, and customers, i.e. any individual, group or organisation that may affect, or be affected by, the performance or image of the company, including the stakeholders.

A considerable part (though not all) of public relations activity is directed at obtaining favourable presentation of the company and its products or services. Whenever possible, presentations through independent third parties are sought. The third party is acting, to a degree, as an endorsement of the company and its product and services. The credibility of any communication is increased if the third party is perceived by consumers to be acting as an *independent* authority, and not as a spokesperson for the company. For example, Rentokil is a company which specialises in killing rodents, insects and pests of all kinds world-wide. It uses sophisticated products to ensure that pests do not return to industrial and domestic property. Rentokil is an international company which uses public relations activity to give a favourable image of the company to the quality press such as *The Times* and *The Guardian*. They enjoy free mentions in a credible media, which attracts investors to their shares.

Public relations activity can be carried out in a number of ways. Here we consider the most common examples.

Press releases provide articles and stories on an organisation or its products that the press may consider newsworthy, e.g. a new social use to which a product may be applied:

- A company may write a press release saying that its lorries and trucks have been chosen to deliver supplies to the starving in Africa because of their ability to stand up to the rugged terrain;

- Other firms may issue press releases if their products are used to help alleviate suffering after a natural disaster.

Meetings and visits can provide opportunities for positive communications. Some firms organise escorted tours of the company and meetings with the chairman and managing director for shareholders and/or financial journalists. These are designed to maintain goodwill and to communicate with key financial analysts in the hope of keeping share prices buoyant. This is now very important as the integrated nature of the world financial markets means that corporate financial information is studied in detail. It is very susceptible to being undermined by competitive activities such as mergers and alliances.

Press conferences are used to announce newsworthy events to journalists, e.g. the launch of a new car, the opening of a new factory, or an alliance with another firm. When the Japanese open a new car factory in the UK (such as Nissan in the North East), they take advantage of the media interest by holding a press conference.

Local community relations and events are designed to maintain goodwill with the local community and local organisations.

Many companies make **donations to charitable causes**, e.g. to medical research, hospitals, voluntary organisations and charities. Although the donations are made for altruistic reasons, companies hope to benefit indirectly by generating goodwill through being seen to display social concern and responsibility.

Testimonials from personalities and satisfied customers contribute towards a favourable brand or corporate image.

In-house journals are used to promote a team spirit, an integrated work-force and a sense of purpose. The Ocean Shipping Group produces its own 'Ocean Mail' magazine for this reason. Similarly, British Airways produces an in-house magazine.

Sponsorship is a popular form of public relations activity. A company may decide to sponsor an event, a personality, an organisation or long running competitions in order to establish favourable associations and to obtain editorial coverage in the media. Sponsorship also provides an opportunity for advertising at the event. For example, Littlewoods Pools has recently taken over the sponsorship of the FA Cup.

Publicity and press coverage

One very important role of public relations is to generate favourable publicity for the organisation. This can take the form of publicity about the company policy on major issues, product launches, charitable donations and good works, unusual achievements of employees and so on. The organisation tries to use favourable publicity as a key aspect of its overall approach to communicating with its stakeholders.

> !?! **Publicity** is a non-personal stimulation of demand for products, services or businesses by offering commercially significant news about them to the media. This is then used, or not used, at the discretion of the media. The exact nature of the publicity generated depends on how the original news items are used by the media.

Newspapers, magazines, television and radio stations may comment favourably – or unfavourably – on a company's activities or products as part of their normal reporting activities. Reports on companies may also be made by other parties, e.g. institutes, associations, and government bodies; the general public may accept their comments as being more trustworthy, unbiased and credible than those coming from the company itself. They would expect the company to put very positive messages forward at all times.

The nature of the media coverage has a direct impact on consumers' perceptions of a company and its products. So, the public relations department (or a public relations consultancy) attempts to ensure that the media receive favourable information about a company and its products. It will attempt to redress unfavourable press reports. In many companies, this task is regarded as so important that a publicity manager is employed specifically to fulfil this aspect of public relations. Publicity managers regularly send letters to the editors of newspapers and television programmes pointing out any unfairness or bias they feel has been shown against them. For example, the main political parties monitor their news treatment very carefully, and are quick to complain about unfair coverage.

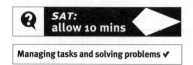

Q SAT:
allow 10 mins

Managing tasks and solving problems ✔

ACTIVITY 2

Imagine you are employed by a company as its publicity manger. How would you use publicity to the benefit of the company? If you are employed, you can think about how your company uses publicity to its benefit. List three benefits that a company might obtain from press coverage.

Commentary...

Favourable publicity can make important contributions to a marketing communications campaign. A company seeks favourable press coverage:

- ○ to improve the company's image

- ○ to improve the product line/brand image

- ○ to announce new products and services and encourage trial purchase

- ○ to encourage the purchase of the company's products and services

- ○ to overcome resistance by sections of the community to the company and/or its products and services

○ to develop other aspects of the company, such as interest in the company's public flotation.

It is important for public relations personnel to have (and to project) an acceptable level of integrity if they are to be credible in their role. They need excellent written and spoken communication skills and have to be tactful and diplomatic at all times.

In explaining the company view of, say, a pollution incident which has attracted a great deal of negative publicity, the spokesperson would have to emphasise the organisation's concern. At the same time, he or she would attempt to put over very positive messages about the company. Here are two examples of what the spokesperson might say to the media:

○ This is the first incident of this kind that the company has been involved in, and I would point out how quickly the organisation responded.

○ Although our record is the best in the industry, we are determined to improve our systems to ensure that this unfortunate and isolated incident does not happen again.

To obtain the most effective results, it is important for firms to integrate organisational communications. Public relations and marketing are related functions, but they are not subsets of each other. Marketing covers a very broad spectrum of functions (as discussed in Section 1); public relations activity concentrates on developing positive relationships with stakeholder groups via open and effective communications from the organisation.

In communications of any kind, the following five aspects are critical:

1. Message **content**: What is the company trying to say?

2. The **audience**: Who is the company saying it to?

3. What **frequency** is needed? How often should the message be repeated?

4. What **media** should be used – the press, television or posters?

5. What **effect** does the communication have? The response to the communication has to be measured and evaluated.

This outline model can be applied to advertising, personal communications or press releases. We concentrate on press releases here, as they form an important part of public relations activity. The problem with press release is that there are so many; in the UK, about 125 million a year are sent out, but less than 5 million are used.

All companies want to develop communications synergy, and carefully managed media relations can play an important part in this process. For example, the UK advertising campaign for Häagen-Dazs ice-cream cost about £300,000 – not a great deal in advertising terms. However, the controversy around its sexual nature generated free editorial coverage in terms of press column inches worth £750,000, which was a remarkable success and, indeed, much of the coverage was very positive.

It is important to remember here that while editorial coverage is 'free' (although there are costs involved in hiring consultants, postage, wordprocessing the press release and photographs, etc.), the company has no control over the message. So although the press coverage worked for Häagen-Dazs, it does not benefit all companies. The article 'Goodbye to all that' (see Resource 1 at the end of the book) describes the departure of Gerald Ratner from the family jewellery empire. This example explodes one great communications myth – that all publicity is good publicity.

The next activity involves drafting a press release. Remember the golden rules. Editors are busy people so you should keep the message quite short and make it factual, but not dull. You should stress the newsworthy events, and the wider consequences or implications. (For example, a school football match is not newsworthy but, if it is played to raise money for a charitable cause, it could be.) You should have given the full names and job title (if appropriate) of any people named and put your name, business address and contact telephone number on your wordprocessed document, checking it for spelling and style. An example of a company press release is shown in Resource 2 (see the resource section at the end of this book).

ACTIVITY 3

Since privatisation, the water companies have on occasions received unfavourable publicity. There has been controversy over the salary increases awarded to directors and senior managers. Some companies were criticised during the hot summer of 1995 for failing to do more to prevent unnecessary leakages from the water supply system.

Identify the key stakeholders for a privatised water company. Are there potential conflicts of interests between different groups? Using the material in this session on the stakeholder model, suggest reasons why the newly privatised water companies have received critical media coverage.

Now consider a scenario for Middle England Water. The company wants to build a new reservoir in an area of outstanding natural beauty as part of its long-term investment programme. To finance its programme, it is seeking permission from the regulator to increase its tariffs.

Identify potential opposition to Middle England's proposals. Suggest arguments that the company could use to convince all its different stakeholder groups that it is acting in their interests. As part of your answer, draft a press release designed to gain favourable media coverage about the proposals.

Use a separate sheet of paper to record your answer. Summarise your findings in the box below.

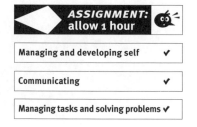

ASSIGNMENT:
allow 1 hour

Managing and developing self	✔
Communicating	✔
Managing tasks and solving problems	✔

summary

This session has been concerned with the firm and its stakeholders. It has looked at the ways in which firms communicate with key stakeholders.

▶ Stakeholders are the different groups with a legitimate interest in the activities of a company. They include shareholders, employees, the local community, customers, suppliers and minority groups.

▶ Stakeholders have a wide diversity of expectations and a business must arrange its activities to achieve a correct balance as far as possible, so as to satisfy all its stakeholders.

▶ Because the power of the various stakeholders differs, a company may have to compromise between the interests of different groups.

▶ Companies must build their image and the image of their products and services to improve sales and to develop customer and brand loyalty.

▶ Public relations is the deliberate, planned and sustained effort to establish and maintain mutual understanding between an organisation and its stakeholders.

▶ Companies try to gain favourable press coverage by issuing press releases, organising visits for journalists and opinion shapers, by community relations and events, by sponsorship and by support for charitable causes.

Responsibility to society

MARKETING ETHICS

ETHICAL ADVERTISING

SOCIETAL ORIENTATION

SOCIAL VALUES AND BELIEFS

ENVIRONMENTALISM

CONSUMERISM

Objectives

After participating in this session, you should be able to:

▶ outline the arguments which relate to the ethics of marketing

▶ discuss the issues of ethical advertising and market behaviour

▶ realise that marketing relations with society is both voluntary and regulated

▶ explain the potential impact of values and beliefs on businesses

▶ show that companies must be environmentally aware and responsive

▶ understand that companies must formulate credible responses to consumerism.

In working through this session, you will practise the following BTEC common skills:

Managing and developing self	
Working with and relating to others	✔
Communicating	✔
Managing tasks and solving problems	✔
Applying numeracy	
Applying technology	
Applying design and creativity	

Marketing ethics

> **\?/ Marketing ethics** are moral principles that allow companies to pursue activities that are generally acceptable to all stakeholders. These principles guide the conduct of a firm and the values it will uphold in certain situations.

Over the years, surveys have been taken to discover the objectives which firms pursue. The more recent ones, including those by organisations such as the Chartered Institute of Marketing and the Henley Management Centre, show that ethical responsibilities are being given a greater weighting. There is increasing evidence that ethical responsibility is a significant objective of most businesses. It is suggested that being ethically responsible improves financial performance in the long term, and this gives an extra incentive to firms.

If a company has a poor corporate image, then a strategic decision made by its senior executives to improve the company's image should improve profits in the long run. This could entail taking a stronger ethical stance on issues such as advertising or working practices. The main objective of many companies is to make sufficient profit to guarantee a future for the company – most strategic decisions are made with this objective in mind.

Some businesses are led by people who see the business itself as a force for good if its actions are carefully controlled. This goes beyond financially based reasoning. Many leading businessmen, both past and present, are **corporate philanthropists** who give large sums of money to worthy causes. For example, in the past, American entrepreneurs such as Rockefeller and Carnegie and, in the present, Richard Branson spring to mind.

However, even corporate philanthropy has its critics. These include economists, such as Milton Friedman, who argue that the key aim of business is to create profits and reward shareholders who risk their money in the company. Socialist economists (following the ideas of Karl Marx in the nineteenth century) argue that corporate philanthropists are merely trying to ease their consciences over the exploitation of their workers. They argue that individuals should not have been allowed to accumulate vast sums of wealth in the first place. Critics also point out that the workers in the companies that generated the profits for the philanthropists are often not well paid and that, in effect, corporate philanthropy is not as socially and ethically responsible as it might appear.

Companies must realise that the public of today are better educated. They are more aware of the finite resources of the world, the fragile balance of the global environment and the effects of certain chemicals and methods of production on the local environment. For example, the Exxon Valdiz oil spill disaster in Alaska showed that even the most remote, ecologically well preserved and precious environments are not safe from the activities of business.

Organisations and managers show a variety of responses to the societal issues. These can be grouped into two broad categories:

1. **The business of business is business,** i.e. the only social responsibility of business is to increase its profit. Followers of this school of thought believe that it is not the duty of the business to be concerned about social issues, but that this responsibility lies with government who should legislate the constraints. However, while placing the onus on government, this group resents any government legislative interference in business affairs. For example, tobacco companies point out that the individual should be free to choose whether to smoke or not. Quarrying and mining companies point out that the demand for their products has to be satisfied despite the environmental damage which may be caused. They argue that the net benefits to society outweigh the problems.

2. **Companies must respond to society's concerns.** Business people who take this view argue that it is basic economic common sense to respond to trends in the social climate, as measured by market research, in a careful and selective manner. Provision is made for sponsorship or welfare in the same way as any other investment or promotional expenditure. For example, many businesses have introduced crèches into the workplace to enable female employees with young children to work. Royal Insurance has invested heavily in sponsoring the Royal Shakespeare Company, which shows a desire to be seen as a company that is concerned with the arts. In both examples given above, the businesses hope to gain from their actions as well as allow others to benefit.

The second approach is often called **enlightened self interest**. The positive benefits from being seen to be a socially responsible organisation justify the decision to be socially responsible. Firms gain favourable publicity and avoid breaking laws.

A growing school of thought believes that businesses ignore social issues at their peril. However, conflicts can arise. For example, companies must strike a balance between pollution control and jobs – the cost involved in controlling pollution could lead to uncompetitive costs and thus threaten job losses and factory closures. Clearly, each company has to achieve a balanced decision in such cases.

How much any organisation can invest in the social good often depends on its financial reserves. Dedication to social responsibility may be interwoven into the objectives set by the company to a greater or lesser degree and incorporated into investment strategies, market entry decisions, and location and product policy.

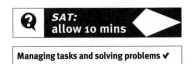

SAT:
allow 10 mins

Managing tasks and solving problems ✔

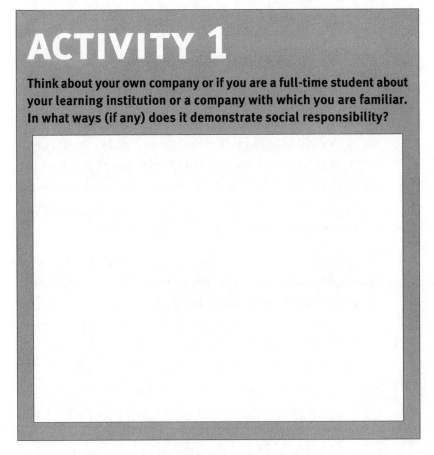

ACTIVITY 1

Think about your own company or if you are a full-time student about your learning institution or a company with which you are familiar. In what ways (if any) does it demonstrate social responsibility?

Commentary...

There are numerous ways in which companies demonstrate the social responsibility:

- having good working conditions and terms of employment

- safely disposing of waste

- locating noisy or smelly factories and plant away from centres of population

- screening production facilities, e.g. nodding donkey oil rigs are often screened by fast-growing hedges

- introducing more efficient production processes to preserve energy.

A college or university might show its social responsibility by:

- allowing unemployed people to pay lower enrolment fees

- providing crèches so mothers with young children may follow courses of study

- encouraging staff to give talks/presentations on their subject areas to outside bodies.

BRITISH PETROLEUM (BP) AND SOCIAL RESPONSIBILITY

In 1994, BP launched a new press advertisement. It shows a map of the River Thames flowing past the Isle of Dogs in London with a caption saying: 'Where BP is exploring for the UK's most vital sources of energy.'

The advertisement proclaims the commitment of the company to the policy of higher education for young people, particularly those from inner cities. It particularly mentions the need for inner city children to have role models who can act as tutors to them. The interested reader is invited to write to BP Educational Service for further details. The theme of this advertisement is clear. It announces that BP is clearly behind schemes which help to increase the knowledge and skills of young people because that ultimately increases the competitive ability of UK companies armed with a highly skilled work-force.

In effect, it proclaims that BP is interested in a societal approach to business. This stresses acceptable relationships and compromises, and a long-term approach.

Ethical advertising

Companies often try to demonstrate their environmental and social responsibility in their advertising and public relations. The BP case study above is a good example of this approach. However, companies need to be careful about the claims they make in their advertisements. The next two activities consider some of the ethical issues involved in advertising.

ETHICAL ADVERTISING

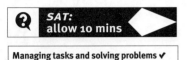

Managing tasks and solving problems ✔

ACTIVITY 2

Read the article 'Healthier ads could catch cold' in Resource 3 (see the resource section at the back of the book). This reviews some of the ethical issues in advertising the health benefits of breakfast cereals.

What would you do if you were the marketing manager of a large company marketing oat-based cereals? Specifically, would you take notice of the complaints, or would you decide that your approach was ethical?

Commentary...

You may have made the following points.

Porridge oats are perceived by the public as a natural healthy product which contain no salt or sugar but the link between oat bran and cholesterol takes the claims into a specific area where medical opinion could differ.

One could argue that the claims are neither ethical nor unethical, but merely incomplete. One sensible point could be to give contextual dietary information on the packet, e.g. to show the ingredients of a low-fat diet. As a marketing manager you would not want to be accused by the Trading Standards Authority of misleading food labelling, and so the above action could be a sensible solution.

ACTIVITY 3

Now consider a second example. Read the article 'Advertising "encourages motorists to race police"' (Resource 4 in the section at the end of this book). Is this ethical advertising? Jot down your thoughts below.

Commentary...

Clearly, in this example, the claims made by Vauxhall, that the campaign had met with a positive response by a police authority, should be investigated. If found to be true, then the claim made by Peter Stephenson-Wright gains credibility.

What the advertising agency is saying via the advert is that the car has one main unique selling proposition: speed. They could stress overall performance better by showing a well-known motor racing driver endorsing the product because of its handling ability, comfort and so on.

What is light-hearted to potential buyers may be seen to increase its appeal to joyriders to steal it. Perhaps, on balance, the comments are insensitive because joyriding is a serious crime against property which threatens the lives of car thieves and innocent people. It could be argued that the advert could benefit from less emphasis on speed and the police car without losing its appeal to its potential buyers.

Societal orientation

This concept is one of the most recent to be examined by marketeers. Firms with such an orientation recognise that they have additional responsibilities beyond making profits. These include the welfare of staff, the concerns of other stakeholders and a wider concern for the planet, e.g. by conservation of both energy and raw materials.

There have been many examples of unethical marketing behaviour; undoubtedly, there will be many more. Such actions can involve taking advantage of the lack of knowledge of consumers to sell products which they would not buy if they knew everything about them. In the 1970s, African mothers overfed their babies with concentrated baby food from Europe, which had inadequate usage instructions and was promoted using free gifts and incentives. The success of the product was obtained to the detriment of children's health. Some babies died. The companies selling the baby food received (and suffered from) extensive criticism.

In recognition of their wider responsibilities, many companies have modified their approach to include a societal emphasis. Some include explicit references to social responsibility in their mission statements or published reports. See, for example, the statement by British Nuclear Fuels below.

> **The nuclear industry is a safe industry for our employees, for the public and for the environment in which we all live. A safe and well-managed nuclear industry has a vital role to play in supplying essential energy to a world which must pay increasing attention to environmental safety, conservation of dwindling raw materials and nature habitats, and sustainability for future generations.**
>
> British Nuclear Fuels Ltd, 1992, *Environmental Care Report.*

Firms with a societal orientation do not seek profit as their primary purpose but as a business requirement. Their purpose is to gain and keep customers; the best way to do this is by meeting customers' requirements without unduly compromising the environment, exploiting workers or using unethical practices of any kind. Naturally, to develop and maintain this enlightened approach requires a tremendous change in corporate culture.

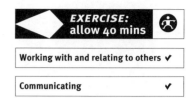

ACTIVITY 4

In small groups, discuss and evaluate these three statements:

1. **The first social responsibility of business must be to make enough profit to cover the costs of its future.**

2. **Firms have to realise that there is more to business than making profits.**

3. **A company develops a social conscience at the expense of the shareholders.**

Summarise your discussion in the box below, listing the main points of disagreement and debate.

Commentary...

The statements are not as contradictory as they might appear at first. One could argue, for example, that if a company is in the private sector, its best chance of making profits is to act in a socially and ethically responsible manner to increase consumer confidence in the policies it adopts and the products or services it markets. Of course, the business must be run efficiently and with a marketing orientation – but this does not have to mean that ethics are secondary.

Shareholders are stakeholders. They have a financial stake in the company, and they realise that any company that ignores ethics and social responsibility may reduce its profitability; society constantly questions the actions of firms, and expects higher standards from the business community as a whole.

People want to live and work in comfort while preserving the environment. They want to be secure in the knowledge that they are involved in a partnership with their employers which is part of a wider partnership aimed at securing the continuing success and prosperity of the planet. Consumers will modify their spending habits to take these considerations into account, and it seems that a proportion of people will pay increased prices for products such as organic food and dioxin free soap powders. However, there is no doubt that many people regard this as too high a price to pay.

Where business has failed in its responsibilities to society, watch-dog bodies are often set up. We have already mentioned the Advertising Standards Authority. Regulatory bodies have been introduced to prevent exploitation where monopoly situations exist, e.g. the bodies regulating the water and electricity companies. When severe problems arise, breaching acceptable standards, legislation may be enacted. The Health and Safety at Work Act (1974) protects the employee stakeholders, and legislation governing pollution emissions and noise is designed to protect the environment.

But the marketing of products and services is also governed by a voluntary code – the Chartered Institute of Marketing Code of Practice. You may find it instructive to visit a library and read through the code.

Social values and beliefs

> **\!?\! Social values** incorporate the goals that most members of a society consider to be important, while placing the preferred ways of achieving those goals as equally important.

Success is desirable and widely admired, but only if it is earned on the basis of skill and effort, rather than crime. Individual hard work and skill benefits society but crime does not. Of course, not every member of society shares the same set of social values. Social values reflect abstract ideas about what is good, right or desirable and what is bad. For example, we are taught to tell the truth, and not to lie or steal.

The following list is considered to be important social values in the UK by the majority of people (Henley Centre, newspaper opinion polls). Politicians from the major parties talk about them in election manifestos, social scientists talk about these issues in reports.

- Freedom of the individual

- Happiness

- Achieving a measure of success in education and employment

- Having a strong work ethic

- Equality of the sexes and races

- Individual responsibility

These social values set the ethos within which both individuals and organisations operate, and they form a context within which individual beliefs are formed. A **belief** is a conviction concerning the characteristics or existence of something. Individuals working within organisations have their own set of beliefs. A person's desire to achieve promotion might be tempered by his or her belief that family life should take priority over work.

People in different countries have different social values and beliefs according to the cultural context within which they have been reared. For example, in Japan, society is very ordered. In a business context, this is illustrated by the formal approach to initial meetings, and concern over the presentation of business cards. A serious, sincere and professional approach is highly valued. Displays of anger and emotion are considered to be in bad taste, while sincerity, modesty and quiet authority are highly valued. Any businessmen seeking business in Japan must realise how important the formal greeting process (aisatsu) is to the Japanese.

Other examples of different cultural traditions are given below:

- In the USA, businesses are very concerned that meetings run on time. In Spain and Latin America, time is considered as elastic (mañana) which means that delays are common and this often frustrates foreign businessmen.

- Gift giving is considered a normal part of business life in many parts of the Far East, especially in countries such as Taiwan and

Korea, but most Western companies would feel that much of the gift giving was bribery by another name.

○ In Middle Eastern countries, the traditional way of conducting business is by standing or sitting very close to the person one is dealing with and then sealing a deal with a handshake. Many businessmen from America and Europe feel intimidated when people (particularly of the same sex) stand or sit very close to them and they are used to signed contracts and formal agreements.

We have seen how the values and beliefs of societies can differ. It is therefore important to study the actions of individuals and companies in the context of their history, traditions, language, customs and cultural norms, if products and services are to be marketed more effectively.

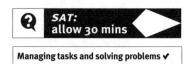

SAT:
allow 30 mins

Managing tasks and solving problems ✔

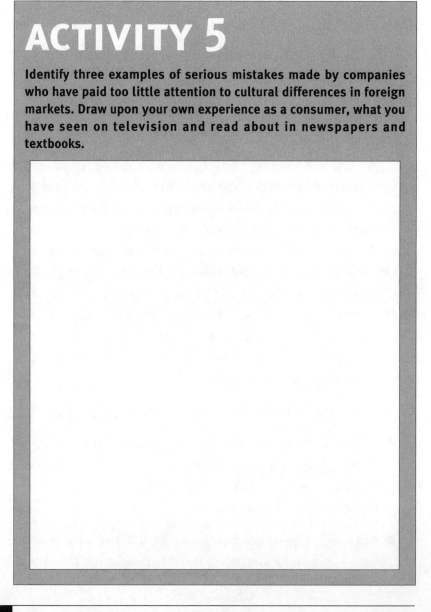

ACTIVITY 5

Identify three examples of serious mistakes made by companies who have paid too little attention to cultural differences in foreign markets. Draw upon your own experience as a consumer, what you have seen on television and read about in newspapers and textbooks.

Commentary...

Here are examples of some of the mistakes companies make by failing to research fully cultural differences.

- Inappropriate names are very common. The Rolls-Royce Silver Mist had to be renamed in Germany because mist means 'dung' in German. The American Chevrolet Nova had to be renamed in Spanish speaking countries because nova means 'no life' or 'will not go'.

- Misunderstanding how people read or gather information is a common error. Many toothpaste companies and headache pill manufacturers have designed poster advertisements for Saudi Arabia assuming that people read from left to right – but Arabic is read from right to left. So a series of three pictures showing, from left to right, dirty teeth, the product, then clean teeth, is interpreted as: 'We have clean teeth, use the product and our teeth become dirty!' Similarly, a series of three pictures for a headache pill could show a person with a hangover, a picture of them taking the product and then one of them feeling great. This is interpreted as: 'I feel great, I take the product and then I feel awful!'

- Misinterpreting how messages are translated is another big problem. For example, 'come alive with Pepsi' translated into German reads 'come alive out of the grave'. In many languages, a phrase such as 'I love New York' can only be interpreted as: 'I like New York' or 'I have a sexual relationship with New York'.

- Causing offence by using inappropriate symbols and colours is a very common mistake. A leading British shoe manufacturer developed an advertising and promotional campaign in Indonesia based around the idea of showing just socks and shoes 'dancing'. In many parts of Indonesia, feet are considered to be the most hated part of the body. Producers who use a green logo to imply environmental concern, experience problems in Asia; for Asians, the colour green frequently denotes danger, often from mosquitoes and so on in forested areas.

- Totally misunderstanding what attributes people value is another problem. For example, an American company advertised a microwave in Mexico with the slogan 'Think of all the time you will save'. This caused offence to many Mexican women who value their cooking skills highly; it went against the idea of mañana – that time is elastic and there is always more of it. In Africa, cigarette companies rapidly realised that rather than dwelling too much on the qualities of the product, it was important to show well-dressed people using the product in advertising. For many poor African men, the fact that the males in cigarette advertisements tended to wear very smart suits showed that they were wealthy, intelligent and attractive to women. Thus, they wanted to be like the men in the advertisements.

Environmentalism

It is important to consider the growing importance of environmentalism. This has implications for what firms can do legally. It also has a big impact on the way that consumers evaluate the overall performance of the firm.

Environmentalism is a word which is becoming increasingly used and understood at all levels of society. Environmentalists argue that the physical environment has to be taken into account if firms are to pursue strategies that are ethical and credible to consumers. Increasingly, consumer awareness of green issues has put pressure on manufacturers to respond. For example, manufacturers of products with CFC-based propellants (refrigerators, spray cans and so on) have been forced to look for alternatives as consumers become aware of the link between chloroflurocarbons and the depletion of the ozone layer.

An important adjunct to this process is provided by voluntary schemes such as the embryonic eco-auditing regulation from the European Commission, which aims to encourage firms to undertake regular audits of their environmental policy.

Firms already have to comply with the Environmental Protection Act (1990). The outcome is that firms are having to reposition not just products but their whole business entity. They must ensure that they are not perceived as laggards in the move to environmentally friendlier marketing practices. No business can contemplate a long-term profitable future if it chooses to ignore environmental issues. Firms can either move, or be driven, by consumer power, competitive responses and legal regulations.

!?! An **eco-audit** is a systematic appraisal of every environment related aspect of a business.

BRITISH GAS

British Gas used a full-page press advertisement as a vehicle to establish its green credentials in September 1990. The company hoped to gain a certain amount of credibility by letting various experts write, in an informed manner, on subjects such as the ozone layer, deforestation and global warming. By clipping a coupon at the bottom of the page, an interested reader could send for a copy of the information in leaflet form. Having built up a collection of leaflets, the interested reader was then sent a copy of the British Gas environmental booklet.

The 'expert press campaign' was timed to coincide with the Government White Paper on the Environment in September 1990. British Gas wanted to contribute to the environmental debate at a time of heightened awareness of the topic. The advertisements were targeted at a well-educated high-income audience in the quality press, and the company received over 30,000 responses for one or more of the 14 specially produced booklets. British Gas eventually used this database of environmentally concerned readers to send out copies of its Gas and the Environment booklet. Over 75,000 copies of this booklet have been distributed so far. The main target audiences the company hoped to influence were:

- schools – teachers and children who are future consumers and potential employees
- property developers – the company hoped to establish the 'green credentials' of gas through communications with the people who will build the homes of the future
- environmentally aware members of the general public.

British Gas is in a difficult position on the subject of the environment. The product is less damaging to the environment compared with other fossil fuels. Its production and use generates less 'greenhouse' gases such as carbon dioxide. Yet, the production and use of gas, as well as gas exploration, is still detrimental to the environment. The key for British Gas is to position the company as satisfying an acceptable compromise – it needs to ensure that society perceives that the benefits of gas have not been gained at too high an environmental cost.

Richard Cassidy, the business issues manager of British Gas (in an interview with the author), pointed out that: 'British Gas does not want to overplay the environmental hand because we know we are not perfect.' Two years ago, for example, British Gas was criticised by the Advertising Standards Authority (ASA) for the wording of its 'Burning Greener' campaign. The ASA insisted that instead of being the 'earth's cleanest fuel', gas should be called the 'cleanest fossil fuel'.

British Gas realises that it has to be seen to be acting in an ethical manner towards the physical environment if it is to achieve its global corporate objectives. For example, exploration concessions frequently depend upon a company's previously established record on the environment. Also, in a world-wide consultancy capacity, its green credibility is a key issue. For example, British Gas has links with Turkey, where it is advising the government on the introduction of natural gas to Ankara. It has recently acted in an advisory capacity to the Greek government over reducing air pollution.

The company has had set-backs on the environmental front. It bought oil drilling rights in central and southern Ecuador from Tenneco who operate

ENVIRONMENTALISM

under stringent USA standards. However, in northern Ecuador, unscrupulous oil exploration had left rich areas of natural rain forest irreparably damaged and the company felt the backlash of being seen to be an opportunist at the cost of the environment, even though it was not itself operating unscrupulously. (The company is no longer involved in Ecuador.)

In the UK, British Gas has constantly tried to prove that it can operate in an acceptable manner in environmentally sensitive areas. For example, the Wytch Farm oil-field set in the Dorset heath land, which British Gas operated in 1982–83, was subject to intense environmental scrutiny because the site was of internationally recognised importance due to the abundance of rare species of birds, flowers and insects. The company has since sold its interest in Wytch Farm.

Other examples of the company's environmental awareness occur in the New Forest and Morecambe Bay where the company constantly monitors the environmental impact of its operations. It knows that it is under scrutiny from government bodies, environmental groups and an increasingly environmentally aware public.

British Gas has undergone a test eco-audit, and a full study is now being undertaken by independent environmental consultants to ensure impartiality. The results have been publicised in the company's annual report as part of the openness policy on this issue. British Gas clearly hopes to be perceived as early adopters on the issue of environmental concern.

Richard Cassidy (in the interview quoted) sums up the British Gas position on the environment: 'The price, reliability and security of our products are of paramount concern to our consumers. Environmental strategy is not the most important part of our marketing strategy, but it comes very high up on our secondary list. Nobody wants to feel that they work for an environmentally dirty company, so there is an internal as well as an external environmental push. The company is committed to environmental awareness.'

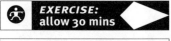

EXERCISE:
allow 30 mins

Working with and relating to others ✔

ACTIVITY 6

In small groups, debate whether you think the British Gas approach is an effective response to environmental challenges? Could it do anything more to improve its image and run a more effective communications campaign?

List the main points raised in the discussion in the box below.

Commentary...

These issues are a matter of judgement. It is quite acceptable to argue that only time will tell. Certainly, the company has had success with its approach. It has built up a great deal of expertise in managing environmentally sensitive sites, and in developing cleaner technology for extracting and using the resource. The issues with the ASA and with the Ecuador situation, shows how complex these issues can be. Mistakes attract a great deal of adverse publicity and perhaps the company still has some way to go.

Maybe the quote 'environmental strategy is not the most important part of our marketing strategy, but it is very high up on our secondary list' will not be considered an acceptable response in the future. No company can ever be complacent about environmental issues.

McDonald's provide another example of a company which has had to think hard about its marketing strategy in view of the environmental debate. The company had to combat two very serious claims from environmentalists before it could be considered to have established a measure of green credibility.

1. There was the claim that CFCs in packaging were contributing to the depletion in the ozone layer – McDonald's decided to remove CFCs from its packaging.

2. There was the perception that the fast-food hamburger companies are actively supporting the destruction of the Amazonian rain forest by providing a market for cheap Brazilian beef from deforested areas such as Rondonia. There is a vicious cycle to this process. The cleared rain forest is used to graze beef herds which eventually leads to the land becoming

desert. More rain forest has to be cleared to allow the process to begin afresh, and so the cycle goes on. Ultimately, there is only wasteland. Clearly, McDonald's could not allow such a perception to remain unchallenged, as to do so would implicitly give the claim validity.

It chose to put out an informative two-page newspaper advertisement which showed pictures of rain forest creatures, such as the pangolin, and stated that as no beef is imported from former rain forest areas, the company is in no way responsible for the destruction of the Amazonian ecosystem.

Both British Gas and McDonald's illustrate attempts to minimise the negative perceptions of a company in order that corporate communications, both in controlled advertising messages and in publicity terms, will be assigned a higher environmental credibility. When such credibility has been established, consumers will give the messages more attention. The importance of this process is clear, given that consumers are more aware and informed than ever before, and will increasingly review the corporations in a holistic sense before trusting them with long-term loyalty and support.

One firm which successfully followed an environmentally aware policy is Varta, the German battery manufacturers. Varta's decision to be the first to market mercury-free batteries in the UK coincided with a rise in market share from 2 per cent to 13 per cent in the late 1980s. The company received favourable editorial comment for its pro-environmental stance and made its environmental commitment the subject of a full-page press advertisement. Of course, factors such as the quality and price of the batteries must be integrated with the environmental stance to understand fully the reasons for the increase in market share.

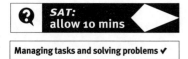

SAT:
allow 10 mins

Managing tasks and solving problems ✔

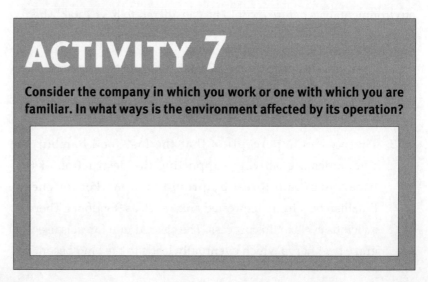

ACTIVITY 7

Consider the company in which you work or one with which you are familiar. In what ways is the environment affected by its operation?

Commentary...

Your answer will vary according to the product or service your company supplies. Examples of the ways in which the environment is affected by certain products include:

- soap powder production leads to pollution of waterways
- transportation of goods generates exhaust emissions
- quarrying produces noise pollution and dust
- confectionery production involves the use of usually non-sustainable energy resources.

You should remember that almost everything that is manufactured is produced at some environmental cost. The ethical approach of companies is to keep the cost to a minimum.

In a strategic sense, it is clear that the pharmaceutical and chemical businesses will never be considered environmentally friendly. The quest for credibility revolves around individual firms removing the perception that profits are going to be achieved whatever the environmental cost. The problem for high profile chemical companies such as ICI is that mistakes, such as toxic waste pollution of waterways, receive a great deal of adverse media attention. This creates a climate of opinion in which ICI's real environmental achievements – such as its award-winning clean ammonia synthesis technique and expert systems (computer systems which take the role of experts and can be questioned) to advise farmers on safe use of pesticides and agrochemicals – are harder to publicise effectively. It needs to break through the barrier of scepticism that has been established.

It is clear, having examined some of the corporate strategy issues which environmentalism raises, that the subject is at the heart of current marketing thinking. Whatever the specific response of individual companies, it is apparent that no business can afford to ignore the issues. Environmental credibility, a key tenet of corporate credibility, can only be achieved by showing hard evidence to consumers to back up claims.

In 1989, the Henley Centre made a prediction: 'In the future, for many, environmental friendliness will be a prerequisite for purchase, and those that do not address these issues will find their products increasingly rejected.' In addition, it might be said that firms which fail to address the crucial issues and develop synergistic solutions will find themselves spiralling to corporate oblivion due to environmental and strategic short-sightedness.

Companies that are environmentally hostile will find it hard to market their products with a premium price and quality strategy. Equally, they will find it increasingly difficult to recruit well-educated, environmentally aware people. In short, they could become a corporate underclass, ignoring long-term strategy and relying on crude short-term tactics to survive. Their future is bleak within such a scenario.

Consumerism

> ¡?¡ **Consumerism** is the organised movement of consumers, backed by legislation, which aims to strengthen the position of buyers in relation to sellers.

Here are several examples showing the growing importance of consumerism:

- The UK consumer magazine *Which?* regularly provides authoritative reports on best buys and unacceptable practices.

- Television programmes such as *That's Life* and *Watchdog* report on companies which attempt to exploit consumers.

- The Advertising Standards Authority regularly monitors complaints from the public with regard to television programmes or commercials, with the aim of ensuring that they are 'legal, decent, honest and truthful'.

- Greenpeace began as a very small low-key group who engaged in 'stunts' to bring environmental issues to the public attention.

It is now a large, professionally run organisation. Two of its main successes have been the vast reduction in whale hunting since the 1960s and the move to CFC-free fridge and freezer production within Europe (especially Germany).

It might appear that the presence of consumer movements shows the failure of the marketing concept – critics of the marketing concept argue that firms have exploited consumers and thus forced them to take action to protect themselves. For example, in America in the 1960s, Ralph Nader led the consumer movement with a series of very high profile attacks on corporations and their products, notably the Ford Car Corporation.

Consumerism has taken off in the UK, Scandinavia, Holland, Belgium, France, Germany and Japan in the last 20 years as consumers have increasingly demanded their rights – they want to be fully informed about product ingredients, advertising claims and so on.

Specifically, consumerism has:

- led to widespread introduction of ingredient and nutritional labelling on food products

- led to the introduction of sell-by dates on food products

- made firms demonstrate what they are doing to remove toxins and reduce pollution from their production processes

- encouraged greater ethical standards in advertising and promotion, e.g. in terms of avoiding claims which cannot be supported.

This is not to say that there is not still much to be done. Despite the fact that the legislative network relating to trades descriptions, sale of goods, safety and public health, helps to protect consumers, certain companies still operate in the 'grey' area. This means that what they do is not strictly illegal, but it is not in the consumer's best interest.

For example, critics argue that banks have underpaid account holders for years by not informing them of higher interest generating new products. With a lack of information, customers leave their money in low interest accounts – this is said to save the banks millions of pounds each year. Now, however, consumer pressure is forcing them to inform existing customers when new products are launched.

Does consumerism spell the death knell of the marketing concept? Undoubtedly, the answer has to be: 'No' What will happen is that

CONSUMERISM

firms will have to pay ever more attention to consumer issues and trends for the backlash from aggrieved consumers is very damaging, particularly as the media is keen to highlight consumer concerns. The forked-tail effect can be very damaging – remember Gerald Ratner?

Consumerism can be seen to represent the ultimate aspirations of the marketing ethos, as it forces a strong customer orientation. Alan Toffler, a noted futurologist, described the consumer of the 1990s as a **'prosumer'** who understands the power they have, will be very selective given the wide choice available, and will not hesitate to form groups aimed at enforcing legislation or pressuring firms to cease anti-social and unethical practices.

Companies should not be defensive in their response to these issues. By formulating credible responses to consumerism, accepting in many cases that the consumer groups are often right to take their stand on issues, they can strengthen their relationships with consumers who are likely to stay loyal to them. Once again, this is an example of relationship marketing at work for every threat also presents a commercial opportunity. For example, the soap and detergent companies have identified a growing market for environmentally friendly washing powders which they now supply.

summary

This session has considered a company's responsibility to society.

▶ Ethical responsibility is seen by some companies as a significant objective. Other companies believe that the only responsibility of a business it to increase its profits. Increasingly, companies are responding to trends in the social climate in a careful and selective manner.

▶ A societal orientation recognises that a firm has additional responsibilities beyond making profits. This includes the welfare of its staff and the need to conserve energy and raw materials.

▶ When business fails in its social responsibilities, watch-dog bodies or regulatory bodies are set up, and new legislation may be enacted.

▶ Firms must take account of a society's values, beliefs and cultural traditions in order to market their products and services effectively.

▶ Firms increasingly have to take into account environmental issues as consumers become aware of green concerns.

▶ It is essential that business forms credible responses to the consumer movement in order to strengthen their relationship with customers.

Analysing the market

Competitive position

Objectives

After participating in this session, you should be able to:

▶ explain the ways in which markets can be segmented

▶ identify the variables which are used

▶ describe the concept of lifestyle segmentation

▶ show how positioning affects consumer behaviour

▶ identify the bases for product positioning

▶ outline the cycle of adoption of a product.

In working through this session, you will practise the following BTEC common skills:

Managing and developing self	✔
Working with and relating to others	✔
Communicating	✔
Managing tasks and solving problems	✔
Applying numeracy	
Applying technology	
Applying design and creativity	

Market segmentation

> **⟨?⟩ Market segmentation** is the process by which a market is divided into smaller, distinct sub-markets.

A company that segments a market does so to target its efforts more effectively and hence, to make higher profits. For example, there is a general market for cars but a more specific market for high performance cars. The market can also be segmented for demand by age, occupation, location or by other factors. One way of understanding the concept of market segmentation is shown in figures 1.1–1.4.

⟨⟩ = a customer

FIGURE 1.1: *The unsegmented market.*

Figure 1.1 represents a general market with customers and a wide range of goods. Food would be an example of this.

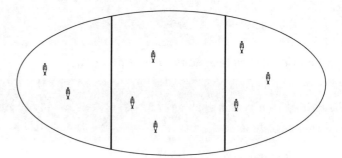

FIGURE 1.2: *The partially segmented market.*

Figure 1.2 represents specialisation within the market by customers and suppliers. In the case of food, the three segments could be fruit, vegetables and meat. Customers would look to fulfil specific needs and suppliers specialise in a segment of the market.

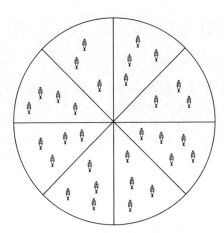

FIGURE 1.3: *A market with many segments.*

Figure 1.3 shows a further involvement of segmentation. Suppliers and customers could be found for more closely defined types of produce. For example, a poultry market would be a segment of the general meat market, and within the poultry market there would be specific segments based on specific types and weights of poultry demanded by consumers.

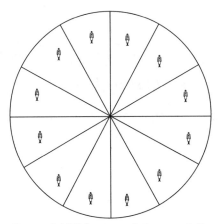

FIGURE 1.4 *Ultimate market segmentation.*

Ultimately each customer could become the focus of a specific segment. In figure 1.4, we see the exact opposite of figure 1.1. For example, a magazine company could produce a product aimed at an individual consumer, but it would not be profitable for it to do so. There has to be a balance between the degree of segmentation achieved, and the rewards to be gained.

SAT:
allow 10 mins

Managing tasks and solving problems ✔

ACTIVITY 1

Consider the market for investments or financial provisions. List five different types of financial product aimed at meeting the investment needs of consumers. Consider if any of your choices are subject to intense competition.

Commentary...

Here are some of the most common financial products:

- Unit trusts

- Life assurance

- Stocks and shares (equities)

- Ethical/green investments

- Offshore investments

- Child savings plan

- Investment trust

- Endowment mortgage

- Personal pension

- Regular savings plan (banks and building societies have various ones offering different rates of interest)

- TESSA (tax exempt special savings account)

- ELSA (equity linked savings account)

Notice that, within each of these segments, there is intense competition. For example, performance tables of specific unit trusts or TESSAs show consumers which are the best performers over a period of time.

Before a market is segmented, four key questions must be asked:

Is the segment measurable?

Companies have to be able to measure the size and purchasing power of the segment. Many youth segments are difficult to measure as the lifestyles of young people make it difficult for companies to use conventional advertising and market research techniques to gather data on them. An example is the so-called 'rave' scene. Until very recently, this was largely banned in the UK and took place illegally. As a consequence, it was very difficult for companies to define the 'rave' segment in terms of the various segmentation variables (see later in this section for a discussion of segmentation methods) that were relevant to the people who constituted it.

Is the market segment accessible?

The market must serve its customers effectively, and this is difficult to do when access to the market is limited. For example, it is difficult for insurance companies to gain access to potential customers in countries with poor infrastructures and high illiteracy rates.

Is the market segment sustainable?

It must be profitable for companies to target the particular market segment. A bicycle for people over seven feet tall would not be profitable because the target segment would be too limited.

Is the market segment actionable?

Suppliers must be able to formulate programmes to attract and serve the market. It would be pointless for an airline company with only two small planes capable of flying from the UK to Paris or Amsterdam attempting to define a segmentation policy aimed at serving the needs of first class passengers wanting to travel to the Far East. The company has to take account of its resources.

It is crucial to note the difference between a segment and a niche. A **segment** is quite broad – the sports car segment for example. A **niche** is a very specialised part of any segment – in the sports car segment, Morgan Cars of Wales occupy a specific niche producing medium-priced sports cars to suit the particular needs of clearly identified Morgan car enthusiasts.

The more precisely targeted the niche is, the greater the chance the company has of owning the niche – that is, of having no (or few) competitors. The danger of niche markets is that they can close quickly due to changes in consumer taste, competitive activity or poor performance by niche owners.

Small companies often find specific niches, but big companies need to reach broad sections of markets. The Germans call small companies aggressively pursuing niche markets 'niche jaegers' – niche hunters, a very apt description.

MAJOR SEGMENTATION VARIABLES

Customer variations are an important factor in segmenting the market. There are three key components of any analysis of customer variations: geographic, demographic and psychographic (or lifestyle). Below are the general variables that can be used within each of these three categories.

Geographic:

- region

- county

- city

- density of population (urban/rural/suburban).

Demographic:

- age

- sex

- family size

- life cycle (longevity)

- occupation

- income

- education

- religion

- nationality.

Psychographic (or lifestyle) analysis:

- social class

- lifestyle

- personality

- activities, interests, opinions (AIOs).

Geodemographics is a very important segmentation variable now. This is an analysis of where people live based on postcode addresses. Because of factors such as the price and mix of housing, the quality and type of leisure amenities and so on, postcodes reveal a lot about the people who live in those areas. Postcode areas are usually given a phrase which sums them up by analysts, such as 'golf clubs and Volvos' for a prosperous area or 'back streets and pubs' for a run-down one.

The key to effective segmentation is to use more than one segmentation variable to give a rich picture of the segment under investigation. Consider a bank that wants a better understanding of its existing customers' requirements and wishes to appeal to new customers. It would be beneficial to use a mixture of geodemographics and psychographics to identify specific customer segments. This would tell the bank: where customers live, who they are, their lifestyle and what issues are really important to them. On the basis of this information – which must be kept up to date by regular use of questionnaires and so on – a bank can segment its customer base.

A bank could use this information to target different market segments with specifically designed financial products:

- For those customers with an above average income, few financial commitments (e.g. they might have paid off their mortgage) and an above average desire to take financial risks, they could launch a personal equity plan (PEP) with an above average return on investment potential but a high degree of risk. (Risk, in this sense, means that investors might receive less than they invested if the PEP performs very badly.)

- For those wealthy well-educated customers with young families (e.g. married couples in their early 30s with three children under the age of ten), there could be an opportunity to target them with products which fit their lifestyle profile. An example would be a special school fee savings scheme.

○ For poorer customers in rented accommodation in run-down inner city areas, the key market opportunities could be loans for university or college education for mature people (wanting to better themselves) and easy-to-understand mortgages for first-time homebuyers.

THE DEVELOPMENT OF SEGMENTATION

In the early days of segmentation, markets were divided up geographically. Companies chose to sell their products in selected parts of a country. This method was forced on companies by the poor infrastructure in many countries. It had little targeting potential.

As countries developed, brands started to go national and the number of products and brands on the market grew rapidly. After the Second World War, there was a social revolution with living standards going up, incomes rising and more leisure and recreation time. The style of advertising at the time made people more fashion conscious. All these factors helped to produce more discerning consumers with a larger choice than ever before.

There was obviously a need for marketing people to recognise the individuality of choice and, out of this realisation came demographic segmentation, the splitting up of a market according to variables such as social class, sex, age and religion.

Companies now had a clearer idea of who purchased their products. Knowing this, they could tailor products and services to particular groups of people. It became apparent that the consumer was becoming a much more informed and educated individual. Marketeers realised that they needed to know not only *who* purchased their products but also *why* they did. Psychographic or lifestyle analysis is a theory and method designed to solve the problem: the identification of the reasons why.

Today, this is more important than ever. Information is being continually directed at the consumer by manufacturers, through television, newspapers, posters and radio advertising, at a faster and more voluminous rate than ever before. Consumers can only take in a limited amount; they will only retain information that is seen as relevant. Other information will be discarded. Geodemographics is still an important segmentation technique but it only gives half the picture, a group of consumers with similar incomes will contain a huge range of different lifestyles. Psychographic segmentation variables need to be applied to ensure the right message or product reaches the right people, at the right time. The more segmentation variables that can be used to analyse and appraise customers, the greater the likelihood of accurate targeting of products and services.

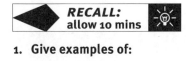

RECALL:
allow 10 mins

1. Give examples of:

   (a) an unsegmented market

   (b) a partially segmented market

   (c) a market with many segments.

2. Explain the difference between a segment and a niche.

3. List the three major market segmentation variables.

Lifestyle segmentation

We each have an idea of what the word lifestyle means and we often use it in our everyday language. We say things like: 'I have an active lifestyle.' or: 'She has a very unconventional lifestyle.' For use in marketing, we need to be more specific than this. To put it simply, we could say that lifestyle is an individual system of **activities, interests** and **opinions** (AIOs) that, together, are a major influence on a person's pattern of living and spending.

Lifestyle is not static; it changes significantly over time and to an extent these changes are driven by the media and the market. The media is very clever at creating convenient lifestyles, that have a whole set of AIOs peculiar to them. Recent media creations include **yuppies** (young, upwardly mobile professionals) and **dinkies** (double income, no children).

The two important things to remember about lifestyles are:

1. The type of lifestyle people lead dictates the way they respond to different events and situations.

2. Lifestyle influences an individual's purchasing pattern. People tend to select those products or services which match or enhance their lifestyle.

Lifestyles are learned by individuals as a result of many influences: culture, social class, groups to which they belong and the family. Lifestyle is also derived from an individual's personality and values, so it can be seen as a combination of personality and social influences.

LIFESTYLE AND GROUPS

Lifestyles are adopted (or followed) by broad and specific groups. People in those groups develop a set of values that are a variant of the national culture. This idea of **'group membership'** is very important to the individual and also to the marketeer. People with similar lifestyles often form groups, which makes it easier for firms to target them with particular products and services.

Each group to which a person feels a sense of belonging (known as a **reference group**) has symbols which represent it, and the consumption of certain goods becomes a mechanism by which you are marked out as belonging to a group. For example, faded jeans and rucksacks are commonly associated with students travelling.

Within any reference group, there are individuals who tend to strongly influence group decision making in terms of purchasing decisions. All companies have to understand how strongly this process determines the demand for their products and services. They must try to target messages at the **opinion leaders** within a specific reference group.

> **\?!** **Opinion leaders** are the small number of people in each reference group who exert a strong influence over the purchasing behaviour of the rest of the group. This is because their opinions are valued and respected.

The opinion leaders in each reference group are different. Opinion leadership is not linked to social status – knowledge and credibility seem to be critical. In a group of computer enthusiasts, for example, an opinion leader could be the one with the most specialist technological understanding.

ACTIVITY 2

What groups influence you? Write down examples of reference groups to which you belong.

How far does your membership of these groups influence your lifestyle. What groups are the most influential?

Commentary...

Your specific answer will vary according to the groups you have chosen. Here is an outline answer to act as an illustration. Typically, we belong to groups like:

- family

- work groups (formal teams or informal groups of workmates)

- college lecture and tutorial groups

- sports-related groups, such as a football team

- social groups – a music appreciation society.

The family group is important as this strongly influences your values, your behaviour and attitudes. Your family has a strong effect on your lifestyle, and your aims in life. For example, the degree of parental control and restriction has an important influence on teenagers; how late they can stay out, influences their lifestyle.

College groups (based around studies) influence the way in which people value achievement, how hard individuals work, and how they blend work and relaxation. For example, the group may only decide to have a night out when they have successfully finished their work; alternatively they will decide that enjoyment is given top priority. Generally speaking, the groups that are most influential to a person are those to which they feel the greatest sense of belonging or need to belong to.

Groups to which individuals feel a need to belong to are called **aspirational groups**. For young sports people, an aspirational group might be a group of first team players; for hard working students, an aspirational group might be the people in the class who are the brightest and earn the highest marks.

PSYCHOGRAPHICS AS A MEASURE OF CONSUMER BEHAVIOUR

Marketeers are trying to find a relationship between their products and brands and specific lifestyle groups; they can then aim a brand more definitely at one type of lifestyle. The lifestyle concept involves the idea of demographics to make predictions more accurate. It allows us to see a person as an individual; if someone's personality is known, along with AIOs, more of a profile of the whole person is drawn.

Psychographics is a principle technique used by consumer researchers as a measure of lifestyle. It seeks to provide a quantitative measure of a consumer's lifestyle, in contrast to qualitative research from group interviews and similar techniques. It centres on a person's activities, interests and opinions.

Activities are described as being an action such as viewing a certain medium, shopping at a particular store and so on. Although these acts are usually observable, the reasons for the actions are not often subject to direct measurement.

Interests may be in some object, event or topic or, for example, dancing or computers.

Opinions can be verbal or written statements that a person gives in response to situations in which a question is raised, e.g. anticipation about future events and the consequences that will result from alternative actions.

Candidates are presented with questionnaires, which seek to measure these AIOs. Many of the questions are in the form of agreement or disagreement, e.g. 'I usually dress for fashion, not for comfort.' or 'I often have a drink before dinner.' The data gathered is then analysed on a computer to determine the distinctive lifestyle groups. Table 1.1 shows the major dimensions used to measure the elements, it also includes the individual's demographics.

Activities	Interests	Opinions	Demographics
Work	Family	Themselves	Age
Social events	Job	Politics	Income
Holidays	Community	Business	Occupation
Entertainment	Recreation	Economics	Family size
Club membership	Fashion	Education	Dwelling
Community	Food	Products	Geography
Shopping	Media	Future	City size
Sports	Achievements	Culture	Stage in life cycle

TABLE 1.1: *The major dimensions used to measure AIOs*

GENERAL AND SPECIFIC LIFESTYLE SEGMENTATION

General lifestyle is about overall patterns of living. For example, 'I usually stay at home on a Saturday night.', tells you something about a person's general lifestyle. It defines overall patterns such as satisfaction with life, family orientation, self confidence and so on. A **specific lifestyle** approach is about the product class or brand, the frequency of use of a product or service, or the media from which the information is sought. A question like 'Would you consider changing your daily newspaper?' seeks information about a person's specific lifestyle.

A marketing department or research agency can use the lifestyle theory to identify general lifestyle groups or take a more specific approach and identify how lifestyles influence the marketing of a brand or product. Having identified various lifestyle grouping (e.g. among women aged 45 and under) a marketing manager has clear options open concerning price, distribution and promotion. If a company has a product which appeals to the more affluent women, then there may be opportunities for premium pricing. An example would be Vivienne Westwood designs.

Similarly, specific magazines will be bought by women who have a certain lifestyle. For example, one group of women who are home centred may buy the magazine *Family Circle* but they might not buy *Harpers & Queen* or *Tatler*. This has obvious implications for companies trying to direct messages at different types of women.

Lifestyle is one of the things that influences where you shop. Products that match a certain lifestyle will be sold through an outlet that best caters for that lifestyle; for example, the most expensive Alfred Dunhill toiletries are only sold in exclusive stores. The company is aware that wealthy people who are frequent international air travellers are likely to be key customers, so they have outlets near the major world airports.

As well as giving indications of the type of products people buy, lifestyle segmentation can also help to identify the price a lifestyle group is prepared to pay, the place it will go to buy it and the media via which they see the advertisement.

Like any theory, lifestyle segmentation has both advantages and disadvantages.

The advantages of lifestyle segmentation

- Lifestyle segmentation provides a simple and valid summary of the major variables used in buyer behaviour theory (attitudes, perceptions and social influence).

- Demographics provides a 'two-dimensional picture' but, when combined with lifestyle analysis, the whole idea of consumer behaviour is given greater depth, and a 'richer picture' of consumers emerges.

- Products can be placed in a way that will have greater success in reaching an identified lifestyle segment and target market because the media can also be segmented on a lifestyle basis.

- There is a greater opportunity to spot gaps in seemingly saturated markets or to identify totally new markets by the application of lifestyle segmentation.

The disadvantages of lifestyle segmentation

- Time and cost: a detailed study takes time and the research will be expensive.

- Failure to comprehend fully or measure the whole lifestyle may account for apparent inconsistencies in a person's lifestyle. This complicates prediction of consumer choice related solely to lifestyle measures.

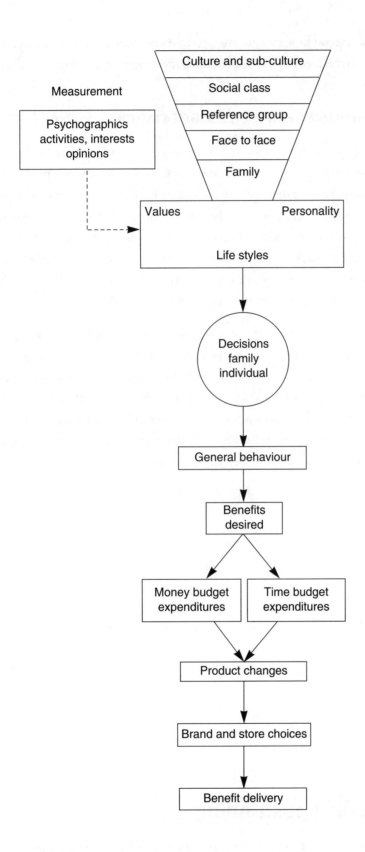

FIGURE 1.5: *Lifestyle influences on consumer decisions.*

○ Lifestyle segments are not discrete; there may be some overlap which could cause problems for specific targeting.

A CRITICISM OF LIFESTYLE SEGMENTATION

Critics of lifestyle segmentation theory may say it is based purely on guess-work. This criticism is too simplistic, but the theory must be put in perspective before we judge its validity. The marketeer works in an environment where knowledge of the market segment and the consumer within the market segment is essential. In this environment, it is not enough to know who buys the product; knowing why can light up previously dark corners. The marketeer is dealing with a consumer who is open to a huge amount of influence.

How are the effects of these influences on his or her consumption pattern measured? The answer is that they cannot be measured totally. The outcome of the analysis of consumer behaviour is a **prediction**. But the word 'prediction' has a completely different meaning from 'guess-work'. A prediction is a **forecast**, based on sound evidence, of what may occur in the future. In this case, the sound evidence is the result of psychographic analysis.

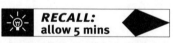

RECALL:
allow 5 mins

1. Explain why lifestyle is important to the marketeer.

2. Explain what the acronym AIO stands for.

3. Give one advantage and one disadvantage of lifestyle segmentation.

Product positioning

Positioning takes place in the consumer's mind, when they locate proposed or existing brands in relation to competitive offerings. It is vital that companies influence the way consumers think about products. For example, a small car could be considered 'cramped' by consumers, so the company should stress its 'nippiness'. A large car could be considered by consumers to be 'extravagant' so a company should stress how 'luxurious' it is.

The key questions that companies must address are:

- What place does the product **occupy** in the market?

- How does the product **rank** against its competitors in various areas?

- What are the consumer's **attitudes** to the product?

HOW DO YOU POSITION PRODUCTS?

The French saying is *'cherchez le creneau'* – you look for the hole. Finding the hole or gap in the market place and the consumer's mind is the key to success. If there is no hole, reposition your competitor and fill its hole. For example, Becks repositioned Lowenbrau: 'You've tasted the German beer that's most popular in the USA. Now taste the German beer that's most popular in Germany'. This stresses the popularity of its product, German beer, with the people who should know, the Germans.

The simple way into the mind is to be the first, preferably with an over-simplified message. For example, 'Shake'n'Vac' was one of the most successful advertisements of the 1980s in terms of raising awareness. Another good example is 'Miller Lite Beer', advertising a product that combines the enjoyment of drinking with calorie consciousness.

When aiming to position products, being the first in the market is extremely useful (providing the gap exists in the market and the mind); being second is considerably less useful. For example, when ICI launched Dulux Solid Emulsion paint in the mid-1980s, it was considered essential to be the first company onto the market with a solid paint. The advantage was that ICI's product would become synonymous with the benefits it gave. These benefits included a 'beautiful finish', which was important given the fact that the main target segment of consumers were young married couples of above average social status – people who dislike the bother and mess of decorating, see it as an unpleasant chore, and who can afford to pay extra for a product which would make the process worthwhile. Having filled that position in the minds of the target consumers, Dulux Solid Emulsion makes it much more difficult for solid paints from competitors such as Crown, Berger or own-label firms to be anything other than a 'me-too' offering. Dulux Solid Emulsion was a premium-priced product directly targeted at people who would willingly pay for the benefits it provided.

GATHERING INFORMATION FOR PRODUCT POSITIONING

Positioning a product can, more often than not, be very expensive, exacting and time consuming. It is far from being easy. Large amounts of time and effort are devoted to research, data collection and interpretation of the measurement techniques used to determine product position.

Before we can develop positioning strategies, we have to collect appropriate information to form a framework that will help us decide which strategy to adopt. The origins of the positioning concept help us to understand where our information has to come from. The concepts of positioning originate from three main sources:

- economists' work on the market structure

- the competitive position of the firm

- the concepts of substitution and competition among products.

However, as the positioning concept has developed, it has become less concerned with the objective economic facts and now focuses on the consumer's perceptions regarding the place a product occupies in a given market. The reason we concentrate on the consumers' perceptions is because the solution to the problem is inside their mind. So this is where our information has to come from.

CUSTOMER PERCEPTION

In the past, when firms have concentrated on the objective features of their products, the customer has not always perceived these features similarly – they have positioned the product differently in their mind. For example, Citroën concentrated on the engineering excellence of their cars, features that consumers did not rate highly or did not add to the perceptions of the product – the result was almost disastrous for Citroën. In contrast, Ford reaped the benefits of providing the features the consumer perceived as being important.

This concept is better understood if we consider the definition of the word **objective:** 'actually existing independent of the perceiver's mind'. So, although the extra features of the Citroën car were real and objective (e.g. advanced suspension), if the consumer (perceiver) does not recognise them (or their overall benefits) then they may as well not be specified features.

In the late 1950s, an American firm thought that they had developed a brilliant new concept in food – old people's food. The basic idea was that old people would enjoy fruit-flavoured vitamin-enriched rusks, because their teeth and digestive systems were not as good as they used to be. When the product was tested it failed disastrously. 'Old' consumers did not feel old, and they resented being seen as infirm or weak. They positioned the product as *hostile* rather than *helpful*.

This illustrates the importance of a strong and positive **brand image**. A brand is normally associated with a mark made on cattle to show to whom they belong – it is burnt on to last. This is the essence of branding companies – such as IBM and Ford – ranges of products (often known as **umbrella branding**) such as Bird's Eye Captain's Table brands, and branding individual products, such as KitKat, Aero, Polo or Bounty.

Whatever approach is chosen, the brand image becomes a complex mix of tangible and intangible attributes which, when developed over a period of time, becomes the **brand heritage** – the unique way in which the brand becomes more valuable than a similar product in the mind of the consumer. Factors such as the ingredients, the packaging, the price and the communication process all combine to give the brand a unique personality.

In qualitative research, people are often asked: 'If product X was a person, who would it be like?' This is an attempt to discover whether the brand is liked, and whether it is being perceived in the way the producers and advertisers want it to be.

ACTIVITY 3

Until recently, Babycham – a light bubbly drink made from pears – was a declining brand aimed at women.

In a small group, discuss how the makers of Babycham could have repositioned it. Jot down your key points in the box below.

Our commentary tells you how Babycham's manufacturers did reposition the brand, so you can compare your ideas.

EXERCISE: allow 30 mins

Working with and relating to others ✔

Managing tasks and solving problems ✔

Commentary...

Babycham has tried to reposition itself towards younger, more socially active drinkers who might appreciate its light, bubbly qualities and drink it in preference to beer or spirits or other wines. The perception that Babycham had to overcome was its image as an old-fashioned drink. The manufacturers have attempted to change this perception with new advertising – with its presentation of young fashionable males and females drinking Babycham – and by repackaging the drink into bigger bottles. The brand image has been strengthened by showing male and female opinion leaders ordering the product and finding it tasted good. In a night-club, the other members of the reference group are shown saying: 'I'll have a Babycham.' They are the opinion followers.

CUSTOMER PREFERENCE

Another approach to obtaining information from the consumer is to consider the consumer's preference for your product in relation to those of your competitors. Not just the overall preference, but preference under various conditions. For example, liquid soap is shown in advertisements as being very hygienic; it is convenient for people who have to wash their hands frequently and want to avoid coming into contact with a bar of soap that has been handled by other people. Target markets include surgeons, chefs and people working in the home (cleaning, cooking and so on).

Ideally, a mix of both types of data, customer perception and customer preference, provides the best information. The reason for using both types of data is based on the premise that customer behaviour is a function of both perception and preference, and the recognition that buyers may differ with respect to both their perceptions of products and their preference for products. This means that two customers may perceive the same ideal point, for example they both want the same balance between sportiness and prestige in a car. However, how they rank specific cars in this market, to meeting the ideal point, may vary.

DECIDING ON WHAT IS THE MARKET

Before we can collect our perception and preference data we have to decide on the boundaries of the market within which our product is competing. All the relevant products and brands that operate within the boundaries have to be identified. This identification of the various products and brands within the market can be done by marketing experts, based on their experience and analysis of existing information. It can also be undertaken from unstructured in-depth interviews carried out on consumers (known as **qualitative research**).

Identifying a broad set of competing items is crucial, since it constitutes the set of **stimulus questions** which will be set for the positioning study. So, when designing a stimulus set of questions, it is sometimes desirable to include two types of products and brands: first, brands in the same product class; and, second, brands outside the product class that may be used by consumers as substitutes. For example, in a study of soup, one could include a set of different soup brands as well as home-made soup. And second, a set of soup substitutes such as salad, sandwiches and coffee.

A BRAND NEW CHOCOLATE CONCEPT IN THE 1980S

This case study looks at the development of 'Spira', a new chocolate product developed by Cadbury which has been available nationally since 1989. The case study is based on information supplied by Cadbury. By tracing the development of Spira, from the first stages of development back in 1984, we show the importance of each stage in the project.

The Spira story starts with a major technological breakthrough. A new production process was devised capable of extruding chocolate into different shapes and textures without the use of moulds. The next stage was to channel this new expertise into a new product which would enhance Cadbury's product range, strengthening a perceived area of weakness.

Analysis of Cadbury's strengths and weaknesses relative to the market and competition showed the strength of the Cadbury chocolate brand heritage but weakness in countlines (bars originally sold by number rather than weight), particularly in teenage lines.

Cadbury decided to launch a competitive attack in the milk chocolate segment. Milk chocolate is the biggest market segment and is Cadbury's main strength, so Cadbury's Dairy Milk was the obvious chocolate choice in a countline format.

The product brief

Cadbury's research and development department was presented with a clear brief to build on Cadbury's Dairy Milk heritage in a pure chocolate countline format, exploring all possible textures, configurations and resultant product possibilities – known in the trade as 'eats'.

Three products were chosen from the many research and development concepts. These were developed for consumer research. Concept boards presenting the product idea, positioning and target audience were produced, plus new pack designs. These were researched through qualitative research – small informal groups of around eight people took part in an in-depth exploration of the issues considering product appeal, relationship to other brands, imagery and distinctiveness. Findings were critically analysed and the field was narrowed down to one product: 'Rollers' a twisted shaped bar with a cart-wheel interior, was considered easy to eat, a convenient 'one-handed eat' and definitely different. The name was not right though, and much more work needed to be carried out.

Quantitative research

The product was reformed. The name 'Spira' was agreed and the presentation was targeted at the teenage sector. This time the research sample was larger, discussions were not in-depth, interviews took place in halls followed by an in-home trial. What was the strength of the appeal? Would Spira take sales from other Cadbury products? What sales volumes could be predicted? The answers to these questions would be crucial to the success or failure of the product.

The appeal was confirmed very strongly, especially among 15- to 24-year-olds; the product concept matched perfectly with the target – it was young, active, trendy, convenient. The scene was set for a test market to assess Spira where it really counts, in the open market place.

A £1 million investment in a test market plant at Bournville was agreed with a September 1987 test launch date and product build-up started earlier in April.

Test market selection

Granada, in the North, was selected for Spira. The television station reached 12 per cent of the population and had the right demographic profile. Major promotional support was allocated, including television advertising and promotional literature.

Spira was launched very successfully in the Granada area gaining a 6.3 per cent share of the total market and the number two chocolate position, despite problems of supply. Such was the success, that it had to be withdrawn as supply to the test market plant could not keep up with demand. (Withdrawing a successful product from a test market is not an uncommon phenomenon in these days of high technology and high investment production units.)

Spira was moved into a second more compact test area – Television South West, which represents under 4 per cent of the country. It was equally successful. During this time, further investment was made in the Spira plant as the Bournville factory continued to build capacity to meet consumer demand at national level.

Conclusion

From this case study you can see how Cadbury positioned Spira. Although the product concept had become a practical possibility due to advances in technology (which could extrude chocolate without moulds), the development of the product and its positioning in the market was a task for management.

Spira was positioned as a countline aimed at teenagers, but it was developed to compliment and to enhance the Cadbury's 'Dairy Milk' brand heritage. The product would also cover an area of weakness in the product range (known as a portfolio) – the countline segment of the market. Notice how important brand image was to the overall success of the product. Spira was a young, active and trendy brand, and its main consumers were young, active and trendy 15- to 24-year-olds who understood and valued the brand attributes.

Qualitative and quantitative research was used extensively to ensure that the product formed a perfect 'fit' with its target market. Remember that, although the company could try to influence the way that consumers thought about (perceived) Spira, only the consumers could ultimately position it in their own minds.

One final point was that the use of 'real life' test markets was important not just to show the strength of demand for Spira, but to show whether it would take sales away from other Cadbury chocolate products (a process known as **cannibalisation**). Because it was unlike any other Cadbury product, Spira developed its own sales and took sales from competitors rather than other established Cadbury brands.

Positioning strategies

Before discussing a positioning strategy it is essential to give consideration to two areas:

- competition in market segments

- product line factors.

The real value of positioning is revealed only when it is coupled with an appropriate **market segmentation strategy**. A company only occupies one rung on a ladder; its competitors occupy the rest. Implementing a positioning strategy without consideration of the competitors in the chosen market segment is unwise. (We deal with this in more detail, in section 4.)

A firm cannot ignore the place a product occupies in its **product line** as perceived by the consumer. It is a combination of positioning in relation to its own product line and those of competitors in the market segment. For example, 'Alka Seltzer Plus' was positioned to compete with other brands and analgesics, but succeeded instead in taking part of the market share of Alka Seltzer standard form. This is also common in lines such as air fresheners, carpet cleaners and so on. The position must be clear and differentiated from existing brands in order to minimise the problem of cannibalisation.

It is particularly crucial that a company clearly differentiates between its high-quality (expensive) products and any new value brands (which will be cheaper), otherwise consumers may simply shift to purchasing the cheaper product. This is one reason why companies develop a strong, high-value brand image for products in order that consumers pay more for them than a less high-value alternative. Andrex toilet tissue is a product that has been developed to achieve this strong brand image and, over the years, the 'Andrex puppy' has come to be a symbol of softness, strength and quality to consumers. This has allowed the product to be priced above competitive offerings – because it is valued more highly by consumers.

ALTERNATIVE BASES FOR POSITIONING

Now we consider some alternative product positioning strategies.

Positioning on specific product features

Attempts may be made to position products because the features offer an advantage over competition. This might be in terms of anything from speed to size or detailed design to simplicity of use. For example, computer advertisements emphasise memory, functions and so on; household products are packaged in self-styled 'easy-to-use' containers.

A recent computer example is the 'Intel Pentium Processor'. Its advertising stresses the many applications. Another good example, a household product, would be 'Toilet Duck' lavatory cleaner which cleans under the 'U' bend because of its unique shape. Notice that this also adds humour to the brand.

Positioning on benefits, problems, solutions or needs

A good example is television adverts for pharmaceutical products which cure headaches. The potential customer desires the benefit, but has little concern for the product attribute (the ingredients).

Hedex are positioned at the consumer (benefits) and Paracodol are positioned at the National Health Service (product attributes). Although Hedex is more expensive, the products are very similar, but there is a different positioning strategy for the different target markets.

Positioning for specific use occasion

Positioning strategies of this type are the obvious exaggerated marketing creations of Mothers' and Fathers' Day. Perhaps not so salient are newer occasions such as 'Red Nose Day'. First, there was the nose for the person, then for the car, then came the tee-shirts, mugs, hats, etc. No doubt we will all be buying funny (or not so funny!) gifts for each other on Red Nose Day in the near future.

Positioning against another product (the 'against' position)

Campaigns which position against another product may be implicit or explicit. Avis, the car rental company, never mentions Hertz explicitly, but its positioning 'Avis is number two in rental cars, so why go with us? Because we try harder', is an example of implicit positioning. Perhaps an example of explicit against positioning was Flymo's 'Its a lot less bovver than a Hovver' garden mower advert. This also had the effect of repositioning the competitor's product in the consumer's mind, thus attempting to poach a gap which your competitor already occupies by filling it more specifically in the minds of consumers.

Product class dissociation

By linking your product to what is already in the mind of the consumer and distancing yourself from it, you can successfully carve out a niche in the market. The classic example is 7-Up's 'the un-Cola taste'.

Product class dissociation is also useful when introducing a new product which differs from typical products in an established category. For example, lead-free petrol and tubeless tyres, are the essence of product class dissociation, attempting to break free from established perceptions of what a typical product in that class should be. This avoids being seen as just another product (known as 'me-toos').

Another form of dissociation is achieving a position that nobody else appears to want. Although by default, the VW Beetle achieved success as the 'Ugly Bug', which it then used to reinforce the reliability image with the slogan: 'We'll stay ugly longer.' Perhaps a more recent dissociation, into an area everyone else has neglected, is that of hiring out old bangers. Wrent a Wreck has successfully found an untapped position in the consumer's mind. A wreck will certainly not confer prestige on the driver, but nobody will want to steal it! Perhaps the main issue is whether consumers trust a wreck to transport them to their destination safely.

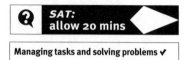

SAT:
allow 20 mins

Managing tasks and solving problems ✔

ACTIVITY 4

Read through the section (above) on alternative bases for positioning and answer the following questions.

How can car manufacturers position on specific product features?

How can breakfast cereals position on benefits and problems?

Give examples of goods that rely on:

(a) specific use occasion

(b) positioning against another product

(c) product class dissociation.

Commentary...

Here are our examples.

Car manufacturers can emphasise features such as airbags, alarms and ABS brakes. Breakfast cereals can promote the healthy benefits of the product against the perceived problems of the alternatives such as high-cholesterol cooked breakfasts.

Specific use occasion products include Christmas cards, birthday cards, wedding dresses and fireworks. Campaigns for butter and margarine use positioning against the other product. Both dispute which is the healthier. Goods which use product class dissociation include tubeless tyres, super lead-free petrol, low-calorie yoghurts and fat-free ice-cream.

Product diffusion

> **\?!** The **diffusion process**, as defined by Rogers (1962) is the 'spread of a new idea from its source of invention or creation to its ultimate users or adopters'.

The rate and ease of adoption of a new product is directly determined by individual consumer characteristics. Some people readily accept change while others are more traditional and are slower to react to change. Innovations take time to spread through the social system. All organisations must pay a great deal of attention to this, particularly if they are attempting to market a very innovative or high technology product.

Let us consider the different types of consumers.

Innovators

These purchasers represent the smallest percentage of the chosen target market that will adopt a new product. They may treat a new product as a status symbol, be fascinated by a technological development, have a deep personal or business need for the product, like to be different, see themselves as opinion leaders or may simply have sufficient income to purchase expensive prestigious products. They buy because they want to and can belong to any class provided they have funds to purchase. They may or may not set a trend, depending on their influence.

Early adopters

These are the consumers (the adopters) who will indicate whether most new products will be successful. They are the opinion leaders or trend setters that other members of the public will follow.

Early majority

This group (with the late majority) represent the majority of adopters. The early majority group may respond to opinion leaders and accept innovations quickly but purchase the product mainly for its usefulness and are, therefore, long-term repeat purchasers. Marketing managers must identify the needs and wants of this large group and introduce products or variations in order to satisfy their expectations and needs.

Late majority

This group tends to react slowly to changes, waiting for the product to prove itself and for the prices to come down before they adopt. Again, they may be long-term continuing purchasers. Allowances for their tastes and needs may also be made through the product mix offered.

Laggards

This the last group to respond to a new product. They value tradition and dislike changes from something well established. They will only adopt once the product has established a track record.

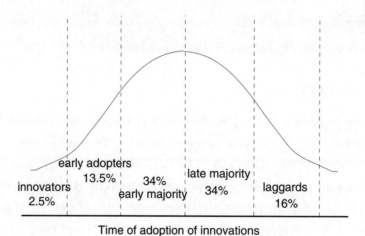

FIGURE 1.6: *Time of adoption of innovations.*
Source: Everett M. Rogers, 1962, *Diffusion of Innovations,* The Free Press.

Remember that the consumer responses will be affected by personal factors (e.g. age and sex), social factors (e.g. occupation and family), cultural factors (e.g. religion and nationality), and psychological factors (e.g. personality and perceptions).

To illustrate the diffusion process, consider as an example the market for television sets. **Innovators** are the consumers who have the income and desire to purchase the very latest state-of-the-art product. For these consumers, very large screens, superb sound quality and interactive facilities are crucial. The television set is likely to be an expensive status symbol for them. They always buy their sets outright.

Early adopters are likely to be very influential on their friends, relatives and associates when the decision to purchase a television set is made. It is almost certain that their sets will have NICAM digital-stereo sound, and that they are aware of the recent developments in picture definition. They have one or two brands which they feel are clearly superior to others, and would consider certain rental deals where they are assured of free service and technical upgrades as they became available.

Early majority consumers buy such products infrequently but, like the early adopters, would want to a set that was advanced technologically and thus likely to last for at least 3–5 years. They listen and respond to the more informed early adopters. The early majority would only consider rental deals which allow them to own the set after a specified number of years.

Late majority consumers are still waiting for the price of NICAM digital sets to reduce. They are more interested in value for money than specific brand names or product functions. Naturally, they own a large colour television, and consider a black and white set to be totally outdated.

Last, the **laggards** are now convinced that colour television sets are superior to black and white sets, although they would wait until the price of technologically advanced sets fell dramatically before they purchased them.

Finally, it is vital to remember that these groups differ according to the nature of the product. Innovators for televisions may not be innovators for cars. Social status, activities, interests and opinions are very important in this respect, as is reference group membership.

PRODUCT DIFFUSION

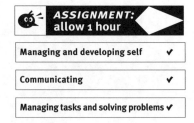

ASSIGNMENT:
allow 1 hour

Managing and developing self	✔
Communicating	✔
Managing tasks and solving problems	✔

ACTIVITY 5

Hotels serve a variety of different customers. For example, holiday makers, business people, individuals wishing to break long journeys all use hotels but for different reasons, perhaps at different times of the week and/or year, and perhaps in different locations.

The (fictitious) Bradshaw Hotel Group is developing a small chain of hotels. The group started with a chain of travel lodges on or near motorways. It now has seven lodges. Recently, it has begun to expand. It now has two three-star hotels in city centre locations and four hotels situated near National Parks. The group has recently acquired a new managing director.

Prepare a brief (500–1,000 word) marketing report for the new managing director. Your report should identify key market segments for the hotel trade. It should clearly explain which markets Bradshaw's hotels are aiming to serve. (Note that there might be some overlap. Certainly, the hotels might be aiming to reach a variety of markets.)

The report should suggest ways in which the hotels might boost trade at off-peak times and in the off-season. Finally, it should outline different marketing strategies for each of the three types of hotel which would identify the features you might use to position each category of hotel more strongly in its particular market segment(s).

Use a separate sheet of paper to record your answer. Summarise your findings in the box below.

summary

▶ Market segmentation allows a company to focus its efforts and target its products more effectively.

▶ When segmenting a market, four key questions must be asked: Is the segment measurable? Is it accessible? It is sustainable? Is it actionable?

▶ Markets can be segmented geographically, demographically and psychographically.

▶ The key to effective segmentation is to use more than one segmentation variable to obtain a 'rich' picture.

▶ Lifestyle segmentation has assumed a particular importance for many marketeers – it provides a simple summary of buyer behaviour which allows products to be placed in a way in which they will have greater success in a target market.

▶ Companies adopt product positioning strategies to try to influence the way consumers think about their products and services.

▶ Product positioning strategies include emphasising special product features, focusing on benefits, solutions or needs, and by developing products for special use occasions.

▶ The rate and ease of adoption of a new product is determined by consumer characteristics. Consumers can be classified as innovators, early adopters, early majority, late majority and laggards.

Types of data

Objectives

After participating in this session, you should be able to:

▶ describe the various approaches to gathering information for marketing research

▶ draw up a research brief

▶ identify sources of secondary data

▶ explain the potential problems associated with secondary data.

In working through this session, you will practise the following BTEC common skills:

Managing and developing self	✔
Working with and relating to others	✔
Communicating	✔
Managing tasks and solving problems	✔
Applying numeracy	
Applying technology	
Applying design and creativity	

Marketing research

> **!?!** What is the difference between marketing research and market research? **Marketing research** is research that is gathered on any aspect of marketing. **Market research** is more closely related to a particular market under consideration.

To manage a business well is to manage its future; to do this effectively requires a diverse range of information on which decisions can be based. Marketing as a business philosophy is concerned with successfully satisfying the needs and wants of specifically defined target markets more efficiently and effectively than competitors and making a profit. To do this, management needs information about its **markets, competitors,** and changes and developments in the **external environment**. Research is an important source of information and can aid all marketing decisions. The following examples are given as illustrations of the different approaches that can be taken to gathering information:

Product research

This is generally concerned with all aspects of design, development and testing of new products as well as the improvement and modification of existing products. Activities would include:

- comparative testing against competitive products
- test marketing
- concept testing
- ideal generation and screening
- product elimination and/or simplification.

Communication research

Firms spend a great deal of money on marketing communications, particularly in consumer markets. Every element of the marketing communication mix, whether it be personal selling, direct mail, exhibitions, sponsorship or advertising, can be better planned and made more effective as a result of research information. Indicative of the type of research carried out in this area is:

- pre-testing and post-testing of advertising

- media planning research

- readership surveys

- testing alternative selling techniques

- exhibition and sponsorship evaluation.

Pricing research

Pricing research techniques can be used to:

- see what kind of price consumers associate with different product variations, packaging, etc.

- assist in establishing a more market-oriented pricing strategy

- establish market segments in relation to price.

Corporate planning

Research information can assist corporate planners by:

- evaluating companies for acquisition

- assessing an organisation's strengths and weaknesses

- providing portfolio analysis

- providing corporate image studies.

Distribution research

Techniques such as the retail audit can monitor the effectiveness of different types of distribution channels and establish any regional variation.

Test marketing

The basic objective of test marketing fast-moving consumer goods is to obtain information on the reactions of consumers in a limited geographical area when confronted by the product in a realistic buying situation. On the basis of the research, a decision is taken as to whether or not the product should be sold more widely. The essential argument put forward to support this is that although the costs of test marketing can be substantial, they can never reach the extent of the losses which are incurred when a national launch and promotion fails.

If a test marketing operation is to be successful, then the test market town or area should possess as many of the following qualities as possible.

1. It should have a **typical range of retail outlets**. Any marked difference from the general norm would distort the overall conclusions drawn.

2. The area should be **remote from other sales areas** to reduce the problem of outside infiltration. The Tyne Tees region is a very popular area, and was used by Cadbury to test their 'Wispa' bar (see case study below) as a prelude to a successful 'roll out' campaign. Another popular region is HTV. Popularity is a double-edged sword, however, and if an area becomes overly popular for test marketing activity, the findings become unrepresentative of the whole.

3. The area should have advertising media that are **compatible with national media**. This can be a problem in some countries but not in the UK. There are regional TV and local radio which can be networked nationally. Some national newspapers will insert an extra page in copies sold in a particular region; popular magazines such as the *TV Times* and Sunday colour supplements, will carry regional advertising in regional editions. Poster advertising can be extended nationally and point-of-sale material, sales promotion schemes and in-store demonstrations can be 'rolled out' after regional implementation. In some areas, local exhibitions can be used to effect, and mail drops can be carried out anywhere. This is not to minimise the serious nature of media incompatibility, rather to point out that it need not be insurmountable.

4. The test area should contain a **typical demographic breakdown** of potential buyers if accurate generalisations are to be made. Ideally, the area should be **representative** both in terms of the general population and in the spread of per capita income.

5. There should be a **previous good record** for a test city as with a region. For example, market research is regularly undertaken in Newcastle and Cardiff in the UK, and Syracuse, Dayton and Des Moines in the USA. Recently, Tulsa has overtaken Des Moines as the most popular test market city in the USA following demographic changes which have made it more representative of the country as a whole.

6. There should be **stability of year round sales**. Seasonal variations in products sales should be carefully noted, e.g. ice-cream, vegetables, fruit and toys.

7. **Marketing research facilities** should be readily available.

One major problem involved in test marketing fast-moving consumer goods is that the perfect test area does not exist – there will always be some bias in the results. Other problems result from any competitive response to the test. When a competitor 'reads' a test market, it means it knows that it is happening and can take action to disrupt it. Companies must judge whether any local counteractives by competitors are representative of what the competition will do nationally at a later date.

TEST MARKETING OF WISPA

Test marketing of the 'Wispa' bar began in the Tyne Tees region in 1981. Norman Hawkins, Cadbury's commercial director, described the reaction as 'fantastic' and recalled scenes of fighting over bars and rationing. Television advertising had to be cancelled after only three weeks as it became clear that the pilot plant could not cope with demand. The decision was taken to withdraw Wispa altogether. Cadbury issued a statement explaining that this was because Wispa could not be produced 'consistently and profitably'. Norman Hawkins admits that this was a justifiable piece of market subterfuge aimed at convincing the opposition that Wispa was a flop while Cadbury geared up for full-scale production on the basis of superlative test market results.

Project Wispa went undercover. A decision was taken to invest 12 million in a new computerised production plant capable of meeting much higher levels of demand. As production began, Wispa was kept well under wraps. Waste paper from the miles of wrapper produced every hour was burnt. Bars were packed in black polythene bags and transported in unmarked vans to specially hired cold stores ready for the relaunch.

Despite the security, the opposition still 'read' the situation. Rowntree Mackintosh installed a new production line in its York factory and, in 1982, the first chunky 'Aero' bars went on sale. Backed by a persuasive modern television and poster advertising campaign, it proved an immediate success. In 1983, 25 million new chunky 'Aero' bars were sold. It was a pre-emptive strike that prevented Rowntree losing out heavily to the onslaught of the Wispa bar.

Wispa was relaunched in the North East in October 1983, and was supported by heavy advertising. Marketing Week reported the cost to be up to £6 million, when the industry spends some 90 million annually on chocolate promotion. With military precision Wispa was progressively 'rolled out' until, by December 1984, it was available throughout the UK, and had been successfully test marketed in America.

Competitors argued that it was still early days and that a lot of trial buying had taken place. Some argued that Wispa's success had been at the expense of other Cadbury lines such as Flake, Double Decker and Star Bar. Cadbury said this was minimal and that Wispa was taking market share off it rivals. Rowntree Mackintosh conceded that 1984 sales of Aero were slightly down on 1983 levels.

Cadbury gained a great deal from the successful test marketing of Wispa. It found it had a 'winner' and this gave a massive psychological boost to the company. It was back in the public eye again and could make investment decisions with confidence. (It needs to be pointed out that 'losers', conversely, detract from the company image and can cause a grave psychological blow.) Despite great secrecy and subterfuge, Rowntree Mackintosh eventually 'read' the situation and acted to revamp Aero. However, the Wispa bar was a resounding commercial success with a demand of more than half a million bars each week. Cadbury hoped 'Wispa' would be worth £25 million annually.

In an insecure world, where up to 80 per cent of new products fail, management needs 'hard' information on which to base its decisions. Even if a product that is launched nationally fails after a successful test market, management at least knows it went about the task in a scientific way. This is an important point, because there is less scope now for inspired hunches and 'flying by the seat of the pants' marketing – people have to be able to justify their decisions.

Test marketing will always be beset with problems such as the lack of representativeness of the test area and competitive disruption of the test – not to mention the 'poaching' of ideas for new products. The advantages of finding out product and distribution 'bugs', eliminating 'losers' before they become a costly mistake and identifying morale-building 'winners' have to be set against the problems of test marketing fast-moving consumer goods. The costs of test marketing these goods needs to be weighed against the potentially disastrous losses incurred if a national launch and promotion fails.

The Wispa bar case study makes the point that marketing information is not free. At times, it can be very expensive to obtain. The object of generating all marketing information is to assist management in making better decisions, collecting unnecessary information represents a serious misallocation of managerial resources. Consequently, strict criteria should be used for evaluating or sanctioning the collection of marketing data. Information should be:

- relevant to the user's needs

- adequate for the type of decision being made

- timely – 'perfect' information is of little use if it arrives late

- cost effective to obtain.

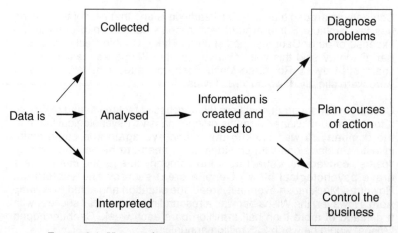

FIGURE 2.1: *How marketing research creates useful information.*

RECALL:
allow 5 mins

Give a brief description of
the five methods of research
discussed above. Then list
five criteria which should be
used for the evaluation of
marketing data.

THE DIFFERENCE BETWEEN DATA AND INFORMATION

> **!?! Information** is data that has been properly processed. It is
> information that helps managers to make decisions.

Data can only become information when it is collected, analysed and
interpreted. Once information is created, it becomes a valuable basis
for decision making. Information is used to diagnose problems, to
plan advertising campaigns, and to control the business. Marketing
research is mainly concerned with strategic decisions.

Marketing researchers should aim for a balanced blend of:

- quantity of information

- quality of information.

It is important to understand the distinction between quantitative
and qualitative information. **Quantitative information** is based upon
the collection and analysis of statistical information such as age,
gender and occupation data. Quantitative data has additive
characteristics – it may be subject to statistical analysis using
techniques such as means, standard deviations, t-tests, analysis of
variance and correlation coefficients.

TEST MARKETING

Qualitative information is not measured along a continuum. It lacks additive properties. Qualitative information would be obtained from responses to questions such as: 'Do you like ice-cream?' or 'Why do you believe that?' Applicable statistical techniques include percentages and chi-squared tests which are concerned with the variation of results around an average.

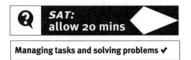

Managing tasks and solving problems ✔

ACTIVITY 1

Cinema chains need information about their customer profile. This information is useful for programming. It is also vital when considering whether (and where) to build new cinema complexes.

Consider a marketing research exercise that might be undertaken by a cinema chain to update its customer information and to build up a customer profile. Write down questions which researchers would ask cinema-goers. Indicate whether each question generates quantitative or qualitative information.

Commentary...

Here are some examples of the questions that might be asked.

1. To which age group do you belong?
   15–20, 21–25, 26–30, 31–35

2. To which income bracket do you belong?
   less than £5,000 a year
   between £5,001 and £7,500 a year
   between £7,501 and £10,000 a year
   between £10,001 and £12,500 a year
   more than £12,500 a year

3. How often do you go to the cinema?
   once a week
   once a month
   once every three months
   less than once every three months
   never

4. What is the best film you have seen this year?

5. Which film did you dislike most, and why?

6. Do you prefer large out of town cinemas to town centre cinemas?

The first three questions provide quantitative information. The last three generate qualitative information.

We have explained the difference between information and data and between quantitative and qualitative information. Market researchers make a further important distinction when looking at data. They make a distinction between **primary data** and **secondary data**.

!?! **Primary data** is new information. It is collected, collated and analysed by yourself. It is data that is being gathered for the first time. **Secondary data** is data that other people or organisations have collected, collated and analysed and which you can use. It is data which already exists.

The market research process

The market research process can be characterised by a systematic series of steps. These are illustrated in figure 2.2.

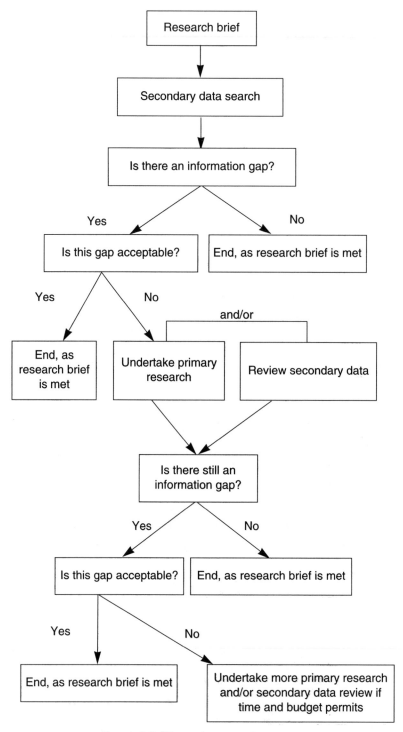

FIGURE 2.2: *The market research process.*

THE RESEARCH BRIEF

The research brief is a **specification**. It gives details of the problem to be addressed, the amount of resources available, the names of the researchers and to whom they report. A specific time deadline by which the research is to be completed is set.

SECONDARY DATA

Secondary data is collected before primary data. Secondary data collection is the cheapest option, because the data already exists. At this stage, there is a check to see if sufficient secondary data has been gathered to fulfil the brief. If the answer is yes, there is no information gap – then the research brief has been fulfilled. An information gap is the difference between the data that has been gathered and that which is needed to satisfy the criteria set out in the research brief. If there is an information gap, then it might be necessary to undertake some research to generate primary data. This is the more expensive option – new market research costs more than looking up existing data sources.

PRIMARY DATA

Primary data is generated in situations where the collection and analysis of readily available secondary data is insufficient to fulfil the research objective. Primary data is more expensive to obtain because it has to be 'unearthed' for the first time. It is possible that a firm will decide that it has enough information, even though the brief is not completely fulfilled.

After primary research has been carried out, there is another check for an information gap. If a gap still exists, then it might be necessary to consult the brief to see if it was soundly set out. Secondary data could be rechecked to see if something was overlooked or the company could conduct further primary research. At some stage, the process must be stopped due to cost factors. It may be impossible to satisfy completely the criteria laid out in a research brief, so an acceptable compromise has to be reached.

Gathering secondary data

When undertaking market research, it is important to research secondary data properly and identify all existing sources including statistics which will be useful to you.

WRITTEN SOURCES

A first place of call should be a college or public library. In the library, reference books and guides to various data sources will be found. These sources include:

- periodicals (newspapers)

- magazines and scholarly journals

- guides to abstracts

- censuses

- guides to associations and manufacturing bodies

- online data information services.

It is often helpful to talk to the library staff especially if they are subject specialists. If the subject under research is not covered fully, the inter-library loan facility can be used.

STATISTICAL SOURCES

Official statistics are one of the most important sources of information. The main provider of government statistics is the Central Statistical Office (CSO). For anyone coming new to government statistics, the first thing to grasp is that each department prepares and publishes its own statistics – through Her Majesty's Stationery Office (HMSO). Some information may later be included in all embracing statistical periodicals like the *Monthly Digest of Statistics* or the annual *Social Trends,* often in a more summarised form.

The necessary information may be found in one of these digests or by consulting the particular departmental publication. If the published source does not yield what is required, check with the department to see if they can help. Most of the principal information can be quickly obtained by major public libraries. As a last resort, refer to the comprehensive *Guide to Official Statistics* which is the standard reference book on the subject.

Trade published data is another major source of information. This data is published by business and professional bodies or the bodies that represent them:

- **Trade associations** exist in most industries, for example Electrical Contractors' Association. Each association usually has an information library staffed with appropriate information specialists.

- **Trade press** is published for most trades. Those of significant size have some journals or magazines relevant to that industry.

- **Professional institutes** are equipped with library and information services available to members.

- Local **Chambers of Commerce** may prove useful if the problem refers to a particular regional location.

Financial institutions provide another source of published data. The major banks, leading stock brokers and financial analysts produce regular reports on various industries, their performance, financial record trends and potential. Note also that the **quality press** and the **financial press** regularly produce industrial and commercial reports on various aspects of business, companies and products.

Businesses are an important source of information. The problem is that much of this information is often regarded as confidential and difficult to obtain unless it is in the public domain. But in-house market research analysts will draw on these **internal sources of information**. This information which can come from various departments:

- The **accounts department** may provide data on value of sales by segments of total customers, total cost of discounts given. This is useful information to a marketeer when considering which customers are essential to the survival of the company or what effect a price change or discounts may have.

- The **sales department** may have information such as dispersion of current customers and total sales for each product in the range. This is invaluable information for understanding what is happening in the market place.

Databases can contain almost any kind of information. One can, for example, obtain very specific census breakdowns, business statistics, market statistics and the actual numerical data used in the preparation of a large number of social science projects.

There are hundreds of **publicly available databases**. One useful example is Spearhead which contains details of progress on the single European market. Like the vast majority of modern databases it is fully relational. This means that the stored information can be accessed in a variety of ways with the aim of producing management reports.

A number of **specialised organisations** exist to provide the type of desk research information obtainable through published sources. These organisations act as **'information brokers'** and produce relevant abstracts and digests of statistics and new items to subscribers.

Using secondary data

Whenever secondary data sources are used, it should be remembered that the data may vary widely in terms of reliability. It is necessary to know whether the data is specific to the particular area of interest, whether it is up to date and the amount of bias it contains. When using official statistics or other data in research, be aware of their weaknesses.

Much of the material is gathered using surveys and questionnaires. These involve some inevitable problems. There can be **clerical errors** – the gathering, collation and presentation can be very tedious. **Truthfulness** is also important in these surveys. If people are asked certain questions, they tend to give the answer they think is expected. For the question: 'Do you take a bath regularly?', the answer is: 'Yes', almost automatically.

It is also important to recognise **who is collecting the statistics**. Consider how many times in the last ten years the method of calculating the unemployment figures has been changed. Statistics are notoriously easy to manipulate or to misinterpret. When trying to persuade the City that it is succeeding in reducing public spending, the government defines sales of assets like British Steel not as income but as negative spending, thus reducing the total spend. But when trying to persuade the voters that it is spending more on the National Health Service, the government adds in the sales of NHS assets as well as assumed 'efficiency savings' within the service; thus spending looks higher.

Even seemingly harmless **conventions** may have implications. Value judgements are contained in such routine decisions as to treat a part-time worker as equal to half of a full-time worker, a child as 'half' a person, or a bathroom as half a room.

SO WHAT USE ARE STATISTICS?

When looking at statistics, beware the danger of feeling that they are hopelessly inaccurate and a waste of time. This is rather like throwing the baby out with the bath water. Statistics are not totally reliable but neither are they totally unreliable. They still have their uses.

The establishment of general trends

This is not to be seen as accurate forecasting but as an attempt to give the general direction of trends. Some trends can be more accurately predicted than others. For example, the number of people over the age of 65 by the year 2000 can be more or less accurately forecast by the number of children born in previous years, whereas the number of children born in 2000 can be predicted only within certain limits. This is simply because those will be 65 in the year 2000 are obviously already alive and can be counted, but the number of new births is more difficult to predict because the birthrate can fluctuate due to a number of factors.

To give a measurement of performance for an organisation

This is easier for commercial organisations where output can be measured in units of production such as cars. For non commercial organisations like the police, this is more problematic. How do you measure performance in areas like 'good community relations'?

Market research surveys on products and service

Increasingly, companies need feedback from customers and clients to judge their levels of satisfaction. NOP and Gallup are two companies who offer market research services to organisations, e.g. to the National Health Service to measure how well hospitals meet the performance criteria specified in the Patient's Charter.

USING SECONDARY DATA

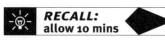

RECALL:
allow 10 mins

List the major sources of statistical information.

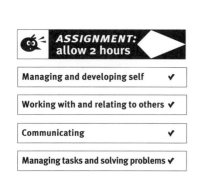

ASSIGNMENT:
allow 2 hours

Managing and developing self	✔
Working with and relating to others	✔
Communicating	✔
Managing tasks and solving problems	✔

ACTIVITY 2

In this assignment, you are required to develop a market research brief, and will need to draw on most of the material covered in this session.

Select a product or service provided by your company or a product or service with which you are familiar, on which you can conduct market research. Retail distribution, for example, is too large a topic – you need to choose a specific product or service.

Now, develop a research outline. You need to consider the following:

- **What** are you researching?

- **Who** is the report for?

- **Where** – which area are you interested in? Are you concerned with national trends or regional phenomena?

- **When** – what is the time-scale of the study?

- **Why** are you studying this problem?

When you have completed this exercise, set out ways in which you might undertake the research. Focus particularly on the information you will need to complete the research brief. Do you need to undertake primary research? Can you obtain data from secondary sources?

Follow this up by visiting a library to identify sources of secondary data which could be of use. During your visit, you should look at *The*

Guide to Official Statistics and list the main government publications which contain information about the product or service you have selected for research. You should also look to see if there are any other data sources that provide information about your product or service.

Produce a 300—500 word report that:

- sets out the research brief

- describes the information needs

- gives the results of your research into secondary data sources.

Use separate sheets of paper to record your answer. Summarise your main findings in the box below.

summary

This session has focused on marketing research.

▶ Management needs up-to-date information about all aspects of marketing: markets, competitors, customers and developments in the external business environment. It uses marketing research to obtain this information.

▶ Test marketing is important as it allows a company to assess the possible success or failure of a product.

▶ Information is data that has been properly processed. Market research information can be used to diagnose problems, plan advertising campaigns and control the business.

▶ The market research process can involve undertaking research to obtain new primary data as well as drawing on published sources of secondary data.

▶ Sources of secondary data include business, government, statistical digests, trade associations, financial institutions, the media and information databases.

▶ Secondary data may vary widely in its reliability. You need to consider whether it is relevant and up to date. You need to be aware of the problems of biased data.

Survey planning

Objectives

After participating in this session, you should be able to:

▼

> ▶ identify the main types of survey

▼

> ▶ describe some of the different approaches to sampling

▼

> ▶ understand the options for conducting surveys

▼

> ▶ outline interview procedures

▼

> ▶ explain the main issues surrounding questionnaires.

In working through this session, you will practise the following
BTEC common skills:

Managing and developing self	✔
Working with and relating to others	✔
Communicating	✔
Managing tasks and solving problems	✔
Applying numeracy	✔
Applying technology	
Applying design and creativity	✔

Surveys

Surveys are a major tool used in market research. They can be carried out by **questionnaires** or by **interviews**. Each has its advantages. For example, interviews are usually used with small groups of people while questionnaires are generally applied to larger groups.

Just as each method has its uses, each has major weaknesses. Interviews can be dominated by the personality of the interviewer or interviewee. Interviewers may (by their body language or emphasis on certain words or questions e.g. 'Do you really agree?') lead the interviewee and create bias in the answers.

Questionnaires can simply not be answered. They may not be taken seriously or they may be done in too much of a hurry. There may be conscious or unconscious biases in the questionnaire which may, for example, seek to prove that sales are going well. Your own biases may come out no matter how hard you try to be objective. Many researchers feel that more than one research method should be used so that you can **cross-check** your results. For example, a large-scale questionnaire can be followed up by personal interviewing.

The use of more than one method can have beneficial results. If you are unsure about what questions to use in your questionnaire, you can conduct a small number of interviews with the questions you intend to use. This gives you a chance to test the questions out, obtain feedback and refine or change them where necessary.

The **pre-test** is a final 'dry run' of the entire survey: the questionnaire, the interview, the instructions and the sampling method. The questionnaire responses need to be analysed for weaknesses and the interviewers should be encouraged to write their own comments — and obtain interviewees' opinions — about the content of the questionnaire. This is known as **pilot testing**.

At all stages, you should be aware of errors.

TYPES OF SURVEY

Researchers frequently use descriptive and attitudinal surveys. In practice, the two are often mixed together.

The purpose of the **descriptive survey** is to count, i.e. to obtain **quantitative data**. When it cannot count everyone, it counts a representative sample and then makes inferences about the population as a whole. Descriptive surveys are important. You will have come across several examples. Any form of public opinion poll is a descriptive survey as are commercial investigations. The job of such surveys is essentially fact-finding.

The advantages of descriptive surveys are that:

- they can tell you how many in a population have certain characteristics, e.g. height above 2 metres

- they rely on facts not attitudes

- they can be used to make predictions.

The disadvantages are that:

- facts may not be so straightforward to gather, e.g. people may exaggerate their height, lie about their age and not know their true weight

- they provide descriptions but no explanations and so they require interpretation.

Attitudinal surveys are attempts to find out the attitudes of groups towards phenomenon. So, for example, an attitudinal survey might seek information about the level of security people feel when going out after dark or the degree of consumer satisfaction with various services. They provide **qualitative data**. This type of survey also tries to find out why these attitudes are held. A typical question is: 'Why do you like/dislike ...?'

Attitudinal surveys have the advantage of finding levels of satisfaction, providing information about consumer preferences and lifestyles. They have the disadvantage that the presence of an interviewer can introduce bias particularly on controversial topics. Also people may not necessarily have formulated opinions or even know about a variety of topics. An example is: 'What do you think of Italian Rugby League?'

Sampling

In drawing up a questionnaire or constructing an interview form, you will have to decide how many people you want to survey. It rarely makes sense to interview the entire target population because:

- the time frame in which decision is to be made is too short to acquire an entire census

- the cost of a full enumeration is prohibitive

- the accuracy of the information may not be justifiably enhanced by a full enumeration

- it is impossible to find the entire population.

You can see from this that it is neither necessary nor desirable to survey the whole of a target population. What normally happens is that we base our estimated values on a **sample**.

THE SAMPLING FRAME

To carry out sampling, there has to be an actual or potential list of all the members of the target population from which to select the sample. This list is called a **sampling frame**. Examples of sampling frames are the Electoral Register and the population census information.

How big should the sample be?

This is the question most often asked by those new to market research. It is possible to estimate the sample size statistically. This is done by first stating what is expected of the sample in terms of desired limits of error. This is a judgement which must be made by the researcher.

The size of the sample is going to be affected by certain practical considerations. These include the total size of the budget for the study and the anticipated cost of each observation. It may also be necessary to increase the size of the sample to convince sceptical executives who do not understand statistical notions that they can indeed have confidence in the results.

A simple example

Researchers need to look at the demand for chicken burgers in a hamburger chain. They survey a sample of customers. They state that this proportion in the sample would need to be within 5 per cent of the proportion in the population. (This is the judgement about desired limits of error a researcher needs to make to which we referred above.) They must also make a guess (as informed as possible) about the proportion in the population which eats chicken burgers. For example, they may know from other studies that this is likely to lie between 30 and 60 per cent of the population.

The estimated sample size, n, is then calculated using the formula:

$$n = \frac{Z^2 PQ}{E^2}$$

where P is the estimate of the percentage of customers wanting chicken burgers in the whole population. $Q = 1 - P$. E is the margin of error acceptable in either direction. Z is a statistical value (taken from standard tables) based on the margin of error acceptable.

In our example, we want the sample to give an answer within 5 per cent of the true answer (i.e. $E = 5$; and $Z = 1.96$) for a 95 per cent confidence interval. Using these figures gives us:

$$n = \frac{(1.96)^2 PQ}{25}$$

So, if $P = 30$, $Q = 70$ and $PQ = 2100$. If $P = 60$, $Q = 40$ and $PQ = 2400$. The value of P in the 30–60 per cent range, which gives the biggest value of PQ, is 50 per cent. This gives a value for PQ of 2500. To be on the safe side, we will use this value. (For convenience, we will round up Z^2 to 4.) So:

$$n = \frac{4 \times 2500}{25}$$

We should therefore use a sample size of 400.

Applying this method to the key variable in a sample survey should produce a desirable sample size. It may be, of course, that your resources and time will not allow you to cover a sample of this size, so you may have to trade accuracy for savings in money or time.

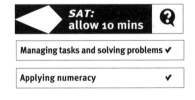

SAT:
allow 10 mins

Managing tasks and solving problems ✔

Applying numeracy ✔

ACTIVITY 1

Consider the example about chicken burgers above. If the estimated percentage of people in the population who eat chicken burgers had been 30–40 per cent, what size sample would you require if it has to be accurate to within 10 per cent (for which Z is 1.68)?

Commentary...

P lies between 30 and 40. Therefore, Q lies between 60 and 70. The maximum value of PQ is thus 2400 (when $P = 40$ and $Q = 60$). $E = 10$ for which $Z = 1.68$. Using our formula, therefore, the sample size should be 68.

$$n = \frac{(1.68)^2 \times 40 \times 60}{100} = 67.73 \approx 68$$

Notice how the limit of 10 per cent requires a smaller sample. This could be useful if expense is a factor but accuracy may become a problem. A tighter error limit of say 2.5 per cent would require a larger sample size. This greater accuracy would increase the cost of the survey.

The method of sampling used above is an example of **probability sampling**. In probability sampling, every member of the relevant population has a chance of being selected and the probability of this selection is known. If there are ten apples and each apple is available for selection, the probability that a particular apple will be selected is one in ten, or 1/10. If three of the apples are green and the rest red, the probability of selecting a green apple is three out of ten, or 3/10. As long as the probability of selection of a particular sample unit can be calculated, you can usually take a probability sample. The accuracy of the samples can be calculated using the methods described above.

Another form of sampling is **non-probability sampling**. Here, the probability that a person or item will be chosen is not known and one cannot measure the sampling error. This may not be important if your priority is to obtain a quick, cheap and rough result.

Other commonly used sampling methods

In practice, researchers may opt for one of the following sampling methods based on convenience and cost.

Convenience sampling

In the simplest kind of sampling, a researcher questions anyone who is available. This method is quick and cheap but there is no way of knowing how representative the sample is, nor how reliable the results are.

Quota sampling

This form of sampling is often used in taking public opinion polls. Here, one first determines the important characteristics of the particular research population. If 15 per cent of the study population are between the ages of 60 and 70, then 15 per cent of your sample should be in this age group. But, the selection of subjects within a defined group is not random. The researcher simply has to find people with the required characteristics. The quota method can produce samples which are based on characteristics like income, education and occupation.

Dimensional sampling

This is a variation of quota sampling. In dimensional sampling, one takes into account several characteristics — gender, age, income, residence, education or whatever characteristics might be appropriate and then ensures that there is at least one person in the study to reflect any relevant combination of these characteristics. Whether the quotas are based upon a single characteristic or on more, the selection of members of the sample is not done randomly. Instead the researcher just finds enough people in each of the important categories.

Dimensional sampling is the form most widely used. Basically, an interviewer is told to obtain views from ten people who between them cover various cross categories. The most general categories would be age (given in four or five age ranges), and 'social class of the chief wage-earner'. There are a number of ways used to define social class. The most commonly used classification comprises six socio-economic groups defined by the Institute of Practitioners of Advertising.

Institute of Practitioners of Advertising Grouping		
Social class	Percentage of population*	Description
A	2 per cent	A successful business or professional person, such as top civil servant, physician or person of private means
B	10 per cent	Senior but not top professional people, such as a university lecturer, pharmacist, or employed accountant
C1	24 per cent	Tradespeople and non-manual workers in administrative or supervisory posts, such as teachers, bank clerks, insurance agents or clerical officers
C2	32 per cent	Skilled manual workers, such as bricklayer, plumber, fitter or welder
D	22 per cent	Semi-skilled and unskilled workers, such as a ticket collector, traffic warden, shop assistant or army private
E	9 per cent	Casual labourers, old age pensioners, widows on state pension and any who are little above subsistence level incomes

* Adds up to 99% due to rounding

TABLE 3.1: *Socio-economic groups*

Conducting surveys

There are three ways in which surveys can be conducted: by mail, by telephone and by personal interview.

MAIL

Sending out questionnaires can seem an inexpensive option. However, postal questionnaires usually generate very low response rates. We know that low response rates reduce the statistical validity of the sample and non-responses can also add bias into the data. If the 5 per cent who respond to a customer satisfaction survey are generally content with a product or service, how can a firm be confident about the 95 per cent who have not done so?

If only 100 postal questionnaires are sent out then a response rate of 5 per cent would produce only five returned questionnaires. Samples of less than 30 are not usually statistically valid. So, to obtain 30 responses it would be necessary to send out 600 questionnaires in the post. This extra cost in time and postage would at least yield a viable sample size.

Postal questionnaires should be as short as possible to extract the data required. Pilot test them to check wording and layout and always send a stamped envelope for the reply. Remember to thank the respondent in a covering letter, which you put in with the questionnaire.

TELEPHONE

Telephone surveys are becoming increasingly popular. As telephone ownership increases, this method of sampling no longer adds a major bias to a sample. Most people – of all social classes – now have a phone as a necessity.

The advantages of telephone surveys are speed and the possibility of increasing response rates. (Researchers faced with a poor response from a postal sample will often phone the people who have not responded in the hope of carrying out a telephone interview.)

However, telephone surveys can be difficult. People dislike unwanted telephone calls, so a pre-call to book a mutually convenient time for the interview is vital. The caller must give some clues to his or her identity to reassure the respondent. However, this can be a problem if the sample is to be an anonymous one.

Some people are more outgoing on the telephone. The interviewer effect is reduced as they cannot respond to the appearance and manner of the interviewer as they would in a face-to-face interview. However, qualitative feedback is reduced because visual clues and body language cannot be noted and the use of the telephone disadvantages respondents who are not very articulate. Importantly, the costs of telephone surveys are far less than personal face-to-face interviews.

PERSONAL INTERVIEWS

This is still the most popular method of collecting survey data. However, there are problems involving both the interviewer and respondent. The respondents might try to please the interviewer by saying what they feel the interviewer wants to hear; the manner, tone of voice and dress of the interviewer can affect the way in which the respondents answer the questions.

Although this method allows a mixture of qualitative and quantitative data to be gathered, it is relatively time-consuming. It is labour intensive and it is the most costly of the three methods considered here.

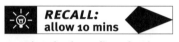

RECALL:
allow 10 mins

1. List the benefits of using more than one research method.

2. Describe the ways in which descriptive and attitudinal surveys differ.

3. Explain the main difference between probability and non-probability sampling.

Interviewing

Interviewing is often used as a means of gathering survey data, and as it is an important technique, we deal with it in more detail.

TYPES OF INTERVIEWS

When we talk about interviewing in a survey situation, we can classify interviews into different forms or types.

Standardised schedule interviews

These are the most formally structured type. They are used where the same information is required of each interviewee. Each person is asked the same questions in the same order. The form on which these questions are written is called the **interview schedule**. It is a type of questionnaire.

You would use this type of interview in particular situations such as:

- when you are interviewing a large number of people

- when the people being interviewed tend to share the same characteristics and outlooks

- when you know what is important to ask and how to ask it, because you already know enough about the subject, and the kinds of people that are to be interviewed (perhaps because you have field tested the questionnaire).

The disadvantages of this type of interview are that the questions that are used are 'closed'. Consequently, the selections of answers are limited. For example, the question: 'Do you like coffee?' is likely to be restricted to a 'Yes/No' answer.

Standardised interviews, no interview schedule

This type of interview is based on the assumption that it may take the same type of questions but put in different order to obtain the same information from different people. You proceed with any approach which is useful to convey to the interviewee the sense and meaning of what you want. Managers, for example, may be asked questions on overall organisation policy first, but shopfloor workers may be asked about working conditions first.

Unstructured interviews

Here, there is no set order or wording of questions, no interview schedule and you are not looking for the same information from each person. For example, you might be interviewing a number of people about their army service. Individuals will remember different kinds of things. Some may have been happy, and some unhappy; some will remember a lot, some a little. You want from each interviewee, his or her own perspective.

This form of interview is often used at the beginning of a research project, when you know so little that you do not even know whether you are asking the right questions, let alone the possible answer categories. Asking the widest, most general questions and allowing the interviewee to develop the subject the way he or she wishes may give you a sufficiently general picture that you can then decide which specific topic of study you would like to follow.

This type of interview has the advantage of encouraging a free flow of ideas. It allows the interviewee to control the situation more and to express a point of view more easily. It has some disadvantages, however. For example, the interviewer must be skilled and avoid leading questions; he or she must be able to make the subject relax and be truthful.

INTERVIEW TECHNIQUES

In addition to choosing the appropriate type of interview to use, it is also important to conduct the interview effectively. This involves interview techniques. If you are a natural communicator and speak easily with people, a discussion of interviewing techniques may not be necessary. But not all of us have these natural talents. We need to acquire and develop them to a greater or lesser extent.

To begin, you should tell the interviewee the purpose of the interview. This should cover:

1. the name of the organisation or group you represent

2. what the study is about, presented in such a way that interviewees see its general relevance and, if possible, its relevance to them

3. how they came to be selected for interview.

You should reassure the interviewee that you will maintain confidentiality, if required.

There are also a number of other basic guidelines you can follow to improve your technique. For example, you should engage in some small talk to **put interviewees at their ease** but try not to create the impression of being too inquisitive. Remember to **give people time to answer;** do not rush through the questions. Listen to the person who is talking to you. Ask the respondent to explain if you do not understand what they have said or ask for an example. **Do not ask leading questions:** 'What do you dislike about...?' Instead, **ask open-ended questions:** 'What sort of food do you like?'

ACTIVITY 2

Select a work colleague or friend who is willing to be interviewed. Find a quiet place and conduct an unstructured interview on the topic of smoking in the workplace. You should prepare for the interview by jotting down questions you intend to ask in the box below beforehand.

SAT: allow 45 mins ❓

Managing and developing self	✔
Working with and relating to others	✔
Communicating	✔
Managing tasks and solving problems	✔

Commentary...

You should now ask your interviewee to fill in the evaluation form below. Request that it be answered honestly.

Yes/No

1. Were you told the purpose of the interview?
2. Were you put at your ease? Did you feel comfortable during the interview?
3. Were you given time to answer the questions?
4. Did you think the interviewer was listening to you carefully?
5. Did you have the chance to explain your answers?
6. Were you asked leading questions?
7. Were you asked open ended questions like 'why do you think people smoke'?
8. Do you think the interviewer established your attitude to smoking at work?

When the form has been completed, check the responses carefully. Compare them with your own thoughts on the interview. Did your perceptions coincide with those of your interviewee? People often read the same situation differently.

You should, as a result of carrying out this activity, have developed a better understanding of interviewing techniques and have developed your skills.

THE STAGES OF AN INTERVIEW

You should appreciate that while it is necessary to conduct a 'seamless' interview, to ensure continuity an interview is, in fact, divided into distinct stages.

Introduction and opening remarks

The purpose of the introduction is to establish rapport and to put the interviewee at ease. Introductions should be made, the reason for the interview established and the topic introduced in general terms, e.g. starting with the question: 'Please tell me about ...'

Probing questions

This is when the interviewer settles down to specifics. You should remember that non-verbal noises can be significant. An 'Oh?' or 'Hmm?' can be quite as revealing as body language in expressing an opinion or attitude. The interviewee should be supported by phrases such as 'That's interesting' and further information should be sought. Questions such as 'Why?', 'Why not?', 'Why do you say that?' are useful here. You should always try to avoid allowing bias to enter the interview.

Closing remarks

It is necessary to close the interview in such a way as not to leave the interviewee 'hanging in the air'. This is best done by summarising the interview. You should use phrases such as 'As I understand it ...', 'Am I right in saying that ...?' to conclude.

Leaving the interview

It is important to close the interview by expressing appreciation to the interviewee. For example, a simple 'thank you for all your help' is usually appreciated. It is likely to create a feeling in interviewees that they would not mind participating in further surveys. The opportunity to follow up should be established by saying, for example, 'May I contact you again, if I need further information?'

Questionnaire design

Questionnaires are the most versatile and widely used method of collecting primary data. They are used for four main purposes:

1. to collect data

2. to make data comparable

3. to minimise bias

4. to motivate the respondent.

The quality of data gathered is highly dependent on the design of the questionnaire and the questions it contains. A poorly designed questionnaire will collect inappropriate or inaccurate data and negate the whole purpose of the research – even though major costs have been incurred.

The main variable in any questionnaire should be the response. This means that the questionnaire should be constructed in such a way that the words used have the same meaning for all respondents and interviewers.

If the questionnaire is being used as an interview 'prompt' to ensure that all interviewers do ask precisely the same question of all respondents, it is usual to instruct them to read out the question from the questionnaire exactly as it is written. If a respondent has difficulty in answering, the interviewer should merely read out the question again and add no words of clarification or explanation.

This procedure only works if the questions are well written and constructed using everyday language. If the interviewer has to assist the respondent with answering, then the questionnaire has failed and the compatibility of the data will be lost. Questionnaire piloting is an essential procedure to ensure that questions 'work'.

In a research interview, **bias** is defined as the difference between the answers given by the respondent and the 'truth'. Bias is minimised by paying particular attention to the sequence and wording of the questions and to the words themselves. The questionnaire should make it easy for the respondent to give true answers. Care is needed to avoid using questions that may 'lead' respondents into giving answers that do not reflect their true opinion.

Answering a questionnaire requires time, attention and thought, possibly to a subject area that may not be of much interest to the respondent. When designing a questionnaire, attention should therefore be paid to the following points.

- The introductory section containing the initial request for co-operation is crucial in gaining the respondent's interest and sparking their motivation to spend some time answering the questionnaire.

- Length should be kept to a minimum.

- Questions should be as easy for the respondent to understand and answer as possible – an uncertain respondent is likely to terminate the interview.

- The format and type of questions used should be varied and interesting for the respondent.

THE 'RIGHT' QUESTIONNAIRE CONTENT

The purpose of the research must be clearly set out before the questionnaire is designed. This, you will remember from your work on marketing research, is done in the research brief. Every question asked must be essential to the research brief. After you have drawn up the questionnaire you must ensure that it meets all the purposes of the brief.

There are three types of data which can be collected using a questionnaire: fact, opinion and motive.

Fact

Factual information can be described as **hard data** because it can be relied upon. It includes 'classification data', facts about respondents that characterise them: age, sex and geographic location. It also includes information relevant to the survey: ownership of a car, video or computer. Facts may also refer to behaviour, e.g.: 'Have you ever gone to the theatre?', 'Have you ever used a library?' Factual information is relatively easy to ask and to answer, providing the respondent can remember. Factual questions give reasonable quantitative estimates for the subject under study, and can form a base for cross-tabulation of results.

Opinion

Included in this category are beliefs, attitudes, feelings and knowledge. An example of a question which fits this category is: 'Do you believe all workers should belong to trade unions?'. Opinion data can be useful to decision makers in giving a background to behaviour but the findings should be treated with more caution than factual data.

In asking people what their opinions or feelings are about a subject, there is an assumption that they hold opinions. If the respondent held no opinion on the subject before the question was asked, an instant opinion may be provided to please the interviewer who will have collected data which appears to measure something but, in fact, does not. The results of opinion questions are an example of **qualitative** or **'soft' data** because they are far less reliable as a base for decision making than factual information.

Motive

Knowing people's reasons for a particular belief or action can be important to those wishing to influence them. It is often difficult to explain why you do, or think, a particular thing. Usually, people will try to give one reason for their particular action or thought, but most behaviour has more than one reason. For example, ask yourself: 'Why are you reading this particular book?' You may be reading it because you have a particular problem at work (such as giving a seminar on questionnaire design) which you hope the book will help you solve, but there will be other less immediate reasons — perhaps you are genuinely interested in the subject matter, or you are preparing for a job change or trying to impress your boss.

This illustrates another problem with questions about motive; the answers are likely to be so diverse that they are difficult to compare and analyse. The results are impressionistic rather than certain. To produce quantitative data about motives, possible reasons for behaviour can be explored using techniques such as group discussions or depth interviews. From these, the categories of reason most relevant to the objectives of the survey can be determined and specific questions can be designed to measure how many people share these motives.

QUESTIONNAIRE DESIGN

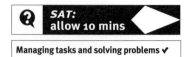

SAT:
allow 10 mins

Managing tasks and solving problems ✔

ACTIVITY 3

To test your understanding of the difference between factual information, opinion and motive, devise three different survey questions which relate to each of the three categories.

Commentary...

An example of an opinion question is: 'Are you concerned about environmental issues?'

An example of a factual question is: 'Which of the following qualifications do you hold?'

GCSEs

'A' Levels

HND/HNC

Degree

Postgraduate

An example of a question about motive is: 'Why did you buy your particular model of car?'

QUESTIONNAIRE CONTENT

Any questionnaire must include three forms of data: identification, classification and subject data.

Identification data

This section is usually completed by the interviewer, and centres on one particular interview. It contains the date, time, length and place of the interview (if relevant). This data is required in case any check back is necessary, either to ensure that the interview took place or if answers were missed out or incorrectly completed. These questions are normally asked at the end of the interview when sufficient rapport has developed between the interviewer and the respondent.

Classification data

This is the data required to classify the respondent and is used as the basis for analysis of the subject data sought in the main body of the questionnaire. It includes data like age, gender, occupation, income group, and any other items considered relevant. If the interviewer has to select the respondent for a quota sample, then it is necessary to ask some of these questions at the outset.

Subject data

This refers to information being gathered to meet the survey objectives and forms the major part of the questionnaire. Care must be taken to plan the sequence of the questionnaire, especially when different questions need to be asked of different respondents. For example, a question like 'Have you visited the library in the last five days?' might be followed by two options:

If YES, go to Question 2.

If NO, go to Question 6.

This type of question is described as a **filter question** because it filters into, or out of, subsequent question sections.

It is important to remember that the respondent's reaction to the first few questions will determine whether he or she will decide to co-operate throughout the interview. These early questions should, if possible, be of interest to the respondent and be easy to answer. Once the respondent realises that the questions are easy to answer and within their sphere of knowledge, they will relax and their confidence to answer will develop.

COMMON PITFALLS

We now turn our attention to look at a number of common pitfalls associated with questionnaires.

Meaning

It is necessary to be sure that the words selected have the same meaning for the respondent as they have for the researcher. Even the most common of words can be a source of misinterpretation in the context of a questionnaire. For example, 'dinner' may be an evening meal, or a meal in the middle of the day; it may be different for children and adults, and different on Sunday from the rest of the week.

When a respondent is being asked about a particular piece of behaviour, the issue must be clearly defined. It is often useful to apply the 'who, what, where, when, how and why' checks to each question, and if these questions cannot be answered, then the question needs to be reworded so that it is more specific about exactly what is required.

For example, consider the question: 'How many times have you personally attended a conference, of any kind, in the UK in the last six months?' This question makes it clear to *whom* the question refers (you personally). It makes it clear *what* information is sought (attended a conference of any kind), *where* the relevant behaviour occurred (in the UK), and *when* it took place (in the last six months), and *how* many times. In this example, *why* the individual attended any such conferences could be the substance of a subsequent question.

Ambiguity

Ambiguous questions should be avoided. Where there is the potential for ambiguity, a definition must be included. Consider a question like: 'Do you read a newspaper regularly?' What does 'regularly' mean? For some it might mean 'everyday', but a person who regularly buys a newspaper every Sunday might answer: 'Yes'. Similarly those that buy a paper on particular days — for specific jobs advertisements or the football results - might also answer: 'Yes'. To avoid this ambiguity, a qualification is usually added: 'By regularly, I mean three or more days each week.'

Leading questions

Leading questions and loaded words should be avoided. These are questions or words with meanings which invite particular responses. The choice of word must be considered from this point of view. 'Bosses', 'managers' and 'administrators' could all be descriptions of the same group of 'workers' (another loaded term). The selection of the term used to describe them is likely to affect responses to questions about the group. The problem is that all words are 'loaded' in one direction or another. The aim is to select words least likely to bias response.

Status bias

You should always be aware that many factual questions are loaded. They raise questions of status or social expectations. In general, people tend to claim that they read more than they do, are taller than they are and have sex more often than they do.

Generalisation

A common problem in wording questions is the use of generalisations. Consider a question like: 'On average, how often do you go to the library in a week?' This question is likely to produce bad data since respondents are being asked to generalise about behaviour. Interviewees could respond on the basis of last week's behaviour or they could pluck some hypothetical figure out of the air. It is better to ask 'On how many occasions have you visited the library during the last seven days?'

Uni-dimensionality

Most questions of the form 'Why did you choose this particular product or service?', have two possible lines of reply. One relates to the perceived attributes of the course, product or service; the other describes the circumstances leading up to its choice and how the respondent came to hear about it. It might, therefore, be better to use two questions, 'How did you first hear about this product or service?', and 'What do you like about the product or service?' Uni-dimensionality refers to the need for each question to ask only about a single point.

Sometimes it is necessary to ask more than one question. As well as asking 'What names of airline companies can you recall?' it would be useful to ask first, 'Do you ever travel by air?' Analysis of recall among travellers and non-travellers could then be carried out. A check should always be made to ensure that the question is only asking about one dimension.

Jargon questions

Be careful about words which have one meaning to the professionals in your field and a different meaning (or no meaning at all) to the public. Niche marketing, rational behaviour, privatisation are examples of such jargon words. They cannot be used as if all respondents shared a common understanding of the meaning you intend.

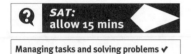

Managing tasks and solving problems ✔

ACTIVITY 4

Below are a number of survey questions. They illustrate a number of common mistakes in questionnaire design. Drawing on the material above, identify the particular mistakes in each instance.

1. What is your age?

    under 20   20—30   30—40   40—45   50—60   70 and over

2. What is your marital status?

    Married   Single   Widowed

3. Have you any dependent children?

    Yes   No

4. How long have you lived in this district?

    ..... years

5. Are you against giving too much power to trade unions?

6. How good are the bars and restaurants in your town?

7. What social class would you say you were?

    Working   Lower-middle   Middle   Upper

8. Do you associate restaurants with a class concept?

Commentary...

Question 1: The response categories are not comprehensive, they omit people age 46—49 and 61—69 completely. The response categories are also ambiguous since they overlap. A person aged 30 or 40 could tick either of two boxes. To make these age ranges suitable for analysis purposes they should be 20—29, 30—39 and so on. Also, this kind of question is too intrusive to ask at the beginning of a questionnaire.

Question 2: A person asked 'What is your marital status?' might be baffled; they could even be very insulted. 'Marital status' is a technical term. Far better to ask 'Are you single, or married or widowed?' The questioning of divorced and separated people can be tricky; if they must be asked for analysis purposes, it is best to ask the question quite openly. Otherwise they can be included as whatever category is most appropriate. Note also that the order of the boxes would be more logical if they were arranged 'single', 'married', 'widowed', which is a 'natural' progression, rather than hopping back from 'married' to 'single'.

Question 3: What are *dependent* children? It is far better to use age groups.

Question 4: District is ambiguous. It can mean a few streets or a town.

Question 5: This is a leading question.

Question 6: This is a double question covering both bars and restaurants. People might offer separate and differing views, e.g.: 'In this town there are great bars but the restaurants are lousy.'

Question 7: This presumes that your interviewee recognises the concept of class. It is also incomplete because it gives working class and upper class, but introduces subdivisions with middle class.

Question 8: This is an example of the use of jargon.

ASSIGNMENT:
allow 1 hour

Managing and developing self	✔
Working with and relating to others	✔
Communicating	✔
Applying design and creativity	✔

ACTIVITY 5

Using the material in this session, design a questionnaire to find out more about consumer attitudes to jeans. Your questionnaire should be designed to discover whether the respondent buys jeans and, if so, what kind of criteria he or she uses in deciding which brand to buy and where to buy them. For example, is price an important factor? Are respondents influenced by television advertising?

Structure your questionnaire so that you are able to compare responses. You will need to capture some demographic information (such as age, sex, broad income range) so that it is possible to compare the attitudes of different types of consumers. Think of the kind of age groups that are more relevant for the survey when choosing your sample.

Test out your questionnaire with five or six friends or relations. You may wish to adjust your questionnaire in the light of this pilot testing, if for example one or two questions proved to be ambiguous or poorly understood by the people in your pilot sample.

Produce your final questionnaire on separate sheets of papers. Summarise any findings from your pilot testing in the box below.

summary

▶ Surveys are a major tool for market researchers. They may be conducted using questionnaires, by telephone or face-to-face interview.

▶ When a survey is carried out, an actual or potential list of all members of the target population has to be established and a sample size determined.

▶ Common sampling methods include probability, convenience, quota and dimensional sampling.

▶ Questionnaires are the most versatile and widely used means of obtaining primary data. They should be designed to collect data, allow compatibility, minimise bias and motivate respondents.

▶ There are a number of common pitfalls in questionnaire design. These include bias, ambiguity and leading questions.

Analytical techniques

Objectives

After participating in this session, you should be able to:

▶ explain the need for analytical techniques

▶ calculate mean, mode and median values

▶ describe the measures of spread

▶ discuss time series analysis

▶ highlight the difficulties of association.

In working through this session, you will practise the following
BTEC common skills:

Managing and developing self	
Working with and relating to others	✔
Communicating	✔
Managing tasks and solving problems	✔
Applying numeracy	✔
Applying technology	
Applying design and creativity	

The need for analytical techniques

Marketing research is never carried out for its own sake. It is an expensive tool which must be used for a specific purpose. Companies should always attempt to judge the overall value of the final research finding before providing resources to implement a research brief. This is sound commercial practice. The reason for carrying out marketing research is to turn the data gathered into information to aid decision making.

It is vital that the statistical content of the research is clearly understood. The primary data is gathered from surveys, observation and experimentation. Secondary data is obtained from a variety of sources including, for example, sales records and government reports.

Let us assume that a marketing manager of a company, manufacturing gas cookers in the UK, has the following sets of data.

- a five-year record of total gas cooker sales in the UK

- the company's sales for the same period

- government statistics of consumer expenditure and demographic trends over the same period

- company pricing policy on its various models and company expenditure on advertising and promotion over the same period.

Notice the words 'over the same period'. It is absolutely vital to compare sets of data relating to the same period if any conclusions are to have validity. The marketing manager can now make the following types of statistical analysis:

- **Averages** can be calculated. These are a very basic and widely used measure. For example, what was the average expenditure on advertising and promotion for the period?

- Using averages as a guide, the **spread** of findings can be looked at. Is there a year when something unusual happened?

- Are there any clear **relationships** that occur within the data sets under analysis. For example, is there a relationship between company advertising expenditure and sales volume, or the national economic trends and total UK sales of gas cookers?

- If a relationship between sets of variable exists, it is possible to attempt to **predict** sales behaviour. 'What if?' questions can be asked. For example, would a special sales promotion discount increase sales sufficiently to raise overall profits?

Let us now consider some of the basic methods of statistical analysis.

Averages

The most easily understood single (or 'representative') value used to describe data is the **average** or **central tendency** of a group of data.

- The use of an average greatly **simplifies** a large set of data. Instead of looking at the earnings of sales staff in a firm, the average earnings would be a more concise way of looking at the issue.

- Averages allow **comparisons** to be made. What is the average earnings of sales staff in the Liverpool branch of a company compared to those in the London branch?

- Averages allow **samples** to be used without the need to know all of the individual data items. For example, it would not be necessary to calculate the individual salary of every one of 700 salespersons if you know that the mean annual salary of a representative sample is £20,000. You would be able to estimate that the total annual salary bill for the sales force is £1.4 million (i.e. 700 x £20,000).

Three different **measures of central tendency** are used in statistics: the arithmetic mean, the mode and the median.

THE ARITHMETIC MEAN

> **!?!** The **arithmetic mean** is calculated by adding all the values together and dividing by the total number of values. It is one of the most useful statistical measures.

The arithmetic mean of 3, 8 and 4 is:

$$\frac{3+8+4}{3} = 5$$

A note about notation: The arithmetic mean of a group of values x, is written as $\bar{x}$. The summation symbol Σ is a capital Greek S (sigma) used to mean 'add together'.

Sometimes, we are dealing with data which are 'grouped'. This is often the case when compiling the results of a survey, because they are easier to collect in this form. We can still calculate the arithmetic mean in these cases. For example, look at the data in table 4.1. The data is grouped in classes. First we need to find the mid-point of each class interval. This is done by adding the value of the upper interval to the lower and dividing the result by 2.

Number of telephone calls per hour	Mid-points x	Frequency f	fx
0-4	2	6	12
5-9	7	9	63
10-14	12	5	60
15-19	17	4	68
20-24	22	1	22
Totals		25	225

TABLE 4.1: *Sample data – number of calls received in an hour*

When the data is given as a grouped frequency table, we use the following formula to calculate the arithmetic mean:

$$\bar{x} = \frac{\Sigma fx}{\Sigma f}$$

To find the arithmetic mean, therefore, all we have to do is total the frequency to give Σf and then multiply each mid-point by its frequency (fx) and find the total of these values Σfx. So, in our example from table 4.1:

$$\bar{x} = \frac{\Sigma fx}{\Sigma f}$$

$$\bar{x} = \frac{225}{25} = 9 \quad \text{calls per hour}$$

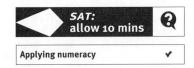

ACTIVITY 1

Table 4.2 shows the range of weekly incomes in a survey group being used for market research. Calculate the arithmetic mean $(\bar{X})$ of these earnings data

Weekly earnings range	Number of respondents
£250 but under £300	10
£300 but under £350	6
£350 but under £400	24
£400 but under £450	30
£450 but under £500	8

TABLE 4.2: *Sample data – earnings of members of market research survey group*

Commentary...

How can we calculate the arithmetic mean weekly income for this group? We do not know where each respondent's earnings are placed within the particular earnings range. Therefore, we have to assume that the individual earnings are evenly dispersed both above and below the mid-point of each earnings range. It follows that the mid-point then becomes the estimated arithmetic mean earnings for all the respondents in each earnings range.

Once we have established the mid-points, we can estimate the arithmetic mean earnings in the manner we have adopted for non-grouped data. The preliminary calculations are shown in table 4.3.

Weekly earnings Range	Mid-point of range (x)	Number of respondents (f)	Mid-point multiplied by respondents numbers (fx)
£250 but under £300	275	10	£2,750
£300 but under £350	325	6	£1,950
£350 but under £400	375	24	£9,000
£400 but under £450	425	30	£12,750
£450 but under £500	475	8	£3,800
Totals		78 (Σf)	£30,250 (Σfx)

TABLE 4.3: *Calculating average weekly earnings of survey group*

So, using the formula for the arithmetic mean:

$$\bar{x} = \frac{\Sigma fx}{\Sigma f}$$

$$\bar{x} = \frac{£30,250}{78} = £387.82$$

The major advantage of the arithmetic mean is that it is widely understood. The value of every item is included in the comparison of the mean. However, there are disadvantages.

- Its value may not correspond to any actual value found in practice. For example, the mean family size is 2.3 children but, obviously, no family actually has 2.3 children.

- An arithmetic mean might also be distorted by extremely high or low values. For example, the mean of 3, 4, 4 and 6 is 4.25, but the mean of 3, 4, 4, 6 and 15 is 6.4. The high value 15 distorts the mean value. In some circumstances, this would give a misleading and inappropriate figure.

○ If the set of sample items is small then the mean becomes less useful.

THE MODE

> ‽ The **mode** is the most frequently occurring item of data in a given set of data.

The mode is used in marketing research to find the most common item in a set of data if a quick result is needed.

Consider the following set of numbers:

7, 6, 2, 8, 3, 4, 5, 7, 2, 7, 7, 1

The **modal value** is 7, i.e. the value that occurs the most.

We can put data into a **frequency table**. Look at tables 4.4 and 4.5. In table 4.4, there is clearly only one modal class – 40 customers between the ages of 41–45. This is not always the case. Look at the data in table 4.5. Notice that 31–35 and 41–45 both occur 30 times. The data is **bimodal** – it has two modal classes. It is common for a single set of data to have many modes – this is called **multi-modal**.

Age group of customer (years)	Frequency
10–15	10
16–20	20
21–25	10
26–30	10
31–35	10
36–40	10
41–45	40
46–50	10
	120 Data readings

TABLE 4.4: *Sample data – a frequency distribution*

Age group of customer (years)	Frequency
10–15	10
16–20	10
21–25	10
26–30	10
31–35	30
36–40	10
41–45	30
46–50	20
	130 Data readings

TABLE 4.5: *Sample data – a bimodal distribution*

The major advantages of the mode are as follows:

○ The mode is particularly useful when we require either a very quick estimate of central tendency or when the most typical value (or values) is required.

○ It is more appropriate than the mean in situations where it is useful to know the most common value. For example, if a manufacturer wishes to start up production in a new industry, it might be useful to know what sort of product made by the industry is most in demand.

○ It is easy to calculate and understand.

○ Unlike the arithmetic mean, it is unaffected by extreme values.

However, its major disadvantage is that it does not take into account all values.

THE MEDIAN

The **median** is the value of the middle item of a distribution when all the data is set out in numerical order.

Consider the following list of values:

2, 6, 5, 1, 5, 4, 1, 1, 3

We can rearrange them into ascending order:

1, 1, 1, 2, 3, 4, 5, 5, 6

The median value of these numbers is 3 since it is the value in the middle of the list. For a list of values with an even number of items, there is no middle item, so the median is usually taken as the mean value of the middle two items.

For example, if we have a list of values:

1.7, 2.3, 4.5, 4.7, 5.3, 6.8

then the median is mid-way between 4.5 and 4.7. The median is

$$\frac{4.5 + 4.7}{2} = 4.6$$

The median can be used to resolve the problem of average earnings. For example, it can answer the question of how much the person in the middle of the earnings ladder receives. Half of the remaining workers receive less than the median and the other half receive more than the median.

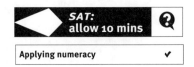

SAT: allow 10 mins

Applying numeracy ✔

ACTIVITY 2

Using the data in table 4.6, calculate the median hotel bed occupancies.

Occupied hotel beds (value)	Number of nights (frequency)	Cumulative frequency
23	1	
25	2	
26	3	
27	4	
28	3	
29	4	
30	3	

TABLE 4.6: *Sample data – hotel bed occupancies*

Commentary...

For data presented in groups, the median may be quickly found by first calculating the **cumulative frequency** of each value. The cumulative frequency of a value is the frequency of that value plus the frequency of all previous values. Thus, for our variable, number of occupied beds:

Value	Frequency	Cumulative frequency
23	1	1
25	2	3
26	3	6
27	4	10
28	3	13
29	4	17
30	3	20

TABLE 4.7: *Sample data – hotel bed occupancies*

So there are 10 values of 27 or below, 13 values of 28 or below and so on. From the cumulative frequency, it can be seen that the tenth ordered value is 27 and the eleventh ordered value is 28. The median is therefore 27.5.

The advantages of the median are that:

- like the mode, it is unaffected by extreme values

- it is useful for comparing changes in a 'middle of the road' value over time

- it is useful in cumulative frequency distributions, for example, 50 per cent of the working population earn less than £9,000 a year.

The disadvantage of the median are that it does not take every value into account. It also ignores dispersion around the median value.

Measures of spread

In our work on averages, we have pointed out some of the disadvantages of using these measures of central tendency to describe a set of data. Averages are a method of determining the central point of a distribution but they give no indication of the spread (or dispersion) of values in the distribution. For this, you need to analyse their **scatter**. In other words you need to measure the **dispersion** of the data above or below its average value.

Measures of spread describe or quantify the dispersion of a variable about its average, the degree of scatter shown by observations or the amount of variability within the data. This is a useful statistic. For example, if a company quantifies the variability of the size of the market in which it operates, it can use this to monitor how profits will be affected by these variations from the average market size.

There are four methods used to calculate dispersion: the range, quartiles, mean absolute deviation and standard deviation.

THE RANGE

> !?! The **range** is the difference between the highest and the lowest observation.

Consider, for example, the two income distributions in table 4.8. It is straightforward to calculate the range. We can see that group B has the biggest range of incomes with £3,380.

	Highest income	Lowest income	Range
Group A:	£10,512	£7,422	£3,090
Group B:	£11,400	£8,020	£3,380

TABLE 4.8: *Sample data – income ranges*

The advantages of the range are:

- it is easy to understand
- it is easy to calculate if there are only a few numbers, and even if there is a larger set of numbers, it is equally easy to calculate provided the data is arranged in order of size.

However, the range has disadvantages:

- The range is affected by extreme values, so it can be misleading. For example, 1,000 is an extreme value in the sequence 1, 6, 9, 10, 1,000. Extreme values are known as **outliers** because they lie outside the normal range.

- The range gives no indication of the spread between extremes; it only reflects the two extreme readings.

- The range is often not suitable for further statistical analysis, because it does not make use of all the values in the distribution.

- It is often more useful to quote the largest and smallest values as a way of giving some appraisal of a set of readings, rather than the difference between the two readings.

QUARTILES

Quartiles offer a method of identifying the range within which most of the values in the distribution occur. The **lower quartile** is the value below which 25 per cent (i.e. one quarter) of observations fall, while the **upper quartile** is the value above which 25 per cent (i.e. one quarter) of observations fall. The two quartiles and the median (the mid-point) divide the distribution into four equal groups.

This, obviously, gives a more accurate picture of dispersion but further refinements can be used. The **inter-quartile range** allows the extreme readings to have less effect on the way the data is interpreted. For example, given the readings

3, 25, 36, 47, 49, 52, 53, 55, 68, 1,000

It is less relevant to say that the range is 997 than it is to point out that 80 per cent of the readings lie between 25 and 68.

MEAN ABSOLUTE DEVIATION

The **mean absolute deviation** gives an indication of whether the values are spread out from the mean or whether they tend to be close to it. The deviation is the difference between the value of the average and a value in the distribution. The mean absolute deviation is calculated using the following formula.

$$\frac{\Sigma|x - \bar{x}|}{n}$$

where x is a value in the distribution, $\bar{X}$ is the statistical mean of the distribution and n is the number of items in the distribution. The lines $|\ |$ indicate that all of the readings are to be taken as positive.

> **\!?\!** The **mean absolute deviation** is the average of the absolute deviations from the mean. Absolute values (these are values which ignore minus signs) are used because we are not concerned about whether the deviations from the mean are positive or negative, but simply how big the deviations are.

For example, let us find the mean absolute deviation from the mean for the numbers

2, 4, 6, 8, 10, 12

First, we must calculate the mean of this distribution.

$$\bar{x} = \frac{2+4+6+8+10+12}{6} = \frac{42}{6} = 7$$

Now calculate the absolute deviations from the mean.

x	$|x - \bar{x}|$
2	5
4	3
6	1
8	1
10	3
12	5
42	18
(Σx)	$(\Sigma|x - \bar{x}|)$

TABLE 4.9: *Calculating absolute deviations from the mean*

Finally, apply the formula for calculating the mean absolute deviation. Note, since there are six numbers, n = 6.

$$\frac{\Sigma|x - \bar{x}|}{n} = \frac{18}{6} = 3$$

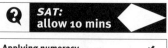

ACTIVITY 3

Table 4.10 gives the incomes of ten people who have been interviewed in a survey on consumer spending. Calculate the mean absolute deviation of income within the group.

Weekly Income (£)	$\lvert x - \bar{x} \rvert$
300	
310	
325	
336	
330	
305	
319	
322	
327	
329	

TABLE 4.10: *Sample data – weekly income*

Commentary...

First calculate the mean for the distribution.

$$\bar{x} = \frac{\Sigma x}{n} = \frac{£3203}{10} = £320.3$$

Now calculate the absolute deviations from the mean.

Weekly income (£)	$\lvert x - \bar{x} \rvert$
300	20.3
310	10.3
325	4.7
336	15.7
330	9.7
305	15.3
319	1.3
322	1.7
327	6.7
329	8.7
3,203	94.4

TABLE 4.11: *Sample income data – calculating the absolute deviations from the mean*

Since there are ten incomes, the mean absolute deviation is:

$$\frac{94.4}{10} = £9.44$$

The significance of this figure is what is says about the spread of incomes. For the researcher, a mean absolute deviation of less than £10 in weekly incomes would, for most purposes, be low enough to consider that the sample group has broadly similar incomes. They could be considered as part of the same income group when, for example, analysing consumer spending patterns.

The mean absolute deviation is a sensible measure of spread – particularly in making a summary of scatter in small sets of data. For statisticians, however, its main drawback is that the mean absolute deviation cannot be used in subsequent statistical analysis of very complex sets of data without laborious calculations. When analysing larger sets of data, they tend to use alternative measures of dispersion such as the standard deviation.

STANDARD DEVIATION

!?! The **standard deviation** is the square root of the variance.
The **variance** is the average of the squared deviations.

The standard deviation is a measure of the average dispersion of the variable. It is the most important measure of dispersion. It is calculated by using the following formula:

$$\sqrt{\frac{\Sigma(x-\bar{x})^2}{n}}$$

Let us take an example to illustrate standard deviations. Find the standard deviation of the numbers

$$2, 4, 7, 8, 9$$

Using the formula,

$$\text{standard deviation} = \sqrt{\frac{\Sigma(x-\bar{x})^2}{n}}$$

first calculate the mean of the distribution.

$$\bar{x} = \frac{2+4+7+8+9}{5} = 6$$

Then calculate the squared deviations from the mean.

x	$x - \bar{x}$	$\Sigma(x-\bar{x})^2$
2	−4	16
4	−2	4
7	1	1
8	2	4
9	3	9
		34

TABLE 4.12: *Calculating the squared deviations from the mean*

Therefore, using our formulae, the standard deviation is:

$$\sqrt{\frac{34}{5}} = \sqrt{6.8} = 2.61$$

Every value in the distribution is used in calculating the standard deviation. It is expressed in the same units as the original data and the arithmetic mean with which it is always associated. The larger the spread of the data is, the larger the value of the standard deviation.

The standard deviation has the disadvantage, however, that it is more difficult to determine than the other measures of dispersion and it also gives undue weight to extreme values in the distribution because deviations from the mean are squared.

ACTIVITY 4

SAT:
allow 10 mins

Applying numeracy ✔

Using the income data from the last activity, calculate the standard deviation for this distribution of incomes.

Commentary...

First, calculate the squared deviations from the mean.

x	$(x - \bar{x})$	$(x - \bar{x})^2$
300	20.3	412.09
310	10.3	106.09
325	4.7	22.09
336	15.7	246.49
330	9.7	94.09
305	15.3	234.09
319	1.3	1.69
322	1.7	2.89
327	6.7	44.89
329	8.7	75.69

TABLE 4.13: *Calculating the squared deviations from the mean*

Using the formula to calculate the standard deviation we have:

$$\Sigma(x - \bar{x})^2 = 1240.1$$

$$\sqrt{\frac{\Sigma(x - \bar{x})^2}{n}} = \sqrt{\frac{1240.1}{10}} = \sqrt{124.01} = £11.14$$

The standard deviation shows a wider range of dispersion (£11.14) compared with the mean deviation (£9.44). For most purposes, it would still suggest that this group could be considered as having broadly similar incomes for market research purposes.

Distribution

Distribution is another feature of data used for analysis. For example, consider the spread of earnings in each of the following three market surveys.

Earnings range	Number of respondents		
	Survey A	Survey B	Survey C
£200 but under £300	12	12	11
£300 but under £400	30	16	16
£400 but under £500	21	20	22
£500 but under £600	17	24	22
£600 but under £700	11	30	16
£700 but under £800	4	11	11
Totals	95	113	98
Estimated arithmetic means	£446.8	£518.1	£500.0
Estimated medians	£428.5	£537.5	£500.0
Estimated modes	£350.0	£650.0	£500.0

TABLE 4.14: *Sample data – income distributions*

In the case of survey A, the arithmetic mean exceeds the median; in survey B, the median exceeds the arithmetic mean; and, in survey C, the distribution is even or symmetrical with both the estimated arithmetic mean and the estimated median in the same position.

These differences in distribution can be shown more clearly by plotting a histogram for each group of data. By illustrating the data for each survey, joining up the values with a continuous line, we can establish three basic shapes. A frequency polygon is formed to show the shape of the earnings range. These three sets of data are examples of three different types of distribution: a **positively skewed** distribution, a **negatively skewed** distribution and a **normal** distribution.

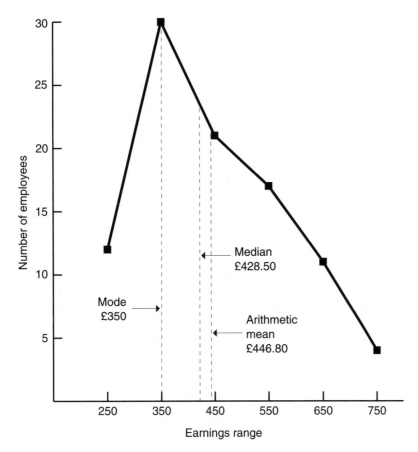

FIGURE 4.1: *A positively skewed earnings distribution (survey A).*

Note that the positively skewed distribution has a long tail to the right and that the arithmetic mean exceeds both the median and the mode.

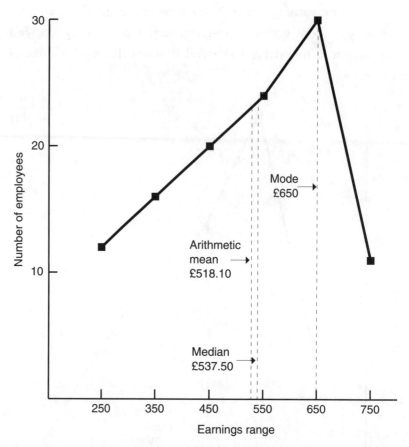

FIGURE 4.2: *A negatively skewed earnings distribution (survey B).*

The negatively skewed distribution has a long tail to the left and the median and mode exceed the arithmetic mean.

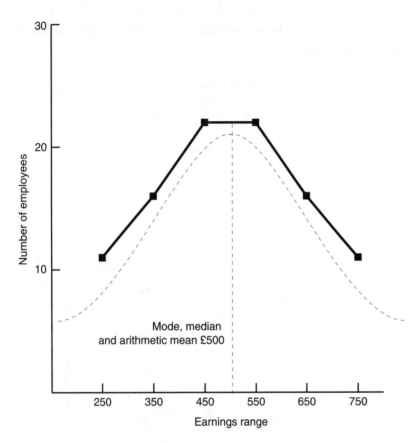

FIGURE 4.3: *Survey C tends towards a normal earnings distribution.*

The normal distribution is 'bell-shaped' and the mode, median and arithmetic mean are identical. The normal distribution occurs frequently in statistics, particularly in those dealing with 'human' data such as height, weight and longevity and can be found in survey data. It is also important for those interested in sampling techniques; the curve has such smooth proportions that statisticians can draw a number of conclusions using very small samples of information.

Some distributions do not lend themselves to the labels of skewed positive, negative or normal. In some cases, the distributions are U-shaped, others are shaped like a Bactrian (two-humped) camel, i.e. with two modes.

Time series analysis

> **!?!** A **time series** is a distribution of data made up of a series of measurements recorded over a period of time.

Time series analysis is a statistical technique which allows us to examine how data has been behaving over time. In doing so, it allows us to look at **trends**.

Examples of time series data include:

- output of a factory every day of last month

- monthly sales over last five years

- total costs per annum over last five years

- retail price index for each month of last five years.

Sales (£s)	Year
174,000	1989
191,000	1990
200,000	1991
208,000	1992
211,000	1993

TABLE 4.15: *Sample time series data – ice-cream sales*

One common way for firms to prepare a sales forecast is to look back at what has happened in previous years. An ice-cream manufacturer, for example, could look back over its sales for the past five years (see table 4.15). This would tell the management several things:

- that sales had risen every year over the last five years

- that sales had risen by a total of £37,000 over the period examined

- that the biggest increase in sales revenue (£17,000) came in the period 1989–1990

- that the smallest increase (£3,000) came in the period 1992–1993

- that increases in sales revenue had reduced in each of the five years.

The management could take a number of approaches to predicting sales of their product for 1994. They could simply take an average of the yearly increases in sales revenue. So, they could assume an average sales rise of:

$$\frac{£37,000}{4} = £9,250$$

On this basis, the 1994 sales forecast would be the 1993 sales plus the average annual sales rise:

1994 sales forecast = £211,000 + £9,250 = £220,250

Alternatively, the management could take the trend towards reducing increases in sales revenue into account. Sales have been increasing at a progressively lower rate since 1990. The management could assume that this trend will continue. So they would assume that the increase in sales during 1993–94 will be less than the £3,000 increase between 1992 and 1993. If they settled on £2,000 this would give predicted sales in 1994 of:

1994 sales forecast = 1993 revenue + £2,000
= £211,000 + £2,000 = £213,000

This assumes that the 1994 sales increase will be £7,250 less than the average annual sales increase based on the last five years' sales. If the company decided that both methods are equally valid ways of predicting sales for 1994, it could take the average of the results of the two methods. So we have a third estimate for 1994 sales:

$$1994 \text{ sales forecast} = \frac{£220,250 + £213,000}{2}$$
$$= \frac{£433,250}{2} = £216,625$$

The company now has three predictions for its sales revenue for 1994. Let us put them in order of size.

1. £220,250

2. £216,625

3. £213,000

EXERCISE:
allow 20 mins

Working with and relating to others ✔

Managing tasks and solving problems ✔

ACTIVITY 5

Imagine that you are the newly appointed marketing manager of the ice-cream manufacturer. The chairman tells you: 'I want you to achieve sales revenue of at least £213,000 and if possible exceed £220,250. Your bonus depends upon it.'

What questions would you have to ask about the figures? For example, has the rise in sales revenue over the last five years been due to price increases, extra sales or a mixture of the two?

In groups of four, decide what factors you would need to consider and the market research you might wish to commission in order to produce a more accurate sales forecast and to develop a marketing strategy. Write your key points in the box below.

Commentary...

You would certainly have to question these figures. They tell you facts but they give no reasons to explain the trends. Without understanding the reason for the trends, you will not be able to develop an effective marketing strategy. Let us consider some of the qualitative factors which must be taken into consideration in this case.

1. How has inflation eaten into the figures over the last five years. Has sales revenue risen in real terms?

2. Has sales revenue varied according to the weather? Are we looking at data which has been influenced due to unusually hot or cold spells?

3. What is the nature of competition? Are we selling more due to competitors leaving the market? Are we selling less due to the strength of competitors? Is the nature of competition stable, or is it easy for firms to enter the market in a hot summer?

4. Are all of the sales obtained during certain months of the year, or do we do well all year round?

5. Can we put all of these factors together and come up with a predicted sales revenue figure for 1994?

6. What are the overall sales trends in the ice-cream market?

7. What percentage of market share have we achieved over the last five years?

You can see how much more complicated this is. Here you are trying to understand the market conditions in order to make predictions. The weather remains unpredictable, but it might be possible to examine data and say: 'On average, we sell £20,000 worth of ice-cream if the weather is good between June and the end of August.' Even this needs to be qualified: What constitutes 'good'? At best, you will arrive at a reasoned estimate; statisticians refer to this as a **forecast**.

Our example above of how to prepare a sales forecast is useful but it is not complete; the internal and external influences that affected the sale performance are not yet shown in the statistics. Let us now look at this complication.

A time series of a product's past sales (Y) can be split into four parts. First, there is the **trend** (T) or long-term underlying movement of sales. This can be illustrated by fitting a straight line through past sales data. Second, there is the **cycle** (C) or long-term variations about the trend caused by booms or slumps. This is more periodic and hence it moves around the overall trend.

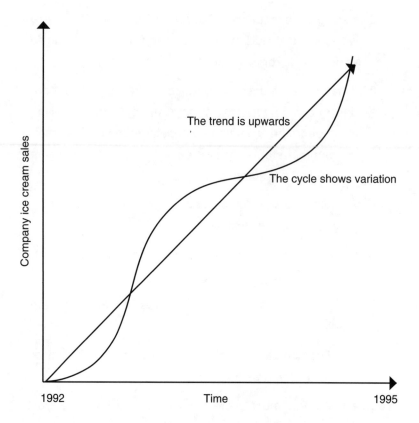

FIGURE 4.4: *Trends and cycles in sales data.*

The third factor is the **seasonality** *(S)*. This would include factors such as the weather patterns and holiday periods. Fourth, is the **erratic** variable *(E)*. These involve unpredictable factors like wars, riots and blizzards. These should be removed from sales data so that a more normal trend can be analysed. So we have these components:

- Past sales *(Y)*

- Trend *(T)*

- Cycle *(C)*

- Seasonality *(S)*

- Erratic *(E)*

Now consider a second ice-cream company. It has sold £12,000 worth of products in 1995 and it wants to predict the value of sales in next December. The long-term trend shows a 5 per cent sales growth per year. So, 1996 annual sales could be predicted as:

1996 sales forecast = last year's sales x 1.05 = £12,600

This gives us a prediction of £12,600 for next year. But, the company's economic advisers predict that there will be a further recession next year. In recessions, the company estimates that sales are only 90 per cent of sales in a normal year. So, if we take the predicted recession into account, we obtain a cyclically adjusted figure of:

1996 sales forecast = £12,600 x 0.90 = £11,340

If sales were equally spaced between months, the monthly sales figures would be:

$$\text{average monthly sales} = \frac{£11,340}{12} = £945$$

However, December is a below average month for sales. In December, the company usually only generates 50 per cent of average monthly sales. Adding a weighting to compensate, we obtain:

predicted December sales $= £945 \times 0.5 = £472.50$

ACTIVITY 6

A paint company sold £150,000 worth of paint last year. It wishes to predict the sales of paint in April the following year. Using the following data, make a forecast for sales in April.

Sales last year: £150,000

Trend: 7.5 per cent increase per year

Cyclically adjusted figure: 105 per cent

Seasonal: April generates above average sales by 12.5 per cent

SAT:
allow 10 mins

Applying numeracy ✔

Commentary...

First predict next year's sales on the basis of the long-term trend.

Next year's sales = £150,000 x 1.075 = £161,250

Adjusting for cyclical factors = £161,250 x 1.05 = £169,312.5

Now calculate average monthly sales revenue and adjust for April being an above average month.

$$\text{April sales } = \left(\frac{£169,312.5}{12}\right) \times 1.125$$
$$= £15,873$$

Correlation

Correlation is used as an abbreviation of the term **correlation coefficient,** which ranges in value from -1 and +1. It measures the relationship between two variables.

A figure near to +1, such as 0.9 shows a small amount of scatter, and thus a strong **positive correlation**. A correlation near 0 such as 0.2 shows little special tendency for two variables to occur with each other. They could do so, or they might not do so. There is a large amount of scatter in the readings. A **negative correlation** of say –0.8 means that a high amount of one variable tends to go with a low amount of another one.

For example, if you used a computer package to measure the correlation coefficient between social class and car purchase, and it came out as 0.1, then there is a very weak positive correlation between them. The weak correlation is indicative, in this case, of the fact that people of all social classes buy cars.

Marketeers find correlation a useful analytical tool. They might use it to investigate:

- the relationship between the price of a product and the demand for it

- the effects of advertising via various media (cinema, television, radio, newspapers, etc.) and sales

- the relationship between age, gender and occupation and attitudes, interests and opinions.

Marketeers need to be cautious, however, in establishing associations. For example, there is a well-known association between drinking and car accidents. A greater proportion of drinkers than non-drinkers have accidents. But non-drinkers also have car accidents, although in smaller numbers than drinkers. There is a correlation between drinking and car accidents, but it is difficult to measure how strong it is.

Let us take another example. A small company producing double glazing generates an average of £50,000 sales revenue each month. It decides to place a series of advertisements in the local newspaper to increase sales and raise awareness levels of the company and its products. If, in the month following an advertising campaign costing £15,000, the company doubled its sales to £100,000 one could conclude that advertising induced a greater number of product sales. However, you need to examine this very carefully.

- Has the increase in demand been partly brought about because the salesforce has been offered greater incentives?

- Has cold weather been partly responsible for some of the extra sales?

- Has an increase in consumer expenditure (perhaps following a cut in taxes) been partly responsible for the extra sales?

It is not so easy to argue that advertising is solely responsible for the increase in sales, although it would undoubtedly be responsible for some of the extra sales.

It is important to recognise that the existence of a correlation does not always show **cause and effect**. To illustrate this we will take an example of false correlation. Each year as the sales of ice-cream rises so do the number of drownings off the coast of England. Here you seem to have a simple correlation (in other words, A causes B – ice-cream causes drowning). But in fact this is obviously a false correlation, there is no casual relationship between the consumption of ice-cream and the number of people swimming in the sea. The real relation is between the numbers of people swimming and the temperature. The more people who want to cool off by swimming the more drownings there will be. Independently, as temperatures soar, more people want to eat ice-cream.

CORRELATION

Nothing is more difficult to prove than cause and effect. This is because there is rarely one single cause for any effect. As we have seen with the double glazing company, a multiplicity of factors probably come into play and it is often impossible to separate out these factors. For example, the decision to buy a car could be related to many factors – the price, age or gender. The use to which it will be put is also variable – long distance trips, local shopping, moving goods about or as a taxi.

> **!?!** Two qualities are **associated** when the distribution of values of one differs for different values of the other.

Marketing analysis involves the exploration of the relationship between two variables to establish the existence of **association**. By calculating measures of association and the strength and direction of correlation, the value of one variable may be predicted from another. Marketing research can involve measuring a number of qualities because marketeers are interested in finding and analysing associations between the markets for goods and services and their customers.

Let us end this session by giving two brief examples to illustrate this point. If a company is interested in launching a low alcohol sweet wine targeted at women under 25, it will look for correlations that might help formulate a marketing strategy. For example, it might be looking for positive correlations between wine consumption and income, occupation, education, lifestyle including social activities, regional and social class variations. These, if found, could be used to target the new wine to the most receptive group. If negative correlations are found, a marketing decision might be to try to overcome these by changing the image of the drink in the minds of potential drinkers. (The relaunch of 'Babycham' with its emphasis on young fashionable drinkers is an example of this strategy, as described earlier.)

The second example relates to lager and how it is targeted at particular groups of drinkers. Manufacturers have found a correlation between age, drinking habits and gender. Lager drinkers tend to be mainly aged 18–30; older drinkers prefer darker beers such as bitter. Lager is consumed mostly by males.

The audience can now be targeted. Lager advertisements are aimed at males in their late teens or early 20s. They stress sociability (males in groups) as this is a very important aspect of life to this target group. Harp lager was presented as being 'sharp to the bottom of the glass' and had a strong appeal based around a young 'Jack the lad' character out with his mates in the pub. The sharp, Jack the lad character epitomised Harp lager, and gave the product a clear identification with sociable, young males C1s and C2s – who are often heavy drinkers of lager.

Many methods exist to measure association: it is outside of the scope of this text to discuss them here. A more detailed coverage is given in a companion volume in this series: *Managing Finance and Information*. If you have access to statistical computer programmes such as *Statgraph* and *Minitab* you will find correlation covered there. Some spreadsheets, such as *Lotus 1-2-3* and *Excel* also produce correlation output.

summary

In this session, we have looked at a number of analytical techniques.

- There are three measures of central tendency: the arithmetic mean the mode and the median.

- Averages determine the central point of a distribution but give no indication of the spread of values in the distribution. For this, you need to analyse the spread or dispersal of the data.

- Measures of spread include the range, the quartiles, mean absolute deviation and standard deviation.

- Another means of analysing data is to consider its distribution. Distribution curves allow statisticians to draw conclusions from relatively small samples of information.

- Time series are distributions of data recorded over a period of time. They allow statisticians to analyse trends.

- Simple correlation is a useful analytical tool which investigates relationships between variables but it needs to be applied carefully when trying to establish associations between sets of data.

The Competitive Process

Market features

Objectives

After participating in this session, you should be able to:

- ◆ classify consumer and industrial markets

- ◆ show how industrial markets differ from consumer markets

- ◆ describe industrial markets in terms of segmentation variables and marketing mix decisions

- ◆ explain what a decision making unit is

- ◆ discuss industrial buyer behaviour in terms of decision process and influencing factors

- ◆ compare consumer and industrial buyer behaviour

- ◆ account for the development of services in the economy

- ◆ discuss the characteristics of services.

In working through this session, you will practise the following BTEC common skills:

Managing and developing self	✔
Working with and relating to others	✔
Communicating	✔
Managing tasks and solving problems	✔
Applying numeracy	
Applying technology	
Applying design and creativity	

Introduction to competitive analysis

Consumers are very demanding in their choice of goods and services. They understand that, together, they have the power to decide which companies will succeed and which will fail. Most private sector companies now realise that they must focus on exceeding the expectations of customers. They must offer value for money if they are not to be deserted in favour of companies who do.

In the public sector, a greater emphasis is being placed upon competition in the form of competitive tendering. Many public sector organisations are now beginning to use marketing techniques for the first time. Even such diverse public sector organisations as job centres, libraries and art galleries are realising that they have to understand the needs and aspirations of their target market if they are to form long-term mutually beneficial relationships with them.

In addition, in the voluntary sector, organisations such as charities now employ marketing managers. There are four reasons why they do this.

1. The main reasons why the public donates money or not, need to be identified, and appropriate plans developed.

2. They must constantly evaluate the business environment for threats. The main competitors need to be identified, and a strategy for overcoming them needs to be developed.

3. They must evaluate the business environment for opportunities. Ways must be found to broaden the appeal of the charity to business, the public and government.

4. In a competitive world, charities must be run in a professional way. Administration costs must be kept down and corporate communications policies must be effective.

For example, the National Lottery is a major threat as it attracts disposable income which might have been donated to charities. Conversely, it is also an opportunity, as it raises money for charity. Charities have to compete to obtain a significant share of lottery profits by demonstrating that they are efficiently run.

It can be seen that competitive analysis for any business is rather like planning a military strategy or playing a game of chess. You are not only thinking about your own organisation, but about any organisation that is competing with you. A manager of any company should constantly be asking the following key competitive questions:

- Who are our main competitors?

- What are their strengths and weaknesses?

- Is the industry we are in, easy to enter and compete in?

- How can we gain a competitive advantage?

- Are we constantly monitoring the business environment?

- Are we paying enough attention to our customers?

SAT:
allow 20 mins

Managing tasks and solving problems ✔

ACTIVITY 1

Choose an organisation in the arts, sport or recreation fields. For example, you might choose a premier league football club, a major theatre company or a record company.

Imagine you are the commercial manager. Who are your organisation's main competitors? What does your company do better than its competitors? How can it be more successful?

Commentary...

Here, we provide some ideas for a premier league football club. Other organisations in the arts, leisure and recreation fields would need to take into account similar factors.

First, consider who are the competitors of a football club. This is more complex than it looks. It would be easy to say that the competition is any other premier league club in the same geographical area. They would be direct competitors. Competition of a more indirect form comes from other leisure attractions such as television, cinema, amusement parks, etc. Shopping, decorating or saving for a car or a holiday offers indirect competition for the hard-earned cash of the fans.

To be more successful – to be better than its competitors – the club should endeavour to:

- be very successful on the pitch

- develop its income from off-the-field activities such as conference and dining facilities, and the club shop

- use its success to be seen regularly on television.

It should develop an effective public relations and corporate communications strategy aimed at developing the unique image of the club and the people who support it. This strengthens its competitive position by attracting even more advertising revenue at the ground, in the club magazine, and in sponsorship.

Types of market

Before a competitive analysis can be undertaken, it is essential for the marketeer to know the market. Markets can be split into two major types (with further sub divisions):

- consumer markets

- industrial markets.

These markets are essentially distinguished on the basis of the buyers' role and motives, as well as the characteristics of the purchased product. Here we are going to present a synopsis of each market before dealing in more detail with industrial markets; consumer markets have already been dealt with extensively in the first two sections of this book.

CONSUMER MARKETS

> ⁇ The **consumer market** consists of all individuals and households who buy goods and services for personal consumption.

There are two common classification schemes for consumer markets:

1. durable goods, non-durable goods and services

2. convenience goods, shopping goods and speciality goods.

This latter classification system is adapted from P. Kotler, 1994, *Marketing Management:* Prentice Hall International.

By classifying on the basis of durable goods, non-durable goods and services, analysts distinguish goods on the basis of their rate of consumption and tangibility.

- **Durable goods** are tangible goods which normally survive many uses (examples are refrigerators and clothing). Durable products are likely to need more personal selling and service.

- **Non-durable goods** are tangible goods which are normally consumed in a short time period e.g. meat and soap. Since these goods are consumed quickly and purchased frequently, they are likely to be available in many locations.

- **Services** are activities, benefits, or satisfactions which are offered for sale, e.g. haircuts and television repairs. Consumer services have the characteristics of being intangible, perishable, variable and personal.

By classifying on the basis of convenience goods, shopping goods and speciality goods, analysts distinguish goods on the basis of consumer shopping habits.

- **Convenience goods** are goods which the customer usually purchases frequently, immediately, and with little conscious choice between alternatives as they have preferred brands, e.g. tobacco products, toothpaste and newspapers.

- **Shopping goods** are those which the customer, in the process of selection and purchase, characteristically compares on such bases as suitability, quality, price and style. The consumer is likely to shop in a number of retail outlets to learn about the available goods and find the right item. Examples include furniture, clothes, used cars and domestic appliances.

O **Speciality goods** have unique characteristics and/or brand identification for which a significant group of buyers are habitually willing to make a special purchasing effort. Examples are specific brands and types of hi-fi components, photographic equipment and men's suits. Speciality goods do not involve shopping effort (since the consumer knows what he or she wants) but only shopping time to reach the outlets that carry these goods.

INDUSTRIAL MARKETS

> !?! The **industrial market** consists of all individuals and organisations who acquire goods and services for the production of other products or services that are sold, rented or supplied to others.

Selling to organisations introduces several considerations not found in consumer marketing:

O Organisations do not buy for personal consumption or utility but to obtain goods and services that will be used in further production, reselling, or servicing.

O Normally, several people are involved in organisational buying, especially for major items, compared to consumer buying which is more individual. The decision makers usually have different organisational responsibilities and apply different criteria to the purchase decision.

O The organisation imposes policies, constraints and requirements that must be heeded by its buyers.

O Buying instruments, such as requests for quotations, proposals, and purchase contracts, add another dimension not found in consumer buying.

There are three main types of industrial markets: producers, resellers and governments.

THE PRODUCER MARKET

The producer market consists of a wide variety of products and services which can be classified in terms of how they enter the production process and their relative cost. Kotler, 1994, in *Marketing Management*, Prentice Hall International suggests a threefold classification of the producer market.

1. Goods completely entering the product – **materials** and **parts,** including:

   (a) raw materials

   - farm products (e.g. wheat, cotton, livestock, fruits and vegetables)

   - natural products (e.g. fish, lumber, crude petroleum and iron ore)

   (b) manufactured materials and parts

   - component materials (e.g. steel, cement, wire and textiles)

   - component parts (e.g. small motors, tyres and castings).

2. Goods partly entering the product – **capital items,** including:

   (a) installations

   - buildings, plant and land (e.g. factories and offices)

   - fixed equipment (e.g. generators, drill presses and lifts)

   (b) accessory equipment

   - portable or light factory equipment and tools (e.g. hand tools and fork lift trucks)

   - office equipment (e.g. typewriters and desks)

3. Goods not entering the product – **supplies** and **services,** including:

   (a) supplies

   - operating supplies (e.g. lubricants, coal, typing paper and pencils)

   - maintenance and repair items (e.g. paint, nails and brooms)

   (b) business services

   - maintenance and repair services (e.g. window cleaning and typewriter repair).

THE RESELLER MARKET

The reseller market consists of all individuals and organisations who acquire goods for the purpose of reselling or renting them to others at a profit. Resellers are intermediaries who purchase finished goods and resell them (without reprocessing) to end users.

For example, an office supplies distributor may buy desks and chairs from one company and personal computers from another wholesaler and sell these products to local companies. Supermarkets, department stores, electrical discount stores and car dealerships are all examples of resellers who sell to the consumer market. Employment agencies – which hire out secretaries, receptionists and security guards – are resellers to the commercial and industrial markets.

Note that resellers also purchase goods and services to enable them to conduct their own operations; i.e. they are also part of the producer market.

THE GOVERNMENT MARKET

The government market consists of central and local government units and public sector organisations that purchase or rent goods for carrying out the main functions of government.

Central and local government buy computers, cars, refuse trucks, desks, uniforms, etc. Institutions such as schools, hospitals and universities are also purchasers of goods and services. Schools and universities require for example furniture, athletic equipment, books, overhead projectors while hospitals buy goods such as pharmaceutical supplies, operating tables, X-ray equipment, beds and food products.

Public sector organisations require services such as laundry, cleaning, catering, security guards and so on.

RECALL:
allow 5 mins

With respect to the producer market, list the types of goods and services that may be categorised under the three headings:

1. goods completely entering the product

2. goods partly entering the product

3. goods not entering the product.

A marketing approach to industrial markets

Let us now look at how the type of goods and services demanded by industry can have an influence on the marketing approach adopted by companies supplying industrial markets. First, we consider in more detail the type of goods required by a manufacturing company.

Installations

Installations are the major items of plant and machinery required for production. Extensive search and comparison is made before buying as this is likely to be the most important and largest single capital investment a company makes at any given time. Price is not necessarily very important when deciding; great emphasis is placed on expert sales advice, technical support and after sales support, e.g. spare parts and service. A complex **decision making unit (DMU)** will form to consider these capital investments as they are costly and critical to the business.

Accessories

Accessories include ancillary plant, maintenance and office equipment. Accessories are less expensive than installations and reduce in value quicker, so fewer people are involved with the purchase. A simpler DMU is involved as the decision has less importance for the company. Compare the choice of an office desk with that of a computer controlled lathe.

Raw materials

Efficient purchasing of raw materials is extremely important. Price fluctuations can have a big impact on a company's profit margins. The quality of the product is also likely to reflect the quality of raw materials. In some industries, raw materials are the vital component. For example, tin is the key input in the food canning business. Cocoa is the vital raw ingredient for chocolate manufacture. Price is not the only factor even in a homogeneous commodity market; delivery, continuity of supply, quality and level of service are all important when deciding on which supplier to deal with.

Components

Component parts help to produce the finished products. The car industry, for example, needs engine parts and replacement items for machinery. A textile manufacturer purchases fabric as raw material but the dyes and chemical finishes are classed as components and should not be confused with accessories. As with raw materials, non-price considerations figure highly in the purchase decision.

General supplies

These are items that are often taken for granted: cleaning items, stationery, general maintenance (other than that required for production plant) e.g. light bulbs, lubricating oil, repairs and renewals. The purchase is often routinely made through wholesalers. The homogeneous (similar) type of supplies and their wide availability means that price is a major factor in the purchasing decision.

Industrial services

This sector has greatly increased in recent years. The principal factor in deciding whether to use outside services or provide service in-house centres on the question of cost effectiveness. If a service is not required on a continuous basis then the outside service means that the firm has a convenient alternative to maintaining under-used equipment or staff. For example, many firms use outside catering, cleaning and equipment maintenance firms, on the basis that it is a cheaper option than doing it themselves.

This classification of industrial products helps when studying industrial buying behaviour. Each category performs a different role for the firm and this knowledge can be used by suppliers in the design of their marketing and sales strategy. In a similar way, so can classification by market segmentation.

INDUSTRIAL MARKET SEGMENTATION

There are some key segmentation variables which specifically apply to industrial markets.

Size of firm

Firms may be classified by size in terms of turnover, capital employed or number of employees. Whatever measure is employed, the important point to note is that large firms use a different criterion for evaluating a supplier and its products than small firms. Partly, this is because the larger firms employ professional buyers. Partly, it is because their scale of purchasing is totally different to small firms. They look for (and obtain) economies of scale.

Type of industry

Different industries have particular requirements in terms of product specifications, price or after-sales service. Consequently, a firm selling industrial valves may require a different marketing strategy and mix for each segment it deals with.

Geographical region

In the UK, some areas, designated as 'enterprise zones' or 'assisted areas', are home to firms that may have government grants or other financial assistance. Marketing to such organisations requires a different strategy especially in relation to price and communication than other areas in the country. A special attempt will have to be made to understand their difficulties in operating in a depressed area where prices must be kept lower than the national average.

Type of buying organisation

Many companies have factories in various parts of the country. They may have either centralised or decentralised purchasing systems. It is important to understand how a company organises its purchases. This directly influences the marketing approach to that firm. A sales representative must find out who has overall purchasing responsibility within the firm.

**A MARKETING APPROACH TO
INDUSTRIAL MARKETS**

When a firm is dealing with a number of different industries, it may be possible to segment by market structure. Some industries may be dominated by a few large powerful firms – such as the car industry or the defence industry – while other industries may be made up of hundreds of small firms. The marketing approach would be different for each industry – large dominant companies would be treated differently to smaller less powerful ones.

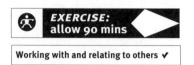

Working with and relating to others ✔

Communicating ✔

Managing tasks and solving problems ✔

ACTIVITY 2

Divide into small groups of three or four.

Choose a company with which you are reasonably familiar which sells to the industrial market. You might, for example, choose a well-known local company. Alternatively, you could choose a national name such as British Steel or Lucas. You should be able to obtain background information about these companies from their publicly available annual reports and from library sources.

In small groups, discuss the marketing mix of your company. You should discuss the mix in terms of:

- **selling**

- **advertising**

- **use of mass media**

- **use of specialised media.**

Make a short presentation to the other groups for comment. Note down the key points of your presentation in the box below.

Commentary...

Direct **selling** from producer to user is common for the following reasons:

- There are usually fewer customers and, in these circumstances, large orders are seen as critical. Relatively few people are needed to establish direct contact with buyers so the ratio of the cost of the salesforce to the value of orders is much less than domestic markets.

- Specialised knowledge is required in the selling process because industrial items are often bought to individual specifications. For example, an engineering company might want a customised lathe to meet its specific needs. Specialist qualifications and training may be important. For example, many salespeople in the pneumatic and hydraulic engineering businesses have specialist qualifications.

- Items of high unit value may require special credit arrangements which may be spread over several years.

- Buyers often prefer direct dealings because of the importance of after-sales servicing and advice. For example, a company that has purchased a computer system may want specialist training and on-tap advice for its staff to help them develop their competence.

Advertising is much less important in industrial markets than in consumer marketing. In general, advertising budgets are low. The budgets typically run into thousands rather than millions of pounds.

Because of the high segmentation in industrial markets, the use of **mass media** is often wasteful. However, some companies do advertise themselves in the national press and on television because it:

- builds up their corporate image

- attracts the attention of executives in the DMUs

- reassures the City that the company is maintaining a high profile; television advertising by the industrial giant Hanson is one example.

Industrial advertising tends to be concentrated in the **trade press** and **specialist media**. Specialist products and audiences mean that trade journals have very low circulations, but they are read by the people who make the key purchasing decisions.

Industrial buying decisions

As we have seen, industrial goods have different market and product characteristics to consumer goods. So, the buying decision is somewhat different for industrial goods. For industrial selling, it is important that the salesperson helps to determine the buyer's needs and shows the buyer how he or she can be fulfilled by the product. The salesperson needs to work closely with everyone who has an influence on the buying decision because industrial selling is extremely competitive, and it is essential that the salesperson understands the nature and roles of the DMU.

IDENTIFYING THE DECISION MAKING UNIT (DMU)

In an industrial situation, identifying who to speak to is not always easy. Salespeople have to determine who they have to see and how much time they need to spend with each person. They must also identify the people who influence the purchase decision and the strength of each person's influence. Such people form the DMU. They may include:

- **initiators** who propose to buy or replace a product or service

- **deciders** who are involved in making the actual decision, such as the plant engineer, purchasing agent and senior managers and directors

- **influencers,** e.g. plant engineer, plant workers and research and development personnel, who develop specifications needed for the product

- **buyers** with the authority to execute the contractual arrangements

- **gatekeepers** who influence where information from salespeople goes and with whom salespeople will be allowed to talk, e.g. receptionists, secretaries and purchasing agents

- **users** who must work with or use the product, e.g. plant workers or secretaries.

The scale of the purchasing decision, and the expenditure involved, determines the size and membership of the DMU. A regular purchase of parts would be carried out by the buyer alone, but a major purchase, such as a new expensive piece of machinery would lead to the formation of a large decision making unit.

Because of the nature of a DMU, it is important for the industrial salesperson to identify everybody involved in the decision-making process. In this sense, it is crucial that the salesperson passes the gatekeepers and talks to the initiators and users, influencers, buyers and deciders. It is important to remember that a person can fulfil more than one role in the buying process. For example, a managing director with technical expertise could be an initiator and a decider.

A practical example

Users of a company's copy machine (initiators) may become dissatisfied with its quality of copies. A secretary (influencer) mentions that Canon makes an excellent copier which the firm can afford. After a conference with several major users of the present duplicating machine, the office manager (decider) confers with the representatives of several competing copy machines and decides to lease the Canon machine. The purchasing agent (buyer) approves the purchase. In this example, the Canon salesperson should have visited each person who participated in the purchase decision and explained the product's benefits to each one.

In conclusion, it is important that an industrial salesperson identifies the DMU because, in many cases, the buyer is often not the only person who influences the purchasing decision. Not only is the decision in the hands of a source or buying centre, but the people in the DMU may change as the decision-making process continues. Therefore, it is important that salespeople recognise the make-up of a source and ensure that the benefits of their products are explained to all the people who influence the purchasing decision.

Managing tasks and solving problems ✔

ACTIVITY 3

Think about your own company or an organisation with which you are familiar and identify the DMU for:

- a significant purchase, i.e. one that is expensive and expected to have a long life

- routine purchases, e.g. computer accessories, machine oil.

Commentary...

The size of your company, say in terms of number of employees, will probably be an influence in the make up of the DMU; the larger the company, the larger the DMU is likely to be. You will probably have found it incorporates a number of people because organisational buying, unlike consumer purchasing, is a group process for significant items. (It also diffuses individual responsibility.) Attempting to allocate roles (initiator, gatekeeper, etc.) often helps to clarify the issues.

In contrast, the purchase of routine items will probably be carried out by one person. For routine purchases, a salesperson needs to find out whether decisions are taken by a buyer or whether the purchasing is carried out as part of the responsibility of another job, e.g. by the production manager or office manager.

SPECIAL FEATURES OF INDUSTRIAL BUYER BEHAVIOUR

Organisational buying is a transaction between a number of individuals rather than an action by one person. Various people within the organisation will be involved in the buying process and those people formally designated as buyers may only be responsible for a small part of the overall process. Key points to note are:

- at organisational level, the decision process is a **group buying process**

- the impact of an unsuccessful purchase decision poses much greater personal and organisational risks than the average consumer decision process, for both groups and individuals involved in the purchase

- there is more interdependence between buyer and seller in industrial markets because there are smaller numbers of goods and customers involved; therefore not only are sellers dependent on buyers for an assured outlet for their goods but also buyers are dependent on sellers for the continued sources of inputs for their processes

- post-purchase processes are much more important, e.g. having sold a company a sophisticated computer system, IBM would ensure that they provided a 24-hour telephone enquiry service to the purchaser in case any problems were experienced, and would also train the staff to use the new system.

As with consumer behaviour, the study of organisational buying centres around the decision process and factors that affect this process. These can be characterised in a number of ways. For example, Kotler has categorised the major influences on industrial buyer behaviour as set out in figure 1.1.

Environmental				
Level of Demand	**Organisational**			
Economic Outlook	Objectives	**Interpersonal**		
Cost of Money	Policies	Authority	**Individual**	
Rate of Technological Change	Procedures	Status	Age Income	
Political and Regulatory Developments	Organisational structures	Empathy	Education Job position	**Buyer**
Competitive Development	Systems	Persuasiveness	Personality Risk attitudes	

FIGURE 1.1: *Major influences on industrial buyer behaviour.*
Source: P. Kotler, 1994, *Marketing Management*

A similar approach is to consider the external factors operating on the purchasing company under several headings:

- **Economic factors,** e.g. interest rates, level of unemployment, consumer and wholesale price index, growth in gross national product are important. In times of recession, firms tend to cut back on purchasing.

- **Political/legal factors** include the government's attitude toward business, international tariffs, trade agreements and government assistance to selected industries. Legal and regulatory forces at the local and national levels affect the industrial decision process.

- **Cultural factors** can be defined as the means and methods of coping with the environment that are passed from one generation to the next and include values, habits, customs and traditions. Corporate subculture also influences the buying decision.

- **Physical influences** can include climate, geography, locations, labour supply and choice of raw materials.

- **Technological advances** will influence the way organisations buy and sell. For example, electronic data interchange (EDI), a system which allows computers to communicate with each other all over the world, can be used to automate the purchasing process.

There are also, of course, organisational factors affecting buying:

- **centralisation** – the physical and managerial location of the focus of influence and decision making authority

- **formalisation** – the degree to which certain rules and procedures are stated and adhered to by the employees of the organisation

- **specialisation** – the degree to which the organisation is divided into specialised departments according to job function and organisational activities.

The problem, then, is to define how these factors relate to the buying process, for the process itself is clearly an important issue. There are a number of stages with clear relations between them. The first attempt to define the industrial purchase process did so in terms of four stages:

1. problem recognition

2. organisational assignment of responsibility

3. search procedures

4. choice procedures.

This logical and rational process clearly shows a series of steps which follow a sequence. Recently, a number of different models have attempted to deal with the complex relations between the factors involved. Each incorporates variables and processes, but this complexity poses severe problems when testing the usefulness of the models. The more complex the model, the less likely it is to be of use in a practical situation.

For example, the American Marketing Association model, shown in figure 1.2, proposes that there are four main influences on organisational buying decisions:

1. influence within the purchasing department

2. interdepartmental influences

3. intra-firm influences

4. inter-firm influences.

Organisation influences	Departmental influences	
	Within purchasing department	Between departments
Intra-firm Influence	Cell 1 Intra-departmental, intra-organisational influences The purchasing agent Social factors Price-cost factors Supply continuity Risk avoidance	Cell 2 Inter-departmental, intra-organisational influences The buying centre Organisational structure Power-conflict processes Gatekeeper role
Inter-firm Influence	Cell 3 Intra-departmental, inter-organisational influences Professionalism Word of mouth Communication, trade shows, journals Supplier purchase reciprocity	Cell 4 Inter-departmental, inter-organisational influences Organisational environment Technological change Nature of suppliers Co-operative buying

FIGURE 1.2: *The American Marketing Association Model.*

The model indicates how these factors interrelate.

- The first cell includes factors relating to the **purchase agent,** including social factors, price, supply and risk aspects.

- The factors in the second cell relate to the **buying centre:** its structure, processes and the role of gatekeeper.

- The third cell relates to **environmental influences** on purchase agents, including increased professionalisation within the purchase function in how communication takes place, how advertising, PR and promotion are done, and suppliers and purchasers are reciprocally related.

- The fourth cell concerns the relation between the **organisation and its environment,** including the rate of technological change and how this influences the way in which the organisation functions.

Although this model emphasises a range of factors, it is concerned with process, and the relationships between factors within a variety of organisational environments. It brings out, however, the centrality of interaction and the behaviour of individuals within the organisation, without satisfactorily dealing with the ways in which these can be used to explain or predict outcomes.

SAT:
allow 10 mins

Managing tasks and solving problems ✔

ACTIVITY 4

Refer to the American Marketing Association Model of organisational buying behaviour and, for each of the four cells, give an example of an appropriate factor. For example, in cell 1, the amount of money available for purchase is a key factor.

Commentary...

- In cell 1, the risk involved in the purchase will be related to how risk-taking the organisation is as a whole. Do they want to be ambitious, or safe?

- In cell 2, two key managers may have a conflict which clouds their judgement and leads them to disagree about a purchasing decision simply because they do not want to agree with each other about anything.

- In cell 3, the level of training which a buyer has had will affect his or her ability to carry out a purchasing task in a professional manner.

- In cell 4, if one or more firms joined together to make a purchase between them (e.g. an expensive machine to be shared between them), then the size and nature of the DMU would need to be modified.

You will no doubt have thought of many other examples.

Consumer buying behaviour

The question: 'What makes people buy?' is a crucial one. The level of importance attached to it can be measured by the volume of literature on the subject, and the range of economic, sociological and psychological models which are used to attempt to explain the buying function. We have already discussed some aspects of industrial buying behaviour. The aim here is to introduce the buying decision, outline some of the main features of consumer buying behaviour and review some of the models relating to the issue. In drawing some broad conclusions, we consider the implications for consumer and organisational buyer behaviour.

Consumer behaviour is determined by a wide range of considerations: economic, psychological and sociological. Non-economic buying motivations are present in the buying of industrial goods and services as well as consumer purchases. While the process of decision may vary in duration, similar stages are observed. First, a general or specific need is felt. Second, a period of **pre-buying activity** follows, such as an investigation of sources of supply which might satisfy the need. Then, a **decision** is taken. This decision could be what to purchase, or whether to purchase or defer purchase. The decision is based on the results of the pre-buying activity and the strength of the need.

No two people perceive things in exactly the same way. People's attitude towards objects, words and ideas is **conditioned** by past experiences and the way in which senses have been stimulated. Accumulated experience builds up, over a period of time, a **perceptual framework** so that one has a predisposition to see or believe what one expects or would like to see or believe. Once a buying need is felt, the perceptual framework is more vigorously activated at a conscious and subconscious level. The potential buyer's ultimate decision is now more likely to be influenced by advertising, displays and personal sales talks, other people's attitudes and opinions.

Some recent work by social psychologists has highlighted the significance and nature of formal and informal social groups and their influence, by their values and beliefs, on individual behaviour. While personality conditions a buyer's behaviour in an individual way, temperament and philosophy, cultural and organisational influences also have a profound effect. Cultural differences arise from values to which individuals have been exposed from birth, allied to other social influences. Importantly, the organisation in which people work is a social institution where irrational values may develop. This complex of influences is brought to bear on both consumer and industrial buying. Additionally, consistent spending patterns may be related to variables such as age, sex, education, occupation, religion, race and income levels.

Two specific fields of study in relation to buying behaviour are lifestyle patterns and attitudes. The concept of **lifestyle patterns** - and their potential application to marketing dimensions - was formulated by William Lazer in 1963. Since then, continuous efforts have been made to identify groups of people according to their **activities, interests and opinions (AIOs),** and to establish if lifestyle data can be associated with conventional demographic information such as age and income. If significant correlations exist between lifestyle and product use, television programme preferences, store choice and so on, the possibilities of devising appropriate products directed towards similar lifestyle groups are opened up.

Attitudes can be defined as predispositions to act in particular ways toward particular people, ideas or situations. They are not innate and are subject to change, although it is difficult to effect changes since many attitudes become deeply ingrained over time. Some attitudes are held with great intensity and, in general, the evidence indicates a positive correlation between attitudes of high intensity, intentions to buy or not to buy and ultimate buying action. As Kotler has said:

The buyer's psyche is a black box whose workings can be only partially deduced. The marketing strategist's challenge to the behavioural scientist is to construct a more specific model of the mechanism in the black box.

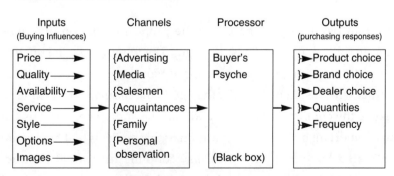

FIGURE 1.3: *Kotler's view of the consumer buying process conceived as a system of inputs and outputs.*

Economists were the first professional group to construct a specific theory of buyer behaviour. The theory holds that purchasing decisions are the result of largely rational and conscious economic calculations. The individual buyer seeks to spend his or her income on those goods that will deliver the most utility according to tastes and relative prices. The antecedents for this view trace back to the writings of **Adam Smith** and **Jeremy Bentham**. Smith set the tone by developing a doctrine of economic growth based on the principle that man is motivated by self-interest in all his actions while Bentham refined this view, seeing people as finely calculating and weighing the expected pleasures and pains of every contemplated action.

Marshall later employed 'the measuring rod of money' as an indicator of the intensity of human psychological desires. Over the years, his methods and assumptions have been refined into **utility theory:** economic man is bent on maximising his utility, and does this by carefully calculating the 'felicific' consequences of any purchase. The essential drawback with this is that it does not take into account the vitally important behavioural factors which influence buyers. One could argue that the model is normative (implying standards) rather than descriptive, and thus provides logical norms for buyers to be seen as rational. Although the consumer is not likely to employ economic analysis in deciding whether to buy a box of Milk Tray or Black Magic, he or she may apply economic analysis in deciding whether to buy a new car. Industrial buyers even more clearly want an economic calculus for making good decisions.

In contrast to this, **'Pavlovian man'** behaves in a largely habitual rather than thoughtful way. Certain configurations of cues will set off the same behaviour because of rewarded learning in the past. For example, a child rewarded for behaving in a certain way is likely to continue to behave in the same way. Although it has no claim to be a complete theory of behaviour, the Pavlovian model is significant in that it could be said to stress the desirability of repetition in advertising.

Freudian psychology is based on the proposition that individuals have an 'id', an 'ego' and a 'super-ego'. The id represents instinctive needs; the super-ego represents social values which tend to lie in conflict with instinctive needs; the ego is the mechanism seeking to resolve the conflicts between the id and the super-ego. Perhaps the most important marketing implication of this model is that buyers are motivated by symbolic as well as economic-functional product concerns. Motivational research has produced some interesting and occasionally bizarre hypotheses about what may be in the buyer's mind regarding certain purchases. It has been suggested that a man buys a convertible as a substitute mistress, and that many businessmen do not fly because of a fear of posthumous guilt – if they died in an air crash, their widows would think them stupid for not taking a train.

The whole concept of symbolic imagery assumes vital significance when one analyses issues such as the corporate image and the influence of advertising. Some companies have a poor image while others enjoy an excellent image in the eyes of the consumer. Our previous discussions on the ways in which some companies promote their concern for the environment in order to improve their image applies here. Certain adverts contain the use of sexual imagery, such as those which imply that certain types of beer are 'manly' and make men appealing to the opposite sex. Parental love for children is clearly demonstrated in the 'Fairy Liquid' adverts; the advertiser attempts to make housewives feel uncaring if they choose not to use it. Certain advertising campaigns assume that the wife is influenced by other members of the family in what she buys, so we have 'Flora, the margarine for men' and other such campaigns.

Thorstein Veblen saw humans as primarily social animals, with their wants and behaviour moulded largely by their present group memberships and aspired group memberships. His hypothesis is that much of economic consumption is motivated by prestige-seeking rather than intrinsic needs or satisfaction. He emphasised the strong emulative factors which aim to equal or surpass others operating in the choice of conspicuous goods like clothes, cars and houses. Although somewhat overstated, the challenge contained in Veblen's work is that the marketeer must determine which social levels are the most important in influencing the demand for his product. Other social-psychological models for analysing buyers include the **McClelland model**, which stressed the theory of achievement motivation, the **Goffman model,** with its emphasis on role theory, and the **Festinger model,** developing the theory of cognitive dissonance (a sense of incompleteness).

Identify the theorists associated with the following influences on human behaviour:

- **lifestyle/attitudes**

- **rational, economic calculation**

- **rewarded learning**

- **group membership.**

ORGANISATIONAL BUYERS

The above-mentioned models tend to stress the role of the consumer rather than the organisational buyer. Many people, however, are engaged in the purchase of goods not for the sake of consumption but for further production or distribution. Their common denominator is that they are paid to make purchases for others. They operate within an organisational environment. There seems to be two broadly competing views as to how organisational buyers make their decisions.

Many marketing writers such as **Melvin T. Copeland** have emphasised the almost 'Marshallian' rationality which precludes their decisions. Organisational buyers are represented as being most impressed by cost, quality, dependability and service factors. They will take special care over rebuy decisions and they are shown as being dedicated servants of their organisation, seeking to secure the best terms. This view has led to an emphasis being placed on performance and use characteristics in much industrial advertising.

Other writers have emphasised personal motives in organisational buyer behaviour. The proposition here is that a purchasing agents' interest to do the best for their company is tempered by his or her own self-interest. For example, they may be tempted to choose among salespeople according to the extent they entertain or offer gifts; they may choose a particular vendor because this will ingratiate the buyer with certain people within the company or they may shortcut their study of alternative suppliers to make his or her workday easier.

In the real world, the buyer is likely to be guided by both personal and group goals. The political model of **Thomas Hobbes** identifies the relationship between the two goals. Hobbes held that man is instinctively oriented toward preserving and enhancing his own well-being. This, however, would produce a 'war of every man against every man'. It is this fear which leads them to unite with others in a corporate body. The corporate man tries to steer a careful course between his own needs and those of the organisation. It is clear that the importance of the Hobbesian model is that organisational buyers can be appealed to on both personal and organisational grounds. Where there is substantial similarity in what suppliers offer in the way of products, price and service, the purchasing agent has less basis for rational choice.

On a more recent note, **Jagdish N. Sheth,** in describing the complexity of his integrative model of industrial buyer behaviour said: 'Organisational buyer behaviour consists of three distinct aspects. The first aspect is the psychological world of the individuals involved in organisation buying decisions. The second aspect relates to the conditions which precipitate joint decisions among these individuals and the final aspect is the process of joint decision making with the inevitable conflict among the decision makers and its resolution by resorting to a variety of tactics.'

David T. Wilson of Pennsylvania State University has endeavoured to represent organisational buying as a decision process model rather as Kotler did for the consumer buying process.

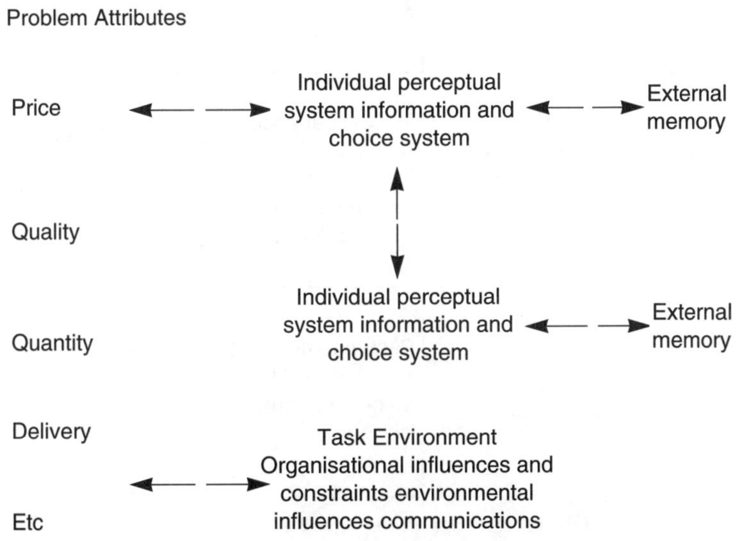

Problem Attributes

Price ⟷ → Individual perceptual system information and choice system ⟷ → External memory

Quality ↕

Quantity Individual perceptual system information and choice system ← → External memory

Delivery

Etc ← → Task Environment Organisational influences and constraints environmental influences communications

FIGURE 1.4: *Wilson's structural elements of the decision process model.*

A basic tenet of Wilson's model is that individuals, not groups or organisations, process information and make choices. The individual within an organisation is subjected to the influences of membership and referent groups, organisational and environmental constraints, but it is still an individual level model. The term 'decision process' includes information acquisition, processing activities, choice processes, and development of goals and other criteria used in choosing among alternatives. Wilson writes: 'The basic elements of the model are an individual in a task environment attempting to make a choice from a number of sets of product–vendor attribute sets. This model is the most parsimonious representation of a complex process. It can be operationalised to describe simple (rebuy) or complex (new task) buying behaviour.'

Figure 1.5 illustrates how the purchasing decision increases in complexity from straight rebuy (the simplest), through modified rebuy (intermediate difficulty), through to new buy (the most difficult). Notice that there may be instances in which a modified rebuying decision is more complex than the original new buy decision. For example, buying a new computer system to replace an old mainframe is more complex because of the massive changes in computer technology.

	Newness of problem	Experience and information requirement	Consideration of buying alternatives
New buy	Problem/ requirement is totally new	Past experience not relevant. Much information is required	Buying alternatives not known. All solutions are considered
Modified rebuy	Problem/ requirement is not new but differs from previous situations	Past experience is relevant – but more information is required before making decision	New alternative solutions will be considered before buying decision
Straight rebuy	Continuing or recurring requirement	Past experience is sufficient – little or no new information is required	Alternative solutions are known but not given serious consideration

FIGURE 1.5: *Classifying purchasing decisions.*

The question of buyer behaviour is one which requires further detailed analysis. Certainly, it is a topic about which few concrete conclusions can be drawn. One could argue that, under certain conditions, at certain times and at certain places, we understand the kinds of things which influence certain types of buyers. Despite the differences which occur when people purchase as individuals rather than on behalf of organisations, many writers stress that the buyer is always acting as an individual to a certain extent, and is thus open to certain psychological, sociological and cultural influences.

Two areas which would well repay greater study are the lifestyle approach and the information processing view of buyers as viewed by writers such as Kotler and Wilson. Many people believe that Kotler is correct when he views the human psyche as a black box which differs from individual to individual. Perhaps he is also correct when, after analysing various models of buying behaviour he says: 'Thus, it turns out that the black box for the buyer is not so black after all. Light is thrown in various corners by these models. Yet no one has succeeded in putting all these pieces of truth together into one coherent instrument for behavioural analysis. This of course, is the goal of behavioural science.'

ACTIVITY 5

In a small group, discuss organisational buying behaviour you have encountered and assess the importance of the approaches presented to you in the text. Jot down your main points below.

EXERCISE: allow 30 mins

Working with and relating to others ✔

Managing tasks and solving problems ✔

Commentary...

You might have picked up some of the following points from the text in this session:

- ◐ Buyer is influenced mostly by cost, quality and service (Copeland).

- ◐ Buyer's interest in serving the company is tempered by his or her self-interest (Hobbes).

You may have discussed the need to reduce personal risk by diffusion of responsibility. You may have found buying decisions affected by conflict resolution through tactical manoeuvring and the conditions and circumstances which bring about joint decision making (Sheth). The latter point about conditions could have been developed to incorporate the fact that some buying (of large, one-off purchases) is governed or influenced by the structure of the DMU.

You could also have made reference to the impact of centralisation and specialisation in the companies you considered.

Marketing of services

A **service** is the provision of an intangible benefit to a producer, intermediary or consumer, in return for payment. This benefit may take the form of:

- ◐ improved access to goods – provided by wholesalers and retailers

- ◐ better transportation and telecommunications

- ◐ repair and servicing of hardware

- ◐ provision of human resources (personnel recruitment and employment agencies)

- ◐ financial resources (banking and insurance services).

The wide range of technical and professional expertise provided by, for example, architectural and engineering practices and management consultancies contrasts with the mechanistic approach to service evident with the fast-food chains such as McDonald's with its 'Have a nice day' slogan. However, many service businesses, including McDonald's, are trying to develop a more professional approach to customer service provision and this means that staff training becomes a priority.

THE DEVELOPMENT OF SERVICE INDUSTRIES

There are two stages of evolution of service industries within an economy:

1. Where the industrial base has not developed significantly due to a lack of investment and expertise, a large part of the workforce must seek employment in providing a service to others, often at low wages or on a self-employed basis. Countries with a warm climate and a tourist tradition are typical here. For example, in Hawaii and Bermuda, many people work as tourist guides, bar owners and hotel workers relying on tourism for their employment. It may also be true of a specific geographical region of an otherwise developed economy; so, the North Wales coastal resorts such as Rhyl and Colwyn Bay rely heavily on the influx of summer tourists to boost service sector jobs.

2. Following an industrialised phase of economic growth, the climate is created for more service provision for the following reasons:

   (a) people have more money to spend and look for new ways in which to spend it

   (b) increased leisure time creates extra demand for services

   (c) demographic trends – an ageing population requires more service provision, particularly in health care

   (d) management skill in exploiting opportunities means there is greater corporate presence in services so, for example, though computer companies used to make most of their income from selling hardware (the actual equipment), now software (applications) and the associated training and service provision is vital.

RECENT TRENDS IN SERVICE PROVISION

Moves towards a freer market, through UK legislation and the external forces of European harmonisation, have had a strong impact on professional services. The traditional gentleman's agreement between client and adviser has been replaced by a more commercial contractual arrangement brought about by the forces of competition. In accountancy, the mergers of leading names to form mega-partnerships such as Peat Marwick McClintock, and Ernst and Young, have created the opportunity for economies of scale and the marketing of a range of consultancy services as add-ons to the core activity of auditing. In the legal profession, the increasing incidence of mergers and adoption of the marketing concept has become prevalent.

Both accountants and legal practices adhere to professional standards in the search for new clients and the development of business with existing clients. The Law Society published *Best Practice – Marketing* in 1989. The Institute of Chartered Accountants announced in early 1991 that it was examining the potential conflict of interest where an accountancy firm provides both auditing services and management consultancy to the same client.

There are also other important trends in relation to the area of service provision. First, there is increasing dependence on expertise in a particular functional or resource area. Second, where there is the option that a service can be provided in the public sector (government financed and managed) or the private sector, through the mechanism of the market, then there has been a trend towards using the latter. This has often been achieved by commercial competitive tendering (CCT), a process which invites companies to tender bids for services such as refuse collection.

RECALL:
allow 10 mins

Define a 'service'.

What influence do the following have on service provision:

(a) a partly developed industrial base?

(b) a more fully developed industrial base?

SERVICES AND THEIR CHARACTERISTICS

In developing a marketing strategy, to a certain extent, services need to be treated differently from products. The specific characteristics of services need to be considered.

Intangibility

Services cannot be held or touched. This makes it difficult to sample them. An insurance policy, for example, is a piece of paper which represents the service provided by the insurer. The service offered is security and peace of mind.

Having said that, it becomes absolutely vital that the physical evidence of service provision is well managed. This provides tangible proof of the service delivery and quality.

- A cinema has seats, a screen, snack counter, toilets and cinema-goers are each given a ticket.

- A bank has chairs, tables, cash machines, staff on the counter and a manager.

- In a lecture or a tutorial, the room has chairs, tables, an overhead projector and a dryboard marker or a chalkboard. There may also be a video recorder and a television. The lecturer may use slides, and he or she might give out notes.

The key is to manage the essential physical evidence completely. In our examples, the qualified bank manager or college lecturer are essential physical evidence. A bank statement and a degree certificate are essential physical evidence.

The non-essential physical evidence is of far less importance to a customer. Non-essential physical evidence depends upon the customer. In the bank example, a free cheap pen with the name of the bank on could be considered to be non-essential physical evidence. In the college example, the logo on the outside of the building could be considered non-essential physical evidence.

Inseparability

Services are difficult to separate from the people who provide them. The doctor, dentist, hairdresser and beautician all give a personalised service to each customer. Sometimes services can be provided without the provider being present; correspondence courses of all types, relaxation tapes and pre-recorded telephone help lines are examples.

It can be argued that these distance services are tangibly different from the personalised form, in that they are not customised to meet the specific requirements of individual consumers because of a lack of interaction between the consumers and the service provider. In correspondence learning, for example, the lack of a lecturer to provide feedback when it is required, provides problems for students who find themselves 'stuck with a problem' for days or weeks at a time. Notice how interactive open learning courses try to overcome this problem.

Perishability

Services cannot be stored like tins of baked beans. For example, if a plane seat is unsold on a particular flight, then it cannot be sold again. Early morning train passengers are charged more than later passengers. The early morning trains provide the utility of travel to a destination at the appropriate time for those who have to travel at that time. Commuters could choose to pay less by travelling later, but they would suffer the consequences of being late for work.

Heterogeneity

Services are often difficult to standardise because they are so personalised. For example, a hair cut is styled to suit an individual. The service in an expensive restaurant is personalised but in a different way to the service a catering company provides to a commercial or industrial organisation.

Often, different customers will have different perceptions about the same service. Even if you enjoyed the way a particular lecturer put across the information, it is quite likely that someone else did not; the same waiter who was seen as efficient by one customer could be seen as cold by another. This kind of factor makes services difficult to standardise.

Ownership

Services are often borrowed rather than owned. For example, a hotel room is hired for a specified period, access to a night-club lasts for a certain number of hours and library books have a return-by date. This lack of ownership is important, because consumers become more demanding about service standards. Consumers expect things to be right during the period within which they are consuming the service. For example, a couple celebrating a wedding anniversary with a romantic candle-lit dinner will be unhappy if anything breaks the special atmosphere that they want to create. In a similar way, a company 'buying in' training will complain about anything it regards as poor service such as inappropriate courses or incompetent trainers.

People and process

We have looked at the importance of managing the physical evidence, especially the essential physical evidence, but people and process also play their part.

People are crucial to the professional delivery of a service. Buyers form perceptions of the provider of the service, and this can affect whether they decide to purchase or not. Even if they purchase the service, they may not enjoy it – and they will certainly not become regular customers. Imagine a worker in the company canteen enjoying a burger when the chef walks past. He is unclean, obviously not having bathed for several days. He smokes and has a cough. Suddenly, the worker is not enjoying the meal so much!

Service providers know that only properly trained staff can interact well with customers. People tend to dismiss programmed service delivery, based around slogans like 'have a nice day' or 'missing you already'; they realise it is insincere. Firms look for professional service delivery in which staff feel confident and well informed when they talk to customers and they feel empowered to manage the so-called **'moment of truth'** with expertise and flair.

!?! The **moment of truth** in a service situation is the actual period of time in which consumers are in direct contact with the service provider.

Wherever people are the main instrument of service provision, there will be an associated variation of performance. But competitive forces and the search for excellence means that recruitment and training programmes within organisations are geared to achieving a high degree of uniformity. Forward-thinking companies in the service sector, from hoteliers to construction engineers, have applied for and obtained British Standard 5750 (BS5750) and now use it as an assurance of consistent and high quality of performance. Many small companies find it very difficult to achieve the exacting specifications of BS5750 due to the time and expense involved in documenting and checking procedures; this could put them at a competitive disadvantage compared to larger organisations when quality is a key requirement of a potential customer.

Now let us consider **process** issues. Imagine you are in a lecture. The lecturer reads from a book in a dry, monotone voice. Even if the information is intrinsically interesting, you will probably not remember it – the experience will not have been a good one. Imagine the same lecture being given by a lecturer using only a few well-chosen key points, in a bright, sparkling manner, even with the occasional joke. You will probably remember some of the information for a long time, because the process was enjoyable.

For the customer, satisfaction is an important part of the service delivery. This turns consumers into loyal customers who will return. Airlines strive to make the experience they offer a satisfying one, as this acts as a competitive weapon in their search for, and retention of, customers.

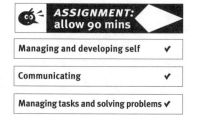

ASSIGNMENT: allow 90 mins	
Managing and developing self	✔
Communicating	✔
Managing tasks and solving problems	✔

ACTIVITY 6

Imagine you are a marketing executive for a major airline. You are deciding how to make the service you provide your first-class passengers (high fare payers) and economy-class passengers (low fare payers) as good as it can be. Prepare a 10-minute presentation entitled: 'Passengers and flying – what is important to customers'. Divide your presentation into two parts, first-class service provision and economy-class service provision. Produce a 500-word report to support your presentation.

summary

▶ Competitive analysis is a key aspect of marketing which requires managers to explore ways of gaining a competitive advantage. It is important to know your competitors, understand their strengths and weaknesses, and to appreciate the potential risk from new entrants to the market.

▶ Industrial markets may be classified by the goods and services provided or by 'demographic factors' such as the size of firm, the type of industry, the geographical regions in which the markets operate.

▶ In operating in industrial markets, companies will use a different marketing mix to communicate with customers. Direct selling and the use of specialist media are likely to be more important than in consumer markets, although some large companies will use the mass media to reach industrial customers and opinion leaders generally.

▶ In supplying industrial markets, salespersons need to understand the buying process. Decisions are often made by groups rather than individuals and a sales team needs to work closely with everyone who has an influence on the buying decision.

▶ In general, buying behaviour is determined by a wide range of economic, psychological and sociological considerations. Perception, group influence, personality and cultural differences all play a part.

▶ In developing a marketing approach for services, companies need to take into account the special characteristics of services such as intangibility, inseparability, perishability, heterogeneity and ownership. The people who deliver the service – and the process itself – are the keys to attracting and keeping customers.

Strategies

Objectives

After participating in this session, you should be able to:

▶ explain the model of industrial competitiveness

▶ understand the strategic planning approach developed by the Boston Consulting group

▶ describe the stages of a product life cycle

▶ outline the strengths and weaknesses of the product life cycle model

▶ explain the strategic decision-making framework of the Ansoff matrix.

In working through this session, you will practise the following BTEC common skills:

Managing and developing self	✔
Working with and relating to others	
Communicating	✔
Managing tasks and solving problems	✔
Applying numeracy	
Applying technology	
Applying design and creativity	

The Porter five-forces model

The Porter five-forces model stresses that the profitability of an industry is not determined by method of production or the appearance of products, but by the structure of the industry. Figure 2.1 shows the model in its most basic form.

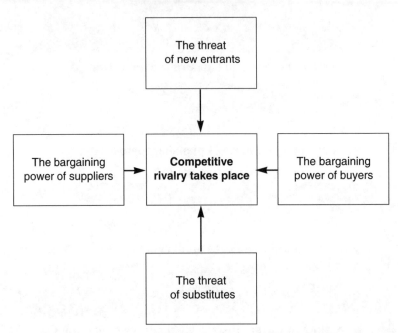

FIGURE 2.1: *The Porter five-forces model of industry competitiveness.*
Source: Michael E. Porter, 1980, *Competitive Strategy: Techniques of Analysing Industries and Competitors,* The Free Press.

COMPETITIVE RIVALRY

Competitive rivalry shows itself in intense competition between companies. Firms can make similar products and sell them in the same market but, in saturated markets, intensive rivalry can lead to price wars which can put firms out of business. (Airlines and newspapers are engaged in price wars at the moment.) Those firms that remain after a price war can increase their prices and build up profits due to the weakening of competition. This gives them the incentive to survive and win.

In oligopolistic market structures, with a few large equal-sized companies, firms often have an unwritten agreement not to compete on price in order to maintain their profits. But they do compete on service, quality, advertising, distribution outlets and other non-price factors. Examples of oligopolies are the oil industry and parts of the chemical industry – large oil companies and the major soap and detergent firms account for the majority of sales in their industries.

Where competitive rivalry exists in an industry, it is manifested by a number of features:

- The number of competitors increases and they employ different strategies.

- There are several firms of equal size.

- Demand is reasonably static.

- There is a temptation for firms to lower their prices to see if this increases demand and boosts overall revenue.

- The similarity of what firms offer to customers means that it is easy for customers to switch between different company offerings.

- Weak competitors in the industry are sometimes purchased by companies outside the industry as a means of entering the market.

- The best companies occasionally attract takeover bids from very large international organisations wishing to strengthen their overall competitive position.

Let us now look in turn at the other four forces in the Porter model.

NEW ENTRANTS

If an industry is easy to enter then, unless demand rises in proportion to the number of entrants, the industry will become less profitable. Economists call this scenario a **zero-sum game** which, quite simply, means that if the market demand is static and new entrants appear, a firm can only take extra market share at the expense of one or more if its rivals.

Firms considering entry to industries typified by competitive rivalry may find a number of barriers to entry which they must carefully consider:

- established competitors with lower unit costs due to economies of scale arising from large-scale operations

- strong brand images and consumer preferences for the products and services of existing competitors

- capital costs of setting up operations

- poor access to distribution channels

- government legislation, including banning or taxing new entrants.

Markets which are easy to enter are those which require very little in the way of **skills, capital** or **experience**. Examples include window cleaning, shoe shining or door-to-door selling. Markets which are difficult to enter are those which require specialist skills, large capital investment and industry experience. This explains why it is virtually impossible for a companies to enter the petrochemicals, nuclear power generation and aircraft manufacture markets.

THREAT OF SUBSTITUTES

A **substitute** product or service is one that satisfies customer requirements in the same way as a product already produced within the industry. Substitutes can become serious competitors for existing products. For example, margarine and polyunsaturates are substitute products for butter. By competing on price and on perceived health benefits, these products have gained a large slice of the butter market.

One question to ask when analysing substitutes is: What are the buyers' switching costs? Consider how easily a consumer could change from one brand of beans to another, then think of the time and expense it would take an airline to change from one make of aeroplane to another.

THE BARGAINING POWER OF SUPPLIERS

Suppliers have power in situations where:

- the input they provide is critical to the buyer

- the suppliers' products are unique and buyers find it difficult to switch from one supplier to another

- the supplier industry is a reasonably secure oligopoly in which three, four or five firms each have a secure share of the market, and are not fighting off competitors at regular intervals. In such a situation, they are able to charge reasonably high prices to the buyers.

THE BARGAINING POWER OF BUYERS

In contrast to the situation where the supplier is dominant, the powerful buyer becomes a major factor when:

- the item bought is not an important input into a finished product, e.g. small components like screws, nuts and valves

- customers find it economical to purchase goods from several suppliers rather than one; this intensifies the competition to keep the order with the customer, and it gives the customer a good deal

- the sellers are large in numbers and small in size

- the buyer is of vital importance to the seller's industry. For example, the car companies are vitally important buyers of the output of many small firms which produce car seats, windscreen wipers and small components. In the same way, Marks and Spencer is a major buyer of foodstuffs and textiles.

SAT:
allow 25 mins

Managing tasks and solving problems ✔

ACTIVITY 1

Marks and Spencer is an internationally known and respected retailing organisation. It has a famous brand name in St Michael. The company does not manufacture any of the products it sells; instead, it buys in from suppliers.

Identify three advantages to Marks and Spencer and, separately, three advantages to its suppliers which arise from this approach. Note them in the box below.

Commentary...

For Marks and Spencer, three critical advantages are:

1. the ability to search out those suppliers who can match or exceed their exacting quality specifications

2. the freedom to specialise in retail marketing rather than move into areas (such as manufacturing) in which it does not have any experience or expertise

3. the power over its suppliers by virtue of its size and success. Suppliers must remain competitive on the key issues of price, quality and delivery times if their contracts are to be renewed.

From the suppliers point of view, there are three advantages:

1. They have a secure outlet for their products because Marks and Spencer is unlikely to go out of business. Indeed, the company intend to expand into a global retailing operation and this increases the opportunity for its suppliers, as larger volumes will be needed.

2. The contracts are regularly renewed and are likely to be fair. It is not in Marks and Spencer's best interests to force its suppliers out of business by paying low prices for its supplies. A mutually beneficial relationship is formed and the suppliers do well as long as they meet specifications.

3. When such a relationship exists, Marks and Spencer and its suppliers can plan for growth and development in, for example, new products. In this way, a small supplier has access to the commercial expertise of a leading retail organisation. For example, a farm manager will regularly discuss business issues with one of the UK's leading vegetable buyers from Marks and Spencer.

As a general point, if all of the forces in the industry are strong, competitive rivalry is intensified and industry profitability will be quite low. This means that several firms may be forced out of business during this process. On the other hand, if the five forces are weak then industry profitability should be above average.

In the competitive fight that takes place in industries, firms battle to influence the five forces through the strategies they pursue. For example, when ICI launched Dulux solid emulsion paint in the mid

1980s, it was the first to market a new product aimed at young, ABC1 social class, married couples who were inexperienced decorators. By being the first to the market with non-drip paint, it was able to set a premium price due to the lack of competition. Over time, Crown, Berger and own label solid paint became available. Crucially, however, ICI wanted to make its product synonymous with the task it performed. This would give the company a competitive advantage which would be difficult to overcome.

Other examples of this kind of customer identification with a brand product are Hoover (people think of 'hoovering' not vacuuming the carpet) and Tippex (people say 'pass the Tippex' rather than 'pass the erasing fluid'). These are very effective ways of making it harder for a competitor to gain market share, which takes time and effort to achieve - product quality and brand image are crucial.

THE TEA INDUSTRY

We shall now apply the five forces model to the tea industry, to illustrate a real-life situation, the impact of threat of entry, power of suppliers, power of buyers and threat of substitutes.

Threat of entry

In the UK tea market, **economies of scale** are not a particular barrier to entry. Small new competitors can take market share from the present manufacturers at low set-up costs, since the basic requirements are tea bushes, ovens and packaging facilities.

Capital requirements of entry for large-scale production lowers the threat of entry, because high investment in such items as machinery, sites and manpower is required.

The high advertising spend necessary to promote and build **brand identity** decreases the threat of new competitors into the tea market. The importance of brand identity is demonstrated by the recent trend in brand valuation. The advertising investment establishing the PG Tips brand over a period of 30 years through the talking chimpanzee advertisements shows the importance attached to brand image.

Access to distribution is an important factor. Distribution sites are ideally situated near to the UK motorway networks increasing the threat of entry, but importation of tea from the tea estates may prove difficult in terms of accessing ships and shipping lanes and this decreases the threat of entry.

Current UK **government policy** does not restrict the number of tea manufacturers in the UK and consequently, the threat of new entrants into the UK tea market is increased. With the advent of the single European market, trade barriers are diminishing, relaxing the export restrictions and this may increase the threat of entry further by exposing the UK tea market to competitors from Europe.

Product innovation by the UK tea manufacturers increase the threat of entry into the new sectors which are created. This is clearly illustrated by the introduction of the first instant tea, Typhoo QT, by Premier teas in 1988. This is ranked as possibly the biggest innovation in the tea market since the introduction of tea bags. Within three years, Brooke Bond's PG Instant (in 1990) and Lyons Tetley's Freeze Dried Instant (in 1991) had entered this new market sector.

Managing tasks and solving problems ✔

ACTIVITY 2

1. Why did tea manufacturers develop instant tea?

2. What benefits does instant tea offer consumers?

3. What problems might tea manufacturers face in creating and sustaining a market for these products?

Commentary...

1. New product innovation is designed to expand markets for tea products and help companies to increase market share.

2. Instant tea offers speed and convenience. It reduces the mess involved in making tea, there is no need to dispose of tea-bags, have a teapot or a tea strainer.

3. Many tea drinkers are very conversative; they need to be convinced that the new products will not be inferior to traditional teas. So companies had to overcome consumer resistance. The QT slogan was 'Try it, you might like it'. Initially, the instant tea market might remain small and not very profitable. In the long term, companies think it might become a strategically important market segment.

The tea industry - *continued*

The power of suppliers and buyers

Suppliers to the UK tea industry comprise **tea suppliers** and **packaging suppliers**. We shall deal first with the tea suppliers.

There are four major tea brokers in the London auction, who buy tea at source and then auction it in London. Most of the UK's tea is purchased at the **London tea auction**. The possibility of inflating prices, due to high demand, for a specific raw tea is reduced because of the large number of different blends that are used to manufacture each tea. (Scarcity can, however, raise the price of raw tea.)

Tea producing countries hold their own auctions but, of course, only sell the tea they themselves produce. For example, raw tea auctions are held India, Sri Lanka, Bangladesh and Kenya.

The major UK tea buying companies - Brooke Bond, Lyons Tetley and Premier Brands - buy the largest part of their tea requirement from the London tea auction and **country of origin auctions**. Brooke Bond, however, has a distinct advantage as they are the only UK tea manufacturer to retain their tea plantations in India and as a supplier, Brooke Bond can influence the market price of their tea.

Packaging suppliers could be a factor. The packaging of tea is formulated from a range of materials. These include pallets, string, plastic, overwrap, caps, film, glass, paper, labels, tea bag paper and cardboard. Despite the major restructuring that occurred in the 1980s, the packaging industry has not increased its control over its destiny. It is caught between rising raw material and other costs and its inability to recover these costs fully in order to profit from technical innovations and increased efficiencies. This is largely due to the overwhelming buying power of the top four multiples which effectively control much of the food and grocery distribution chain. Tesco's and Sainsbury's are particularly important in this respect.

The **power of the buyers** should not be underestimated. There are two distinctive types of buyers employed by tea manufacturers, who are essential in determining the final quality of packaged tea. These are the **tea taster/blender** and the **packaging buyer**.

Tea tasters attend auctions where they bid for tea. They are vital in the buying process as their knowledge and experience is essential to purchase the correct amount of tea, originating from different countries, which they will later blend into various teas. Unforeseen conditions overseas can raise the price of tea and freight transportation costs causing price increases which might ultimately lead to loss of market share. So tea tasters also have responsibility for monitoring overseas conditions of tea harvests, both in terms of political unrest and weather conditions. They buy in bulk strategically in order to overcome the effects of anticipated natural disasters or political instability on tea harvests.

It is the **packaging buyer's** responsibility to source new suppliers both from home and abroad. Sourcing is based on price, favourable discounts and quality, together with suppliers' reputations for meeting lead times for delivery and their ability to hold warehoused stock, to be supplied on a 'just-in-time' basis for production basis, at no extra charge.

The pressure on packaging buyers is to reduce costs of packaging, as savings increase the profit margin for tea manufacturers. It is their responsibility to match bulk buying for favourable discounts against the storage cost for materials. Packaging buyers contribute to new product development in sourcing alternative materials for use in production, to reduce the risk of higher costs in times of scarcity. Packaging buyers exert substantial power over suppliers as they will switch from suppliers if favourable terms cannot be negotiated. The switching costs for suppliers are high as the loss of a major tea manufacturer's account could result in their bankruptcy.

Threat of substitutes

Since the late 1960s, when instant coffee first became available, tea has been declining in popularity, especially with young consumers. Some new innovations within the tea market, such as round tea bags and one cup bags, have recaptured much of the market share lost to the coffee sector. However, since the 1980s, with the consumer trend towards health consciousness, both tea and coffee have declined in popularity with the young who favour caffeine-free soft drinks.

Within the drinks sector, there exists an increasing demand for drinks which are perceived by consumers to be natural with no caffeine, no artificial flavourings, no colourings and with few calories. Consequently, decaffeinated and fruit/herbal teas have become more popular as substitutes for the higher caffeine teas and coffees.

Competition is fierce within the UK tea market. Competitive advantages are only gained through the creation of new market segments via new product innovations. However, the development of products is costly. It requires intensive research and, once launched, massive advertising budgets to acquire a large market share.

Competition also occurs on a price basis between the less expensive own-label products and the more expensive branded products. The latter relies on quality of taste, brand loyalty and heavy advertising to maintain its market share. Advertising is a major determinant in the competitive rivalry and brands compete to attract new tea consumers and cause other consumers to switch brands.

The Boston Consulting Group portfolio matrix

In 1970, the Boston Consulting Group (BCG) developed an approach to strategic planning based on an analysis of a company's product portfolio. The key for organisations is to evaluate whether their mix of products is balanced across the company. If they have achieved a well-balanced range of products and services, they are likely to be competitive. If they had an unbalanced portfolio (product range) they are likely to face various financial and strategic problems.

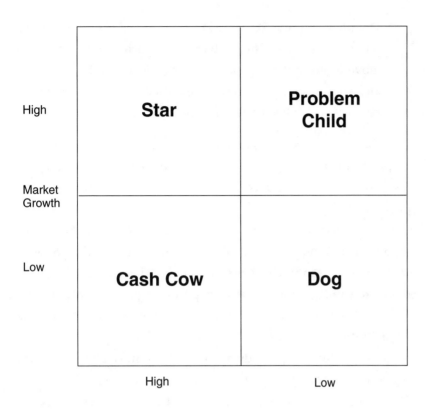

FIGURE 2.2: *The Boston Consulting Group's product portfolio matrix (BCG, 1970).*

The BCG matrix shown in figure 2.2 looks at two measures of performance: market share and market growth. It has four segments: star, cash cow, problem child and dog.

- A **star** is a product with high market share in a high growth market. As the name suggests, it is very successful but it requires funding to advertise and distribute it. The Mars Ice Cream Bar was a star shortly after its launch.

- **Cash cows** are products which have a high market share in a mature market with a low growth rate. A cash cow provides the main financial return in the portfolio but it needs to be carefully tended to ensure its success. A product like Tide soap powder is a cash cow which has had many changes in formulation and packaging to keep it successful. Cash cows bring in revenue which supports products in the other segments.

- A **problem child** is a product with low market share in a high growth market. In the chocolate confectionery market, the product called Drifter was an example of a problem child. The advertising themes ran from cowboys to cool dudes in an attempt to communicate successfully with its target audience.

THE BOSTON CONSULTING GROUP
PORTFOLIO MATRIX

- **Dogs** have low market share in a static or declining market. The manufacturers of Spam are trying to reposition this product to move it out of the dog category. Increasing health awareness and a suspicion of additives have turned it into a down-market product with a low quality image.

The idea of a portfolio of interests emphasises the importance for companies to have products which provide both security and funds (cash cows), and products which will ensure the future of the company (stars and cash cows). Problem children are not doing as well as expected, and this could be due to an advertising problem or inadequate distribution. Dogs need to be evaluated carefully to see if they should be continued. For example, if a dog product brings in enough revenue to cover the costs of producing it and distributing it – the variable costs – then any additional revenue is said to be making a **contribution** to the fixed costs (costs which have to be paid) of the rest of the product range. If advertising expenditure on the dog is kept very low then each pound in revenue generated by a dog is often referred to by accounting and marketing managers as being 'contribution rich'.

Contribution is an important financial concept. A product should not be dropped from the product range just because it is not making a profit. It is important to check whether its revenue covers the variable costs involved in producing it for sale.

Cash cows have a high market share in a relatively low growth market but the low growth rate acts as a deterrent to new entrants. This enables these products to bring in revenues well in advance of their costs. A star makes a lot of sales revenue but at a price. Stars have very high costs in a rapidly growing market which usually attracts new entrants because of the profits to be made.

As a general rule, a company should concentrate on developing stars and turn them into cash cows over time. Products like KitKat, Cadbury's Flake, and Heinz Baked Beans are mature cash cows which have carefully developed over 50 years or more. To illustrate these points further, figure 2.3 shows the BCG matrix applied to Premier teas.

Star	**Problem Child**
Typhoo QT	Typhoo Extra fresh
Typhoo Decaffeinated	Ridgeways Organic
London Herb & Spice Co	
Heath & Heather	
Cash Cow	**Dog**
Typhoo	Ridgeways Premium
Fresh Brew One Cup	
Typhoo One Cup	
Ridgeways Imperial	
Fresh Brew	
Ridgeways Speciality	
Melrose Speciality	
Kardomah	
Glengettie Teas	

Market growth: High — Low

Relative market share: High — Low

FIGURE 2.3: *The Boston Consulting Group's product portfolio matrix applied to Premier Teas.*
SOURCE: Compiled from company and industry reports, 1992.

ACTIVITY 3

Consider Premier Teas product portfolio range as illustrated in figure 2.3. How would you describe this portfolio: poor, reasonable, good or excellent? Briefly explain how you came to your decision.

If you are employed, apply the BCG matrix to your own company's products or services. How does the portfolio compare? Again, describing the portfolio as poor, reasonable, good or excellent. If you are a full-time student, draw up a BCG matrix for a company that you are familiar with or that you have researched for previous activities in this book.

SAT:
allow 30 mins

Managing tasks and solving problems ✔

Commentary...

The answer must be 'excellent'. With nine cash cows and only one dog, the portfolio shows great financial strength. The four stars take up revenue, but there are a lot of cash cows to support them. The problem children could become dogs if they are not carefully monitored but, even then, the portfolio would be in very good shape. Notice how important it is financially to have a balanced portfolio of products. This is the very essence of portfolio analysis.

Product life cycles

The product life cycle is an attempt to apply a biological model to a manufactured product. The essential comparison is that just as human beings are born, develop, mature, age and die so do products.

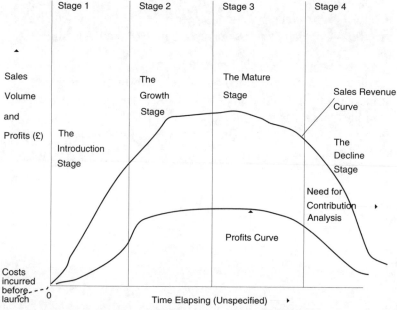

FIGURE 2.4: *The standard product life cycle.*

Figure 2.4 shows the hypothetical shape of the sales revenue curve over the product life cycle covering an unspecified time period. Costs are deducted from overall sales revenue to give profits; the profits curve is therefore shown as lower and flatter than the sales volume curve. Also note that many costs – such as advertising, promotion, production, distribution and test marketing – are incurred before point O at which sales volume begins with the launch of the product onto the market.

There are four distinct stages to this product life cycle:

The introduction stage

The product is launched onto the market. All costs previously incurred would be lost if the product failed shortly after launch, and up to 80 per cent of all new products do fail. This is a dangerous period, for sales often rise slowly and profits are low as customers try the product for the first time. Problem children often stick at this stage.

The growth stage

During the growth stage, a product achieves its strongest and steepest rise in sales. These sales are being achieved by intensive distribution, advertising and promotional activity and so the profits are not as high as might be expected. Many more people are trying the product, and there is some repeat purchasing from consumers who like it. Opinion leaders spread favourable messages about the product. These products are stars.

The mature stage

Here, sales volume reaches a peak and then levels off to a constant plateau. The consumers know and trust the product and repeat purchasing is usual. A positive brand image has been established, and the profits are at their highest level, partly due to the fact that the initial costs of distributing and advertising the product have been met. These products are cash cows.

The decline stage

This occurs when sales volume begin to fall, at first gradually and then very steeply. Profits plummet as this happens until at some stage no profit is made, and a company should examine whether the product is financially viable. If it is not financially viable, the logic of the model suggests that it should be eliminated from the portfolio. These products are dogs.

The main problem with this standard model is that it suffers from over-simplification.

- The idea that a product 'follows' a life cycle is rather far fetched. When we looked at the development of a brand image we saw that it was what management did that was important. For example, companies try to maintain products in the mature stage (cash cows in the BCG Matrix) by varying the advertising, the product formulation and so on.

- A product is introduced and at some stage production of it ceases – but over what time period? Time is unspecified, and there is nothing to stop a product that is declining badly from being regenerated by being repackaged, repositioned at a different target audience and so on.

- In the wider sense, a product which is declining in one market could be sold to customers in a different market to take account of an international product life cycle (IPLC). For example, in many developing countries there is a demand for very basic cars, computers, domestic appliances and so on because the economies are not as sophisticated as in developed countries, and incomes, fashions and tastes are different.

- One of the great skills of international managers is to turn domestic products into global products to protect them against decline in any one market. If we take the drinks sector for example, Coca-Cola makes about 80 per cent of its sales revenue outside the USA which is its home market. A British product such as Boddington's Bitter is a cult beer in Japan, and Newcastle Brown Ale is selling in vast quantities as 'Gentlemen's beer' in China – this name was chosen because to the Chinese, Britain is the home of gentlemen.

- The product life cycle is not a tool which should be used to predict sales volume. If marketing managers use the standard PLC to predict sales, then they will be following a tautological argument (an argument which is a self-fulfilling prophecy) which runs: 'The product life cycle shows that our sales are falling. That is it then, sales must inevitably fall now.' This is not supportable because in statistical terms, the sales volume curve is not an independent variable, it is a dependent variable. Sales volume is dependent upon management skill and management action. Remember the Cadbury's Wispa bar?

> **!?!** A **dependent variable** responds to changes in other variables – it does not cause the changes.

On the positive side, the PLC and IPLC can be useful as part of an integrated series of planning and control tools (including the BCG matrix and the Porter model). For example, they can highlight the need for management action, but they cannot take the place of management action.

In practice, the shape of the PLC varies greatly, owing mainly to the issues discussed above. Figures 2.5 and 2.6 show the product life cycles of some commonly found product types. Figure 2.5 illustrates a **'fad'** product which sees a strong peak and a rapid decline. Examples include yo-yo's and Ninja Mutant Hero Turtle products. Notice, however, that these kind of producers can be resurrected after a period of time and aimed at a new audience. Figure 2.6 shows the cycle for products such as nylon. Just as a decline seems set to occur, a new use is found for the product, e.g. nylon stockings, nylon ropes, nylon in parachutes. This keeps the product alive in new forms.

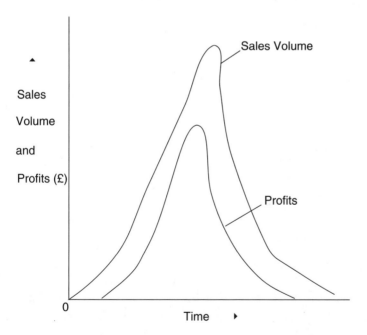

FIGURE 2.5: *The product life cycle of fad products.*

PRODUCT LIFE CYCLES

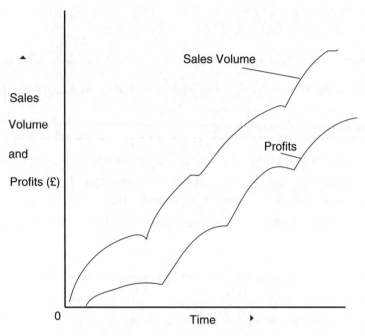

FIGURE 2.6: *The product life cycle of products sustained by new innovations and uses.*

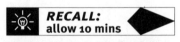

RECALL:
allow 10 mins

What are the strengths and weaknesses of the product life cycle concept? List them in the box below.

The Ansoff product—market matrix

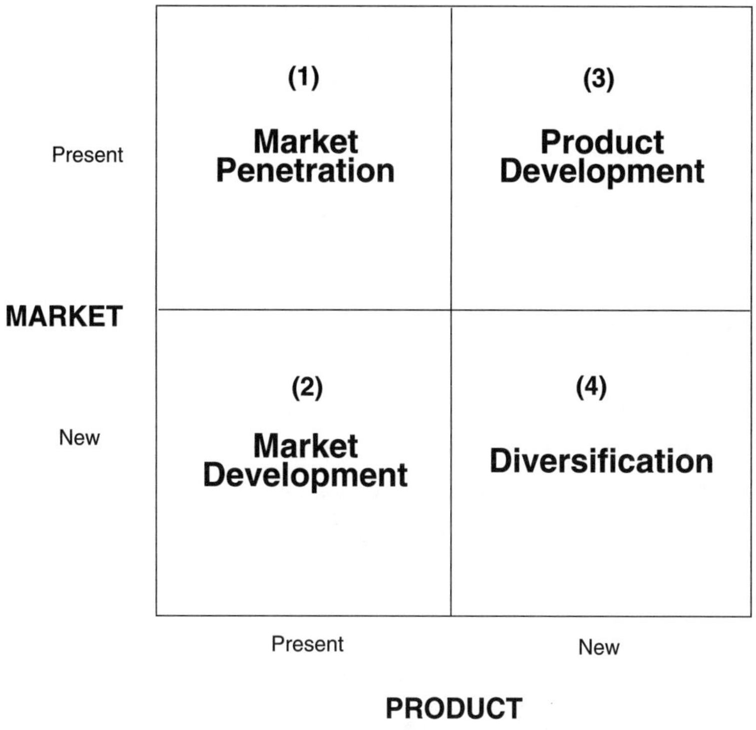

	Present	New
	(1) Market Penetration	**(3)** Product Development
	(2) Market Development	**(4)** Diversification

MARKET — Present / New (vertical)

PRODUCT — Present / New (horizontal)

FIGURE 2.7: *Ansoff's product-market matrix.*
SOURCE: developed from H. Igor Ansoff, Strategies for Diversification, *Harvard Business Review,* September/October 1957.

The Ansoff matrix (shown in figure 2.7) is a conceptual framework developed to aid strategic decision making, assisting companies in the strategic planning of its markets and products. It presents four strategic alternatives:

1. **market penetration** – a strategy of expanding sales of existing products in existing markets which could be achieved by increasing advertising and promotion

2. **market development** – a strategy of expansion based on entering new markets, e.g. firms could decide to export to the single European market

3. **product development** of new products in existing markets which involves launching new products more closely linked to the needs of consumers – most new products are not entirely new, but are adaptations of existing products

4. **diversification** – the option with the most risk involving new products and new markets. Companies very rarely diversify from products and markets which they know well, as they lose the advantage of market knowledge and experience.

**THE ANSOFF PRODUCT
—MARKET MATRIX**

Generally speaking, the options rise in cost, risk and complexity in the order present above, from market penetration to diversification. Market penetration is the simplest in relative terms, while diversification is the most complex. Firms aiming to diversify usually try to develop a policy called near or close diversification. This means that they will move into an associated area to the one with which they are very familiar. For example, a washing machine manufacturer may decide to make dishwashers or refrigerators or a financial services company may decide to offer home loans and so on.

The main advantage of the Ansoff matrix is that it presents a simple, visual matrix of strategic alternatives that companies can follow. Of course, this has the corresponding disadvantage of a lack of complexity. For example, what if a company wants to undertake a proportion of each of the options for varying products in a range of markets? Clearly, reference to the matrix is only the beginning of this process.

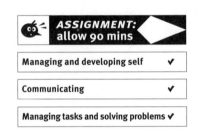

**ASSIGNMENT:
allow 90 mins**

Managing and developing self	✔
Communicating	✔
Managing tasks and solving problems	✔

ACTIVITY 4

Identify real-life examples of each of the four strategies identified in the Ansoff product-market matrix. Explain how the companies pursued that particular strategy. You should carry out preliminary research to help you complete this task.

Write a report of no more than 1,000 words to your tutor. Summarise the key points in the box below.

summary

This session has identified a number of models and strategies used by marketeers.

▶ The Porter five-forces model stresses that the structure of the industry has a strong influence on profitability. The five forces: are threat of entry, power of suppliers, power of buyers, threat of substitutes and competitive rivalry.

▶ The Boston Consulting Group's portfolio matrix indicates that organisations need to balance their mix of products. The matrix describes four product types: star, cash cow, problem child and dog.

▶ Product life cycles apply a biological model to products. The standard model describes four stages in a product's life: introduction, growth, maturity and decline.

▶ Ansoff's product-market matrix presents a simple visual matrix of strategic alternatives a company can follow in developing its business. The four strategies are: market penetration, market development, product development and diversification.

Market structure

Objectives

After participating in this session, you should be able to:

- discuss regulation of business

- show competitive differences between perfect
  competition, oligopoly and monopoly

- identify the consequences of competition within the
  public services.

In working through this session, you will practise the following
BTEC common skills:

Managing and developing self	✔
Working with and relating to others	✔
Communicating	✔
Managing tasks and solving problems	✔
Applying numeracy	
Applying technology	
Applying design and creativity	

Market regulation

> **\?/ Market regulation** is the process by which the government, or a government appointed body, intervenes with the free market mechanism in a given market.

In our discussions of the behaviour of markets, and firms within markets, we have concentrated so far upon markets in which the government does not intervene, i.e. we have focused upon **free markets**. In reality, a number of markets are regulated by government, by government-appointed bodies or even by private organisations. Even recent market-oriented governments have recognised that there are some markets in which free unregulated activity is not desirable. In this section, we highlight markets in this category, focusing upon those in which ex-nationalised industries have recently been transferred to private ownership.

REASONS FOR REGULATION

The principal justifications for government regulation of markets are contained in what is known as **market failure theory**. A detailed coverage of this theory is beyond the scope of this module but, basically, market failure refers to the occasions when markets fail to produce the level of output at which the surplus of benefits over costs to society is maximised.

Since the perfectly competitive model is a theoretical ideal and not a representation of commercial markets, it follows that in the real world the output of markets is highly unlikely to be at that level. Market failure theory recommends that, at least in the more drastic occasions of market failure, government should intervene to move a market's output closer to the desired level and thus increase the ultimate benefit gained by society from the market's production.

More recently however, this view has been opposed by a body of theory known as **state failure theory**. This criticises the market failure theory in two main ways:

1. Governments have insufficiently precise information about the behaviour of markets, so they do not have the expertise to intervene.

2. While moving the level of output to a more desirable level

would be a good thing, government intervention may well involve inefficiencies that outweigh the benefits associated with the change in output. Here, too much bureaucracy is seen as a common problem.

Such views have had an impact in terms of reducing the extent of government regulation and intervention in recent years. However, in the remainder of this section, we concentrate upon markets in which government has seen the desirability or necessity for regulation.

Regulation refers to the imposition of controls and constraints and the application of rules. The rationale in economic theory for the imposition of regulation stems from the existence of market failure. One particular area of market failure provides the main reason for the regulation of market activities generally: **informational market failure**. An understanding of what this involves will help to explain the purpose of the regulation of markets and transactions.

In business, consumers are often poorly informed about the quality of the product they are being offered, e.g.

- in the second-hand car market, a buyer may be given confusing information about reliability, mechanical soundness or running costs

- in the financial services markets, it is very difficult for a consumer to evaluate the claims of competing pension funds or the quality of investment advice.

In situations where consumers are poorly informed about products, it is likely that markets will not function as some economists believe they should, i.e. bringing together buyers and sellers to engage in mutually beneficial exchanges. If customers do not understand a product, they do not know if it is worth the asking price and cannot evaluate the competing merits of products offered at different prices. They may then respond by not buying at all or by making expensive mistakes. This means that net benefits to society would not be maximised.

Of course, consumer uncertainty about product quality is by no means limited to used cars and financial services. Markets for televisions or stereo systems are not characterised by regulation but here consumers are given indirect assurances as to quality by such devices as guarantees and warranties. Competition acts as a stimulus to the provision of quality goods and services because consumers will choose another supplier if they are not satisfied.

Broadly speaking, forms of regulation are divided into two categories: external regulation and self-regulation.

External regulation

External regulation is effected via an external regulatory agency. There are a number throughout the economy. Some have responsibility for a particular industry, e.g. the Office of Telecommunications (OFTEL) has regulated the telecommunications industry since the privatisation of British Telecom. Others have a general responsibility, e.g. the Office of Fair Trading monitors trading behaviour across industries as a whole. In some cases, the external regulator is a government department, e.g. the Department of Trade and Industry authorises and monitors insurance companies.

Self-regulation

Self-regulation can take many forms. Some groups of producers generate self-imposed codes of conduct to deal with consumer concerns about quality and to reassure customers. Self-regulation is a common feature of the professions such as accountancy, where standards of competence and conduct are governed by a professional body to which practitioners belong. The Chartered Institute of Marketing, for example, has a code of practice.

There are, as you may expect, some criticisms of self-regulation:

- Self-regulation is sometimes seen as pursuing self-interest rather than the interest of customers. For example, the British Medical Association has been criticised for protecting its members rather than seeking to uncover malpractice. Professional bodies are seen by some people as unnecessarily secretive in their actions.

- Self-regulation is accused of having a lack of power and authority. This criticism is levelled, for example, at the Press Council in its handling of a number of personal intrusions by the tabloid newspapers.

Explain:

○ market regulation

○ market failure.

REGULATION OF THE FORMER NATIONALISED INDUSTRIES

In the 1980s and early 1990s, a number of state-owned industries were sold to private investors in a process known as **privatisation**. This significant policy served a number of objectives. One rationale was the belief that the performance of privately owned organisations exposed to market forces would be superior to nationalised industries. It was argued that public organisations were sheltered from many of the claimed incentive effects of market forces. These include the need to reduce costs to stay efficient, and the need to recruit highly qualified and experienced staff to manage the businesses.

Market forces generate the most beneficial outcomes when markets are competitive. However, many of the nationalised industries were originally taken into public ownership because competition in such industries was seen as either unfeasible or undesirable. Many were, in other words, **natural monopolies**.

> **!?!** A **natural monopoly** occurs where substantial economies of scale are available and the market is most efficiently served by a single producer.

Economies of scale generally associated with natural monopolies, tend to derive from activities which depend upon a network of pipes, wires or similar, to deliver services to customers, often to their houses. The costs of laying and replacing these distribution networks are extremely high. Examples of natural monopolies achieving economies of scale are telecommunications, gas, electricity and water distribution and railways. The argument concerning lower costs of provision for a sole supplier can also be presented by saying competing companies laying down new networks - for example two sets of water pipes – would simply be a wasteful duplication of expensive capital equipment. One argument was that natural monopolies should be left in place.

Recent experience suggests that the following factors should be taken into account with respect to monopoly:

- It is only activities involving distribution which are naturally monopolistic. For example, in the electricity industry, while electricity distribution is naturally monopolistic, the generation of the electricity to be distributed is not, because it does not have such extensive economies of scale. This was recognised to some extent when the electricity industry was privatised. Distribution was monopolistic, while generation enjoyed some competition, notably between the newly created companies Powergen and National Power.

- While it is cheapest to distribute products such as gas, electricity and water via just one network, it is feasible to have competition for the use of the network. Thus in all major network industries, developments have occurred allowing organisations to compete to supply products distributed by a single network. A single network used by a number of suppliers is said to be operating on a common carriage basis.

- Technological developments in the telecommunications industry have led to greatly reduced costs of network provision and these, along with significant growth in demand for telecommunications, have meant that competing networks in some areas of activity have become feasible. In this instance, technological development has ended the naturally monopolistic status of some areas of telecommunication. For example, the development of digital networks has led to a massive increase in the capacity of telecommunication systems while competitors to British Telecom, such as Mercury, have developed competitive distribution systems to enter the market.

Despite these developments, you should recognise that the existence of network bases of supply means that some industries will contain some naturally monopolistic elements. Certainly, the government may have missed opportunities to introduce competition into areas of non-natural monopoly activity, notably when the whole of British Gas's activities were privatised as a monopoly.

Finally, it should be said that some economists would argue that:

- to reap the benefits of market forces, competition should be introduced wherever feasible

- in areas of natural monopoly, regulation is necessary to protect consumers from the possible abuse of monopoly power which a natural monopoly will inevitably have.

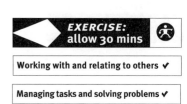

EXERCISE:
allow 30 mins

Working with and relating to others ✔

Managing tasks and solving problems ✔

ACTIVITY 1

In a small group, discuss the benefits of market forces and competition. Review the possible abuse of power in a monopoly industry. List below two examples of benefits and power abuses.

Commentary...

We have chosen to review British Telecom. You can compare your ideas with those below. Benefits of market forces competition in the telecommunications industry include:

- price competition, which tends to result in lower prices for business and household telephone users

- increased efficiency due to exposure to competition

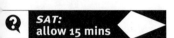

SAT:
allow 15 mins

○ the development of new products and services, which is stimulated as firms use technological innovations to attract and maintain new customers. An example is British Telecom's new system which allows customers to check the telephone number from which the last call to them was made.

Abuses of monopoly power in the telecommunications industry are possible:

○ Throughout the 1970s and 1980s, British Telecom increased the cost of calls to household consumers at a time when it was making record profits. While British Telecom argued that the profits were needed for investment and as a reward to shareholders, customers expressed discontent.

○ The number of layers of management within British Telecom grew during this period. Many economists argued that the company was suffering from too much bureaucracy caused by a lack of competition.

It is to be noted that both of these potential abuses have been largely reversed in recent years, as extra competition and OFTEL, the regulatory body, has forced British Telecom to reduce prices and reduce its numbers of managerial staff.

Competition as rivalry

PERFECT COMPETITION

> ⁉️ **Perfect competition** occurs where the market has a large number of small suppliers, none of which is large enough to have a direct impact on any other firm or the market, and each produces the same type of goods.

When we consider a model of perfect competition, we mean competition in terms of a large number of different firms all producing the same product. The market functions 'perfectly' in that the intensive competition between firms competing for the custom of highly informed consumers would eliminate the inefficient producers who cannot meet the quality and price requirements of the market.

Competition in this form has beneficial consequences, including the fact that a firm had to keep its costs and prices down to the level of its competitors and its quality up to their standards. However, as a reward for providing high-quality goods at competitive prices a company could see an increase in its share of the market.

OLIGOPOLY

> **!?!** An **oligopolistic market structure** is one in which a small number of firms dominate the supply of a particular product or service onto the market. Each of these companies has a similar share of the market.

Oligopoly is defined in general terms as competition among the few. Examples include high street banks such as Barclays, Lloyds, Midland and National Westminster, car producing firms such as Ford, Nissan, Chrysler and Datsun and petrol distribution firms such as Esso, Shell and Gulf.

Technically, an oligopolistic market is a market in which the bulk of the product concerned is supplied by a small number of producers, each of which supplies a significant share of the market. In these terms, the model is quite a realistic one. A major and important feature of competition in these situations is the interdependence of the decision making of the organisations involved.

Imagine you are responsible for the pricing policy of a car company which currently has a 30 per cent share of the market and is seeking to increase sales. In an oligopolistic market, the existence of rivalry for custom makes an exercise such as price cutting virtually impossible because the competitive reaction would be swift. The competitors would wish to protect their share of the market. If they cut their price below yours you would match it, and if this developed into a price war, every company could see their profits reduced. Consequently, companies involved in an oligopoly situation try to differentiate their products and services on a non-price basis, e.g. by free promotional offers or enhancements to the company image by sponsoring good causes, etc.

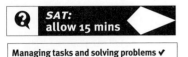

Managing tasks and solving problems ✔

ACTIVITY 2

Identify three examples of how companies involved in an oligopolistic market situation can differentiate their products and services without changing prices. Should the company which employs you operate in such a situation, you should give examples of how it differentiates its products or services.

Commentary...

Answers will depend on the industry; here we use the banks and car manufacturers as examples.

All banks charge similar interest rates on loans and deposits. However, they have competed against each other on the basis of:

- more convenient opening hours

- images established by advertising campaigns, e.g. the listening bank, the action bank and the bank that likes to say 'Yes'

- sponsoring sporting events

- gifts and promotions to attract new customers, particularly students and the young generally. (The student of today could be a prosperous and loyal customer for many years. Think back to the relationship approach.)

If we take car manufacturers, then we see such things as:

- free fitting of safety devices such as airbags

- extended warranties and after-sales provision

- added luxury to interior fittings.

MONOPOLY

> !?! A **monopoly** exists when the whole market is supplied by just one organisation, or one organisation has a high share of the market.

The model of monopoly is the polar opposite of the perfectly competitive model. It assumes that the whole of the market is supplied by just one organisation or that one organisation has a major influence in the market.

In perfect competition, firms earning large profits in the short run have those profits eroded in the longer term by firms entering the market. These new entrants force down prices by increasing the supply of goods offered to consumers. However, the monopolist is protected from this competition by **entry barriers**. These entry barriers can exist for several reasons:

- Cost advantages of the monopolist mean that any entrants would produce at a higher average cost than the monopolist and could not compete price-wise against it. Such cost advantages may come from a number of sources but the most common include the economies of scale available to the monopolist and the efficiencies generated by long experience of producing that product.

- Exclusive access by the monopolist to an essential input into the productive process such as raw materials or a specific form of capital could either make it impossible for other firms to produce this product or give the firm a cost advantage.

- Strong customer loyalty to the existing firm will mean customers are unlikely to switch.

- Statutory barriers such as the award of a patent prohibit the replication of a product for a period of time. Supply may also be restricted to a firm issued with a licence by government. The best known examples of monopolies protected by statute in the UK were the nationalised utilities such as coal, gas and electricity prior to privatisation.

COMPARING PERFECT COMPETITION AND MONOPOLY

The result of these entry barriers is that the monopolist's supernormal profits can, under certain conditions, endure into the long run without stimulating entry. We can now compare this long-run position of the monopolist to the beneficial outcomes that are felt to come from the theoretical perfectly competitive firm in the long run.

1. Unlike the perfectly competitive firm, the monopolist can earn supernormal profits through into the long run. Thus its consumers will pay prices greater than the average cost of production, including the normal profit element, even in the long run.

2. There is no built-in tendency for the monopoly firm to be producing at the bottom of its average cost curve and thus minimise its average costs by utilising its fixed capital approximately.

3. The monopolist does not produce a level of output at which society maximises its surplus of benefit over costs.

In contrast to this, firms operating in competitive markets are likely to exhibit directly opposite features to those above.

Traditionally, many public service suppliers have been monopolists, although as we have discussed, recent reforms have sought to expose public service provision to various forms of competition, e.g. via competitive tendering. Under monopoly, the lack of stimulus from competitors can lead to costs being allowed to rise higher than the minimum feasible. These cost rises are passed on to the consumer in higher prices. There is also lack of incentive to maintain quality and be responsive to the requirements of customers.

Firms operating competitively find difficulty passing on increased costs to customers and they must maintain availability and customer responsiveness or are likely to go out of business.

However, in certain situations, monopolies may produce benefits. If a monopoly's production activity yields economies of scale, this could reduce the monopolist's average costs below those which would be borne by perfectly competitive firms producing the same product. If these economies of scale are great, this could lead to the consumers paying a lower price than they would in a perfectly competitive situation. The monopoly passes on at least a part of its savings. This is the main reason why UK policy concerning monopoly treats each case on its merits rather than assuming that monopoly is necessarily a bad thing. Of course, the central issue is the way in which a monopolist uses this power in the market, and whether this process needs to be tightly regulated.

The directors of a monopoly will often argue that they serve a whole market rather than simply choose to serve profitable segments and, in this case, there is an argument that an element of social responsibility is being performed. For example, British Telecom argue that they maintain rural call boxes at a loss as part of their socially responsible approach and that increasing competition could mean that they will not be able to guarantee this service to rural communities.

Market orientation and the public services

Recent reforms have been introduced to make public services operate in a more competitive, market-oriented manner. **Compulsory competitive tendering (CCT)** was made a statutory requirement in local government through the Local Government Planning and Land Act (1980) and the Local Government Act (1988). This means that local authorities are now required to put certain activities – such as street cleaning or refuse collection, which were not previously subject to competition – out to competitive tender. Outside private-sector companies have the chance to prove they can do the job better and cheaper than providers of the existing services.

The reforms have introduced competition for the right to carry out activities. This reflects the belief implicit in the free market model that competition provides stimuli to cost minimisation and quality. The net result of this competition should be cost reductions and a better deal for consumers.

Similar reforms have been introduced in central government. When organisations in central government compete with the private sector for the right to continue to provide services, this is known as **market testing** rather than competitive tendering. The same stimuli from competition are believed to result. Profit-oriented stimuli are also present when private firms win the right to supply. But under market testing, all central government organisations are required to break even rather than earn a positive profit. It must be remembered that taxpayers fund the services provided by local and central government, and they demand value for money alongside the provision of high-quality services.

This process of market testing and competitive tendering is designed to play an important part in developing a sensible balance between efficiency and the maintenance of services. For example, old age pensioners in remote areas value a meals-on-wheels service. Efficiencies made elsewhere can allow this particular service to run at a loss and still be continued. Whether this is always possible will also depend on the overall funds available, the level of saving achieved and the keenness of the local authority to provide this level of service.

In the National Health Service, market forces have been introduced to the resource allocation process through the **internal market**. The internal market arises from a division of the health service between fund-holding general practitioners and district health authority on the one hand and hospitals who provide the services they purchase. This divides the NHS into **purchasers** and **providers**.

The major publicly funded purchasers are the district health authorities who receive funds according to the size and characteristics of the resident populations. They have a duty to purchase health services for their population which provide the best value for money. In doing this, they have a choice of suppliers open to them:

- local authority hospitals

- hospitals allowed under the new legislation to opt for self-governing or trust status

- hospitals managed by other district health authorities

- private sector hospitals.

On a much smaller scale, fund-holding general practitioners can also choose from a range of suppliers to obtain optimum value for money for their patients. This means that the stimuli of competition has been introduced in the NHS. Suppliers are being encouraged to minimise costs and ensure that they offer value for money and a service which reflects consumer needs. The intention is that resources will tend increasingly to be allocated to organisations that do this most successfully.

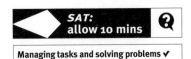

SAT:
allow 10 mins

Managing tasks and solving problems ✔

ACTIVITY 3

The stimulus of competition in the health service is claimed to have achieved better value for money. Identify six ways in which this may have been achieved.

Commentary...

You may have identified the following features:

1. shorter waiting lists to see a consultant

2. more patients seen

3. shorter bed occupancy time

4. waiting time before treatment reduced for patients

5. cost of operations known more accurately allowing assessment of cost reduction possibilities

6. the grouping of certain types of surgery or medical provision in a limited number of locations to reduce costs, particularly where equipment used is of high capital value.

Remember that in cases such as the health service, the supporters of competition may use available statistics to illustrate the benefits they believe they have achieved, but there may also be negative aspects to the changes.

Public sector organisations and customers

Private sector organisations such as banks, brewers, supermarket chains and television companies, spend vast sums of money trying to establish the needs of consumers. They recognise that to compete in highly competitive and mature markets requires a clear understanding of underlying trends within the market and perception of the needs of different individuals. No two individuals have the same needs and an individual's needs change over time.

The public sector provides a complex range of personal and technical services to the whole population. To develop the customer-centred approach requires both a clear definition of what needs are being satisfied and how the needs of different groups of consumers vary for the same service, e.g. tax advice, highways maintenance or housing provision.

It is important that public sector organisations use market research methods to uncover the needs of the different groups of people who use their services; it is only by measuring these requirements, that they can develop programmes aimed at meeting customer expectations of service quality and delivery.

Developing a customer-centred approach within the organisation requires the acceptance of this principle at all levels. It is not sufficient that those at the interface with customers adopt a different approach. This merely transfers the problems that arise one stage further up the organisation. Those in contact with customers need to feel that the whole organisation is committed to improving service quality. Middle management cannot abdicate responsibility for customer satisfaction; they are required to play their part as much as the front-line employees such as counter staff who talk to customers.

Only when the organisational philosophy has changed and the customer-centred management style is in place can the organisation make most effective use of its marketing resources. The framework in figure 3.1 attempts to define the relationship between strategic and tactical decision making within the organisation with regard to customer delivery.

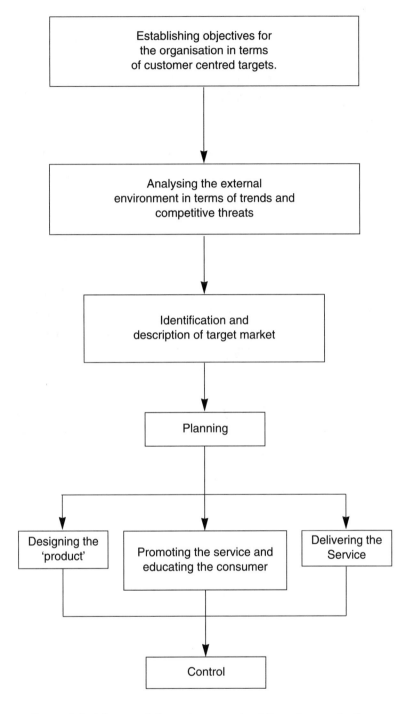

FIGURE 3.1: *A framework for customer service delivery in organisations.*

Notice how the customer is central to this framework. The external
environment can be analysed using DEPICTS analysis (covered in
Section 1, Session 2). The target market can be broken down into
various segments. Plans are developed to deliver the overall service
levels and quality, and a communications strategy needs to be in
place to increase people's awareness of the service. Control is taken
into consideration through feedback from customers and, if necessary,
adjustments are made.

**PUBLIC SECTOR
ORGANISATIONS AND
CUSTOMERS**

Adopting a customer-centred approach within the public sector starts with an organisational response through a change in management philosophy and the establishment of new types of organisational goals. Although there are many significant differences between public and private sector organisations, there is only one marketing theory. Putting the customer first has clear implications for goal setting and a requirement for sophisticated information on consumer behaviour. The danger of believing that the responsibility for this new approach can be left solely with front-line employees is likely to result in internal disillusionment and external criticism.

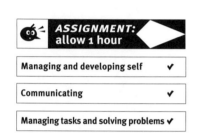

ASSIGNMENT: allow 1 hour
Managing and developing self ✔
Communicating ✔
Managing tasks and solving problems ✔

ACTIVITY 4

Consider a job centre and a public library and in each case consider:

- **the different groups of customers who use these services**

- **the criteria customers apply in judging the quality and efficiency of the service.**

Explain what market research methods you would recommend to assess whether the needs of the different groups of customers are being met.

Write report of no more than 500 words, and summarise your main findings in the box below.

summary

▶ Market regulation is the means by which government or appointed bodies intervenes with the free market mechanism. In a given market, regulation may be external, for example OFTEL, or may be self-regulation by, for example, a professional body.

▶ Markets may be classified as perfect competition, oligopolies or monopolies. All these types of markets bring differing advantages and disadvantages to the customer.

▶ Many public services have been reformed recently to introduce competition which has spurred the development of a customer-centred approach.

Resources

Resources

Goodbye to all that

Daily Express
26 November 1991

Gerald Ratner was last night forced out of the firm he had built into the world's biggest jewellery empire.

He is receiving only a gold-plated handshake. He collects £375,000 – one year's salary. But he held a three-year contract as chief executive.

Mr Ratner paid the penalty for declaring one of his company's cut-price decanter sets was 'total crap'.

He had already been forced to relinquish his chairmanship and now severs all connection with the company he spent 26 years building into a trans-Atlantic giant.

Last night a spokesman for Ratner's said: 'The board would like to record its appreciation of Mr Ratner's immense contribution to the development of the group.'

But he could not explain why the former chief executive was not getting his £1 million entitlement.

Mr Ratner, 43, said in a statement: 'I am obviously saddened to be leaving a business of which I am so proud.'

'However, the continuing negative press I have attracted leads me to believe this decision is in the interests of the group and the people working in it.'

It was while addressing the annual meeting of the Institute of Directors in April 1990 that he repeated a quip he had often made in private.

Referring to the decanter set, he said: 'People ask me how can you sell this product for such a low price. I say it is because it is total crap.'

Customers, staff and shareholders were outraged. The wisecrack came when the company was already feeling the pitch of the recession.

At his peak he had expanded the business from his father's single jewellery shop in Richmond to include the Ratner's shops, Zales, H Samuel, Ernest Jones, Watches of Switzerland and Salisburys.

Profits soared from £4.2 million in 1986 to £112 million in 1990. It grew faster in the USA.

Mr Ratner left school at 16 to join the family firm and prided himself on having done every job in the company, from tea boy to serving behind the counter, buying stock and running the offices.

When he was 34 he organised a boardroom coup to oust his father.

Once in control he used marketing ideas from snooker-playing friends, television magnate Michael Green and advertising guru Charles Saatchi to turn the small firm into a giant. It had 1,000 shops in the UK and another 1,000 in America.

He took the snobbery out of jewellery. The plan was to make anyone going inside a Ratner's shop feel like it was a trip to the sales.

But after his fateful words he struggled to rebuild the damaged business. From being a high-profile character, he became a virtual recluse. He brought in soccer's Gazza to tell the world his jewellery was 'world class' in a series of adverts.

But by that time the recession had set in the group's losses last year were £122 million.

To keep the bankers at bay he was forced to give up his job as chairman and take a huge pay cut.

But the 'total crap' tag continued to haunt him.

RESOURCE 2:

BP press release

PRESS RELEASE

FOR IMMEDIATE RELEASE
JUNE 23, 1995   5/09

BP STATISTICAL REVIEW OF WORLD ENERGY

After remaining level for three years, world energy consumption increased by nearly one per cent in 1994, restoring the pattern of steady growth seen for much of the 1980s. The increase would have been significantly greater were it not for the continuing steep decline in energy use in the Former Soviet Union.

Energy demand in the world outside the FSU grew by 2.8 per cent, but this was largely offset by a 10.4 per cent fall in consumption in the FSU itself, according to the *1995 BP Statistical Review of World Energy* published today.

Growth in the emerging market economies, excluding Eastern Europe, was a strong 5.1 per cent with Brazil, China, India and much of the rest of East Asia all experiencing growth rates in the range of 5-10 per cent. With an increase of over 5 per cent in energy demand, China overtook Russia to become, after the USA, the second largest energy market in the world.

Demand in Western Europe was steady over the year, but there was higher consumption in the USA and Japan, reflecting cold weather and a hot summer respectively. The marked slowing of the decline in energy demand in Eastern Europe, excluding the FSU, continued to reflect successful re-structuring and the beginnings of economic development.

World oil consumption grew by 1.7 per cent in 1994. A fall of almost 15 per cent in the FSU was more than offset by increases in demand in the emerging market economies, Japan and North America. Demand in Western Europe remained almost level in 1994. As in 1993, the greatest growth in oil demand was in Asia, up 6 per cent overall, particularly in South Korea (up 9.9 per cent) which overtook the UK to become the world's eighth largest oil consumer.

Oil remains the world's most important fuel, accounting for 40 per cent of the energy market.

Oil production rose by almost one per cent, despite continuing falls in the USA and the FSU. Output from non-OPEC countries outside the FSU rose by 4.2 per cent, with UK production increasing by 26.6 per cent, and was at an all time high in 1994. **Oil reserves** rose very slightly, with new discoveries of oil and higher recovery rates from existing discoveries more than replacing production. Notable new discoveries were made in Colombia, Argentina and Angola. At 1994's production rate, the world's proved oil reserves would be sufficient to meet demand for the next 43 years.

The British Petroleum Company p.l.c., Britannic House, 1 Finsbury Circus, London EC2M 7BA
For Further Information Telephone 071-496 4324/071-496 4358/071-496 4708/071-496 4344   *More . . .*

Oil prices fell markedly during the year, bringing the average Brent marker crude price for the year down from $17.07 in 1993 to $15.98, the lowest level in real terms for 20 years.

Although there was a healthy increase of 2.9 per cent in demand for **gas** in the world excluding the FSU, the 7.6 per cent fall in demand in the FSU meant that overall global demand fell by 0.2 per cent. The emerging market economies, excluding Eastern Europe, showed strong growth in demand of 6.8 per cent with notable increases in South Korea (up 33 per cent) and Taiwan (up 31 per cent). In Europe, gas has now overtaken coal to be the second most important fuel after oil.

World **coal consumption** rose slightly in 1994, the first rise for four years. Global demand grew by 0.5 per cent, although outside the FSU demand grew by 2 per cent. There was a strong increase of over 5 per cent in coal demand in China, the world's largest producer and consumer of coal. **Hydroelectricity** consumption remained steady while **nuclear energy** use rose by 1.7 per cent in 1994 and accounted for 7.2 per cent of all primary energy.

Notes to Editors:

- Emerging Market Economies (EMEs) consists of those countries previously termed Lesser Developed Countries (LDCs) – Latin America, Africa, Middle East and non-OECD Asia – plus Eastern Europe.

- The *BP Statistical Review of World Energy* was first published in 1953. It initially reported only on the oil industry but has since been expanded to include other forms of energy and increasingly detailed regional coverage. It is also now available on diskette.

- Press copies of the *Review* are available from the BP Press Office (tel: 0171 496 4715).

– ENDS –

Healthier ads could catch cold

RESOURCE 3:

The Times
August 23, 1989

A £5 million advertising campaign launched last week for a new Kellogg's cereal has stirred up what the tabloids are prosaically calling 'a storm in a breakfast bowl'. The controversy centres on Kellogg's claim that its Common Sense Oat Bran Flakes can reduce blood cholesterol, and thus lower the chances of contracting heart disease.

The cereal's packaging, and the newspaper and television advertisements, show a heart shaped breakfast bowl with the slogan: 'The heart of a good breakfast'. Immediately the advertising appeared, experts from the Coronary Prevention Group were said to be indignant that the advertisements did not emphasise that oat bran (a modish product in the United States, where sales have risen by 600 per cent in the past year) must be consumed as part of a low-fat diet to be effective. They also pointed out that it lowers cholesterol only if you eat three or more bowls of it a day.

Responding to the fuss, the Ministry of Agriculture, Fisheries and Food creaked into action, referring the advertising and the packaging to the Local Authority Co-ordinating Body on Trading Standards, which is responsible for ensuring that food labelling regulations are enforced. The matter, it says, is under urgent consideration.

Coming as it does just two weeks after the manufacturers Ever ready and Alberto Culver were censured for misleading 'environment friendly' claims on batteries and hair spray, the oat bran episode raises uncomfortable questions for advertisers and their agencies. Are they, as the Coronary Prevention Group suggested, guilty of cashing in on the popularity of products considered environment friendly and 'natural healthy foods'?

Alberto Culver's VO5 hair spray was advertised with a green sticker marked 'ozone friendly' because it contained no CFCs. But the company omitted to point out that the product contained hydrocarbons, which can damage the atmosphere. The company now admits the label was misleading and will withdraw it.

However, the Kellogg's case is less straightforward. The company, whose cereals account for half of all sales in the £650 million British Market, denies any attempt to mislead, saying 'Kellogg's does not make health claims unless supported by thorough research.'

Common Sense is not the first oat bran product to run into trouble. Jordan's and Quaker already have less heavily advertised products on the market, and a recent Quaker press advertisement, which says its product is 'causing quite a stir in the fight against cholesterol', is currently under scrutiny by the Advertising Standards Authority's Health and Nutrition Committee.

The advertising authority and the broadcasting watchdog, the IBA, admit they are finding the assessment of 'healthy' food claims and green claims a growing problem. The two bodies are now holding discussions about whether a code of practice needs to be introduced for this particular area.

Like Kellogg's, Quaker claims it is advertising its oat bran cereal in a responsible manner. David Lillycrop, the company secretary, says. 'We are the acknowledged oats expert in the eyes of the public, so we feel there is a heavier responsibility on us to get the message about oat bran across in a clear and balanced way.'

He points out that Quaker's advertisement states that oat bran can reduce blood cholesterol, 'when added to a low fat, low cholesterol diet', although he acknowledges that it does not outline the components of such a diet. Kellogg's too, says its oat bran flakes 'can only be effective when part of a healthy diet and lifestyle', although again, it does not say exactly what the diet and lifestyle should consist of.

Stephen Locke, head of policy at the Consumer Association, has been worried about food claims for some time. He says: 'Full nutrition labelling, which we have been advocating for years, would help because then consumers could make sensible, informed comparisons between different foods.'

Unlike some pressure groups, he feels that fault in cases of supposedly misleading claims does not always lie entirely with the manufacturers and advertising agencies. 'New, and often conflicting, discoveries are being made about food properties all

the time, which makes the whole issue very confusing.'

And in the end, should consumers themselves not be prepared to take some responsibility? Philip Circus, legal affairs director of the Institute of Practitioners in Advertising, says: 'I'm not convinced the consumer is as naive in this area as pressure groups would have us believe. And in any case you cannot expect advertisers to outline all the requisites of a healthy diet in an ad for one particular food product. People have to take overall responsibility themselves for what they eat.'

① RESOURCE 4:

Sunday Times
March 26, 1989

Advertising 'encourages motorists to race police'

A poster campaign for a new high performance Vauxhall car is being investigated by the Advertising Standards Authority because of fears that it will encourage drivers to race the police.

The family of a victim of a high speed police chase has joined MPs and road safety groups calling for the withdrawal of the posters, which depict a racing car in police colours.

The campaign for the Vauxhall Astra GTE 16-valve shows a picture of the car with a racing car in police marking poised to give chase. Its launch follows eight deaths in four weeks as a result of high speed police chases. In London there were more than 5,000 accidents involving police cars last year.

Last week, David Marshall, chairman of the Commons' Transport Committee, called for the posters to be withdrawn. "The manufacturers deserve all the criticism they get. There are many better ways to promote their product than in this unthinking manner and if they have any sensitivity to public feeling they must drop the campaign immediately."

Patricia Lawrence, the sister of a victim who died in a Vauxhall Astra

after a police chase earlier this month, said: "This advertisement is distasteful after what has happened. It should not be carried."

Alf Lawrence, an amateur footballer, was killed with two team mates when a joyrider fleeing the police rammed his car.

David Williamson, the ASA's deputy director, said a letter had been sent to Vauxhall, because he believed the campaign could attract complaints from the public.

The £13,000 Astra hatchback, which was launched earlier this year. It has a top speed of 132 mph and accelerates from 0 to 60 mph in 7.6 seconds.

Road safety groups are concerned about manufacturers selling cars on the strength of their macho image and speed appeal. Last June the ASA upheld complaints against BMW and Citroen for glamorising fast driving.

Friends of the Earth, which has conducted a campaign against adverts which they say encourage dangerous driving, said: "There are 5,000 people dying each year on the roads while you get advertisers saying fast driving is socially acceptable and desirable. In the light of recent police chase deaths, this has become even more distasteful and quite unacceptable."

Vauxhall and its advertising agency, Lowe Howard-Spink, said the campaign aimed to play up the car's sporting image while reminding drivers of the need for lawful restraint.

"It is a poster which says this is a fast, high performance car, but be careful and act with responsibility. It is intended to be a bit light-hearted and says the police are ready for it," says Peter Stephenson-Wright, of Lowe Howard-Spink, "I certainly don't think we are being irresponsible. I can't see any link with these recent car chases beyond the fact that we have a police car in the advertisement."

Vauxhall claims the poster was shown to a police authority before the campaign and met with a positive response.